"Professor Beehner offers useful lessons for us all in applying the concepts of systems analysis to the urgent challenge of providing leadership for sustainable development. He rightly sees an appreciation for complexity and a commitment to integrative thinking as keys to the leadership we need that focuses on the whole and on the whole's interconnections to natural systems. I highly recommend his instructive book to all those who seek a sustainable world."

**James Bacchus**, *Distinguished University Professor of Global Affairs, Director of the Center for Global Economic and Environmental Opportunity, University of Central Florida, former U.S. Congressman, and former chief judge at the Appellate Body of the World Trade Organization*

"This insightful book gives one multiple examples into current applications of much needed system leadership and system leaders for sustainability, such as determined (US) local government leaders, who have impact within and beyond their communities. The multilaterally agreed SDGs are end result based. This book guides us on what governance is needed across the board (NGOs, INGOs, different levels of government, businesses, and citizens) to make change real in today's network society."

**Dr. Dorine van Norren**, *ex-diplomat, researcher at Tilburg University, PhD Development as Service, The Netherlands*

"A sustainable future does require system leaders, who orchestrate interactions among multiple stakeholders transcending system and subsystem boundaries. This book clearly presents the how-to of system leadership for business, government, non-profit, and educational organizations. It stimulated me to create new partnerships for local and global action."

**Dr. Dennis Heaton**, *Professor, Sustainable Business MBA, Maharishi University of Management, USA*

"In *System Leadership for Sustainability*, Beehner has zeroed in on the most critical aspect of solving wicked problems: it cannot be done without an integrated, collaborative effort across multiple arenas of influence. Sustainability is such a wicked problem, requiring innovation across boundaries and stakeholders. Beehner explores this holistic leadership approach in depth, with clarity and ample illustrations, exploring both the strengths of this systems approach to sustainability leadership and the barriers to it."

**Dr. Toni L. Blum**, *Associate Provost for Institutional Effectiveness, The University of Texas at El Paso, USA*

# System Leadership for Sustainability

This book is the first to explore the application of system leadership to promote sustainable solutions for contemporary and future environmental and social problems. The combination of synthesized research summaries and case studies of individuals and organizations contribute considerably to the field by expanding system leadership concepts from theory to practical application. System leadership has been identified as a method by which complex societal problems can be addressed, but it has as yet not been applied to sustainability. The first chapters introduce the background and fundamentals of system leadership and its relevance to sustainability. The chapters that propose methods of developing system leadership, examples of system leaders, and practical application of system leadership in industry, academic, government, nonprofit, and NGO settings. Each chapter includes a chapter case, interview, and/or reflection questions in order to stimulate critical thinking and provide instructional tools for academic use and practical application. The book is particularly relevant to researchers and students internationally in the fields of social development and sustainability. It is also relevant to public, private, and nonprofit/NGO management practitioners who are curious about the leadership styles and skills necessary to develop a sustainable future.

**Christopher G. Beehner** is Professor of Business and Information Management, Seminole State College of Florida, USA. He is the author of *Spirituality, Sustainability and Success: Concepts and Cases*. He has also frequently published and presented about sustainable business education.

**Routledge Frontiers in Sustainable Business Practice**
Editor: Satinder K. Dhiman

This Series focuses on the practice of business as it relates to environmental sustainability – making responsible decisions that will reduce business' negative impact on the environment.

It explores topics such as climate change, air and water pollution, water conservation, ecology and habitat, green buildings and eco-villages, sustainable food systems, waste management and recycling, energy conservation and renewable energy, smart manufacturing and the role of sustainable business practice.

# System Leadership for Sustainability

Christopher G. Beehner

Routledge
Taylor & Francis Group
LONDON AND NEW YORK

First published 2020
by Routledge
2 Park Square, Milton Park, Abingdon, Oxon OX14 4RN

and by Routledge
52 Vanderbilt Avenue, New York, NY 10017

*Routledge is an imprint of the Taylor & Francis Group, an informa business*

First issued in paperback 2021



*British Library Cataloguing-in-Publication Data*
A catalogue record for this book is available from the British Library

*Library of Congress Cataloging-in-Publication Data*
Names: Beehner, Christopher G., author.
Title: System leadership for sustainability / Christopher G. Beehner.
Description: Abingdon, Oxon ; New York, NY : Routledge, 2020. | Includes bibliographical references and index.
Identifiers: LCCN 2019035949 (print) | LCCN 2019035950 (ebook) | ISBN 9780367342180 (hardback) | ISBN 9780429324512 (ebook)
Subjects: LCSH: Sustainable development. | System theory. | Leadership.
Classification: LCC HD75.6 .B44 2020 (print) | LCC HD75.6 (ebook) | DDC 658.4/092–dc23
LC record available at https://lccn.loc.gov/2019035949
LC ebook record available at https://lccn.loc.gov/2019035950

ISBN: 978-0-367-34218-0 (hbk)
ISBN: 978-1-03-208357-5 (pbk)
ISBN: 978-0-429-32451-2 (ebk)

Typeset in Bembo
by Apex CoVantage, LLC

# Contents

# Preface

The topics of sustainability and sustainable development emerged in academic literature in the late 1980s, following publication of the Brundtland Commission report by the World Commission on Environment and Development (WCED). Global interest in sustainability further expanded with the introduction of the United Nations Millennium Development Goals (MDGs) in 2000, and the subsequent Sustainable Development Goals (SDGs) in 2015. While a rapidly growing consensus acknowledges the need for immediate, significant, and global action toward sustainability, it cannot be achieved without a concerted, collaborative, and global response. Leaders are needed who can collaborate and influence across boundaries, even when they possess no formal influence. This book is part of a journey that I have undertaken to promote sustainability and to assist individuals in becoming leaders for sustainability.

An article entitled "The Dawn of System Leadership" by Senge, Hamilton, and Kania (2015) provided the inspiration for this text. System leadership originated in the field of education, wherein teachers and principals influenced beyond their schools and districts to entire systems for the purpose of obtaining sustainable educational advances. In their article, Senge and colleagues proposed system leadership as a method by which complex societal problems can be addressed. However, this author was unable to locate any research or literature examining system leadership as a means of addressing sustainability within the context of sustainable development. Moreover, existing literature on system leadership development primarily originated within the field of secondary education (e.g. Fullan, 2005), with limited literature in other fields or disciplines. This apparent gap in literature and theory further influenced my motivation to write this text.

The purpose of this text is to introduce system leadership as a contemporary solution to the sustainability challenges facing humankind and our planet. My goal is to provide a framework and model of system leadership for scholars and practitioners in multiple fields and sectors to address contemporary sustainability issues. The text develops and expands the theoretical base of system leadership into practical application for sustainability in organizational and interorganizational contexts. The first few chapters introduce the background and fundamentals of system leadership and its relevance to sustainability. The chapters that follow propose methods of developing system leadership, provide examples of system leaders, and offer methods for practical application of system leadership in industry, academic, government, nonprofit, and individual settings. The final chapter summarizes the key concepts and themes of the book and identifies future research opportunities, recommendations, and trends. Each chapter includes reflection questions, and several chapters include a chapter case study or personal interview to stimulate critical thinking and provide instructional tools for academic use and practical application. The personal interviews explore how several professionals from diverse sectors have applied system leadership in their careers and organizations to advance sustainability. These interviews provide qualitative support for the premise of the text, as well as content for reflection questions that readers may use to reflect on how they would have responded in similar situations and critique the interviewee's application of system leadership.

The overarching theme of the book is the development and application of system leadership to promote sustainable solutions for contemporary and future environmental and social problems. The combination of synthesized research summaries, personal interviews and case studies of individuals and organizations, may contribute to research and knowledge advancement by expanding the system leadership concept from theory to practical application. This text is intended to begin a conversation that must take place locally, globally, and immediately. While the primary target of this text is academic, a secondary market of public, private, and nonprofit management practitioners may benefit by learning about system leadership and how it may be applied in developing and implementing sustainability initiatives.

# Acknowledgments

I would first like to express my gratitude to Dr. Satinder Dhiman of Woodbury University in Burbank, California, in the United States for his continued mentorship with the publication aspects of my academic journey. I would also like to acknowledge Rebecca Marsh, Sophie Peoples, and the numerous staff members at Routledge who supported me during the publishing process. The proposed system leadership for sustainability model and framework would be less meaningful without the personal interviews of Gerben van Straaten, Robert Franco, and Florencia Librizzi, each of whom demonstrates system leadership for sustainability and willingly shared their experiences with me. I would also like to thank my friend and colleague James Bacchus, former US Congressman and former chief judge at the Appellate Body of the World Trade Organization, for his endorsement of this book. Since my appointment by Jim as a Community Fellow at the Center for Global Economic and Environmental Opportunity (GEEO), at the University of Central Florida, I have learned from and been inspired by his continued sustainability leadership. Finally, and most importantly, I am grateful to my wife Corene and my sons, Logan and Erik, for supporting me during my doctoral studies and career change from industry to academia, and for providing influence and encouragement in the sustainability-focused direction in which my career has since transitioned.

# 1 Introduction to system leadership

## Introduction

Leadership has been defined as the ability to influence a group of individuals to accomplish a common goal (Northouse, 2018). The study of leadership originally focused on traits of known leaders, believing leaders were born, not made. Subsequent theories examined leadership behavior and skills, introducing a perspective that leadership could be developed and taught. Contemporary leadership theorists have examined the role of followers in leadership. Most scholars and practitioners agree that leadership does not require a formal position of authority. Anyone can demonstrate leadership, often without conscious awareness of doing so.

Much of the focus of leadership research, literature, and training has been with organizational leadership. However, researchers have more recently examined system leadership as a form of leadership which transcends organizational boundaries (Fullan, 2004, 2005). A system leader is a unique individual capable of seeing and comprehending the larger system and catalyzing collective leadership to proactively co-create the future (Senge, Hamilton, & Kania, 2015). The system leader exhibits boundaryless leadership, extending influence among stakeholders across entire systems both inside and outside of their organizations, industries, and sectors. According to Timmins (2015), system leaders are distinguished from organizational leaders by their experience "working across" services and organizations, especially in situations involving considerable complexity.

System leadership is not a leadership style, but rather a model or framework describing leadership being applied beyond the immediate influence of the leader. As such, this chapter and book are not intended to introduce a new leadership style for sustainability. Instead, the purpose is to introduce and describe system leadership as a platform on which to develop sustainability leadership. This platform is intended to enhance, not replace, other leadership styles. In this text, I propose application of the system leadership model as a framework for realization of sustainability.

While varying definitions exist for sustainability, a generally accepted definition originated in the Brundtland Report: "Sustainable development is development that meets the needs of the present without compromising the ability of future generations to meet their own needs" (World Commission on Environment and Development, 1987). This definition, which has framed and influenced much of the sustainability conversation for the previous three decades, provides the context for sustainability throughout this text. Sustainability describes an ideal state of mutual existence in which humans and other living entities consistently flourish within planetary environmental limits (Ehrenfeld, 2012). However, sustainability is not a final outcome, but a dynamic objective that is constantly improving (Gaziulusoy, Boyle, & McDowall, 2013), and must exist within planetary boundaries, which define the safe operating space for society (Rockström et al., 2009; Steffen et al., 2015).

The focus of this chapter is to provide a foundation for the remainder of this book. The history, background, and concepts of system leadership are introduced with existing literature summarized and synthesized. Systems thinking is examined within the context of system leadership and sustainability. While the literature contains references to both system leadership and systems leadership, for consistency, the term system leadership is used throughout this book. The scope of this text is to introduce system leadership as a contemporary solution to the sustainability challenges facing the public, private, nonprofit, and NGO sectors. The theoretical base of system leadership will be expanded into practical application in organizational and inter-organizational contexts.

## The origin of system leadership

System leadership first appeared in literature in the early 21st century within the field of education. System leadership was described as an emerging practice consisting of a broad range of responsibilities developed either locally or within individual networks or programs that, when combined, can contribute to system transformation (Hopkins & Higham, 2007). Within the education field, system leaders are administrators who are willing to assume system-wide roles to improve other schools and systems in addition to their own (Hopkins & Higham, 2007). Outside of academia, Timmins (2015) defined system leadership as "seeking to achieve change across organizations where people do not have direct line management responsibility".

Fullan (2004) suggested that a new type of leadership is necessary to challenge business as usual. Because systematic forces have the advantage in preventing system transformation, powerful, proactive action will be necessary to change the existing system and context. Leaders who will enact systemic change must be adept at thinking systemically, because systems thinking can directly and indirectly provide the tools for system change. Achieving organizational and systemic change will require leaders who can connect people and resources from multiple system components. System leaders influence stakeholders across boundaries inside and outside of their organizations, industries, and sectors. In addition, these leaders must be capable of developing other leaders with similar abilities to achieve scale and impact.

In 2015, Senge et al. suggested that "[t]he deep changes necessary to accelerate progress against society's most intractable problems require a unique type of leader – the system leader, a person who catalyzes collective leadership" (p. 27). The system leadership concept built upon Senge's (1990) earlier work in the field of systems thinking. System leadership can be summarized as possessing the following three characteristics.

1 System leaders are not unique, extraordinary individuals but are facilitators of the conditions necessary for successful social change.
2 Any individual in any organization, in any industry or sector, and with any (or no) formal authority can be a system leader.
3 The core system leadership capabilities include the ability to see the larger system, promoting reflection and more innovative conversation and transforming the collective focus from reactive problem solving to proactive co-creation of the future.

(Senge et al., 2015)

System leaders develop these core capabilities, which produce collective leadership (Senge et al., 2015). The collective leadership style and the three core capabilities are further examined in Chapters 3 and 4.

System leaders perceive situations characterized by polarization and considered unsolvable problems to be opportunities for innovation (Senge et al., 2015). They are capable of balancing temporary reactive problem solving with permanent proactive value creation. System leaders positively influence organizational politics, assisting organizational members in recognizing that individual and organizational success is dependent upon the well-being of the broader systems in which they exist.

Although system leaders possess varied personalities and leadership styles, authentic system leaders have an extraordinarily similar impact (Senge et al., 2015). Their deep commitment to the overall well-being of the whole system influences similar behavior in other individuals, and their ability to empathize with people of diverse perspectives creates an environment of transparency and openness. System leaders build relationships based on intentional listening, which encourages development of honest, collaborative networks. The strength of a system leader is often not in what they know, but in what they do not know, which enables them to ask obvious questions and demonstrate a commitment to ongoing self-development that becomes a contagious influence on broader change efforts (Senge et al., 2015). Authentic leadership and other leadership styles appropriate for system leadership are examined in more detail in Chapter 3.

## Systems theory

Because systems thinking is the application of systems theory, it is appropriate that we first understand the principles of systems theory. Kaine and Cowan

(2011) defined a system as a collection of interconnected elements that form a relationship comprising the entirety of the components interacting in a non-linear manner. Systems can vary in complexity, and each system is characterized by circumstances, purpose, association, inputs, throughputs, outputs, and evaluation, feedback, and control processes (Robèrt et al., 2004). System components interact in a manner that results in an outcome greater than the sum of the individual components (Siebert, 2018). These essential systems features provide the foundation for a holistic decision-making framework (Davidson & Venning, 2011). However, understanding system behavior is difficult, because the temporal and spatial interconnections between system variables further complicate decision-making (Kunz, Moran, & Kastelle, 2013).

Von Bertalanffy introduced general system theory (GST) in 1928, defining GST as a collection of components from multiple existing systems approaches (von Bertalanffy, 1968a). Two assumptions influenced existing systems theory: open systems, defined as steady-state processes that remain constant over time, and closed systems, defined as a time-independent stable state, characterized by increasing entropy, and seclusion from the surrounding systems (von Bertalanffy, 1968a). Open systems require constant change to maintain equilibrium, experiencing both positive and negative entropy, while closed systems experience interactions among system components, and not the external environment (von Bertalanffy, 1968a). One of von Bertalanffy's contributions was recognizing GST in biological organisms as open systems, suggesting that an organic perspective was essential for understanding and critically analyzing systems. The open systems model, when combined with systems thinking and acknowledgment of the interaction between internal system and external factors, offers a robust method for examining and changing systems (McNamara, 2006). Systems theory is the result of various researchers' efforts to develop a common field of conformity, providing both a glossary of commonly understood terms for researchers from diverse fields and a shared foundation for presentation and interpretation of phenomena (Ramosaj & Berisha, 2014).

The viable systems approach (vSA) is a systems theory which provides an interpretative model that reinforces a governance methodology for any entity that can be viewed as a viable system (Barile, 2000, 2009; Barile, Pels, Polese, & Saviano, 2012a; Barile & Saviano, 2011; Barile, Saviano, Polese, & Di Nauta, 2012b; Golinelli, 2010; Pels, Barile, Saviano, Polese, & Carrubbo, 2014). The vSA is based on Beer's (1972a, 1972b) definition of a viable system as one that survives, remains intact, is integral, is externally and internally balanced, and possesses processes and abilities for expansion, learning, development, and evolution, thereby increasing system influence within its environment (Barile & Saviano, 2018). According to vSA, every entity (individual, organization, or community) can be viewed as a microenvironment, composed of multiple interconnected sub-components engaged in a common objective (Barile, Orecchini, Saviano, & Farioli, 2018). These networked and interconnected collections of systems provide eco-systemic conditions for any entity existing within them, persuading and being persuaded by their actions. Under these eco-systemic conditions, the structural boundaries among system components disappear when interaction develops (Barile et al., 2012b; Barile et al., 2018).

Systems theory has significantly influenced our understanding of organizations and our ability to achieve organizational change (McNamara, 2006). When applied to organizations, a systems approach can assist in rapidly identifying root causes of organizational issues and determining where and what appropriate response is needed (McNamara, 2006). Systems analysis is the application of systems theory, for the purpose of achieving system improvement by ensuring that all system components work efficiently to accomplish their purpose. Systems thinking is a major systems analysis tool and is the topic of the following section.

## Systems thinking

Systems thinking is a holistic analytical method used to examine how a system's constituent components interconnect and how they function over time and within the context of larger systems (Ambler, 2013). Systems thinking is the study of systems from a viewpoint of the entire system, corresponding subsystems, and the repetitive patterns that occur between the subsystems (McNamara, 2006). Systems thinking consists of:

- A holistic view of situations characterized as a collection of assorted interacting components within an environment.
- Acknowledging that relationships among system components are better predictors of system behavior than the actual components.
- Acknowledging a hierarchy of system levels in which attributes emerge at various levels, with mutual influence existing both within and between levels.
- Recognition that individual behavior within social systems will conform to dissimilar purposes or philosophies.

(Mingers & White, 2010)

The use of systems thinking encourages a broad perspective of systems and their overall structures, patterns, and cycles (McNamara, 2006). Systems thinking is useful for the identification and management of interrelated components, processes, and relationships that occur in systems (von Bertalanffy, 1968a). An important assumption of systems thinking is that system components will change behavior when separated from the system or other system components. The practical application of systems thinking stimulates an exploration of the interrelationships, perspectives, and boundaries of the organization or system (Learning for Sustainability, 2019). Because all systems generate emergent attributes that always differ from the sum of their components, systems cannot be understood by only examining the components (Robertson, 2014).

Systems thinking is not a new idea but rather a new name for a natural, intuitive manner of understanding the world (Siebert, 2018). Systems thinking is the term assigned to the contemporary resurrection of integrated thinking in academic and professional disciplines, beckoning us to follow our instincts, remove barriers, see the broader picture, explore opportunities, and relearn what we already know (Siebert, 2018). Humankind has been observing the interaction between systems and components throughout recorded history, with the ancient Indian Vedic philosophy being a holistic systems thinking tradition nearly 10,000 years old (Siebert, 2018). Although holism is at the foundation of most Eastern cultural and spiritual traditions, the influence of holism in Western culture can be observed in the Pythagoreans, who developed an ideology based on cosmic systems and oneness through numbers (Siebert, 2018). Moreover, numerous indigenous peoples recognize that people exist within a broader complex web of life that must be respected and lived in harmoniously (Siebert, 2018).

Systems thinking encourages a holistic worldview, in opposition to positivist and reductionist thinking (Learning for Sustainability, 2019). Positivism is a philosophical approach wherein every reasonable assertion can be scientifically confirmed or demonstrate logical or mathematical proof, and reductionism involves examining only the system components. However, reductionist thinking, dualism, and narrowmindedness have progressively undermined this ancient method of relating, especially since the beginning of the Industrial Revolution (Siebert, 2018). Systems thinker(s) recognize that while assertions and observations can be confirmed, demonstrated, and proven, these assertions and observations may produce varying outcomes when examined within the context of diverse systems.

Systems thinking is especially beneficial in addressing complex or complicated situations that cannot be solved by any single entity, because complex systems cannot be completely explained from one single perspective (Learning for Sustainability, 2019). In addition, because complex adaptive systems continuously evolve, systems thinking is suitable for organizational and social learning and responsive behavior (Learning for Sustainability, 2019). Systems thinking is helpful when faced with complex and "messy" circumstances, because it assists with understanding the situation systemically, enabling the identification of multiple leverage points that can be utilized to support beneficial change (Learning for Sustainability, 2019). Leverage points are locations in a system where minimal modification can leverage maximum system improvement (McNamara, 2006).

Systems thinking is an appropriate perspective for assisting leaders with understanding the basic structures, thinking, and beliefs that embody their organizations (Ambler, 2013). By focusing on the whole system, sustainability leaders can identify solutions to solve as many problems as feasible (McNamara, 2006). Systems thinking occurs when all organizational members understand the organizational vision and mission (Hadid, Mansouri, & Gallear, 2016). Moreover, systems thinking indicates the presence of relationships between components among centrally located organizational units (Hadid et al., 2016).

Peter Senge popularized systems thinking, defining it as "a discipline for seeing wholes. It is a framework for seeing interrelationships rather than things, for seeing patterns of change rather than static 'snapshots'" (Senge, 1990, p. 68). In his seminal text, Senge proposed systems thinking to be the fifth discipline that integrates the other four disciplines of personal mastery, mental models, building shared vision, and team learning (Senge, 1990). Senge argued that a systems orientation provides the motivation to consider how the disciplines interrelate. Senge suggested the need for a mind shift from viewing ourselves as existing separate from the world to one in which we are connected with the world, resulting in recognition that the problems we experience are the result of our own actions, and not external actors (Fullan, 2005).

The primary assumption underlying the systems approach is that everything consists of interdependent systems and relationships, suggesting that everything interacts with everything else (Ambler, 2013). The complexity of this relationship suggests that introducing change is challenging and risky, and that effective change requires action to alter the fundamental structure responsible for event and trend initiation, ultimately producing alternative results (Ambler, 2013). Action and not reaction to events and trends is necessary for facilitating effective change (Ambler, 2013). Systems thinking requires users to look at the big picture, assume a wider perspective, consider multiple perspectives, peel back the layers of the onion, examine relationships among components, look for root causes and improvements, and challenge and change our paradigms (Siebert, 2018).

Systems thinking has provided multiple tools and methods for analyzing and changing systems (McNamara, 2006). There are several broad categories of systems thinking tools: brainstorming, dynamic thinking, structural thinking, and computer-based tools (Kim, 2018). While each tool can be used individually, the tools can be combined to achieve profound understanding of dynamic behavior. The double-Q diagram is a common brainstorming tool, based on the "fishbone" or cause and effect diagram, and is useful for capturing unrestrained thoughts in a structured format, distinguishing between "hard" (quantitative) and "soft" (qualitative) variables and assisting participants with seeing the entire system (Kim, 2018).

Three common dynamic thinking tools are the behavior-over-time graph, the causal loop diagram, and the systems archetype (Kim, 2018). The behavior-over-time graph is useful for graphing variable behavior over time and gaining understanding of interrelationships between variables. The causal loop diagram uses cause and effect linkages to portray how system variables are interrelated and is useful in identifying reinforcing processes, which reinforce change, and balancing processes, which seek balance. The systems archetype helps users identify and manage common system behavior patterns such as *drifting goals*, *shifting the burden*, *limits to success*, *fixes that fail*, and other recurring patterns of organizational dynamics (Kim, 2018).

The common structural thinking tools are the graphical function diagram, the structure-behavior pair, and the policy structure diagram (Kim, 2018). The graphical function diagram captures the effects of one variable on another, by plotting the relationship between variables over a range of appropriate values and explaining nonlinear relationships among variables. The structure-behavior pair incorporates the basic dynamic structures that serve as components of computer model development, such as exponential growth, delays, smoothing, S-shaped growth, and oscillations. The policy structure diagram provides a conceptual map of the organizational decision-making process, focusing on the elements that influence each decision, and is useful for developing a generic structures library (Kim, 2018).

Computer-based tools include the computer model, the management flight simulator, and the learning laboratory (Kim, 2018). The computer model allows the user to convert all relevant relationships into mathematical equations, which are used to run policy analyses through numerous simulations. The management flight simulator provides management training through interactive computer games, in which users can identify the long-term outcome of decisions by developing strategies to assist in decision-making. The learning laboratory blends active experimentation with reflection and discussion, by using all systems thinking tools (Kim, 2018).

While systems thinking has been used by societies for millennia, holistic thinking appears to have been inhibited during much of the modern Industrial Age (Siebert, 2018). Contemporary industrial civilization is predicated upon the automation and commodification of society and nature (Siebert, 2018). However, systemic change will be necessary for society to overcome the current environmental, social, and economic challenges resulting from such a mechanistic approach. Systems thinking is both useful and necessary for understanding and addressing these major systemic challenges. Leaders who seek to address these major problems and issues will be required to influence across multiple systemic boundaries, with systems thinking providing the foundation for the required system leadership.

## Systems thinking and sustainability

To effectively manage critical societal challenges, researchers and practitioners can benefit from expanded understanding of the dynamic interactions among interconnected systems (Whiteman, Walker, & Perego, 2013). Systems thinking provides a framework for understanding complex economic, social, and ecological systems (Holling, 2001). Because sustainability is a complex economic, social, and ecological system, based upon the triple bottom line of people, planet, and profits, systems thinking offers an essential method for addressing sustainability issues. Systems thinking was previously identified as useful for developing a broad perspective and overall structures, patterns, and cycles in systems (McNamara, 2006) and addressing complex or complicated situations that cannot be solved by any single actor. Since the 1990s, numerous management scholars have recognized that highly complex and interdependent social systems require a systems approach, and that because these systems are situated within natural systems, business is significantly dependent on nature (Gladwin, Kennelly, & Krause, 1995; Marcus, Kurucz, & Colbert, 2010; Roome, 2011; Starik & Rands, 1995; Whiteman, Forbes, Niemelä, & Chapin, 2004).

Achieving sustainability will require changes to how existing organizations and systems operate. Systems thinking is the most appropriate problem-solving framework for sustainability (Siebert, 2018) and may represent the next phase in the evolution of sustainability (Confino, 2012). Systems thinking is appropriate for sustainability because it involves relational learning and thinking, and coordinating a diversity of knowledge, enabling complex circumstances to be understood as adaptive processes (Tarrant & Thiele, 2016). Although systems thinking has been found to be important in the operationalization of sustainability, systems thinking has not yet been widely applied in sustainable development (Davidson & Venning, 2011). Moreover, the failure to use systems thinking results in less effective decision-making processes (Davidson & Venning, 2011; Porter & Cordoba, 2009). The advantage of applying the systems thinking approach to sustainability issues originates in understanding the dynamic interconnections between numerous actors across broad social, economic, and ecological systems (Lozano, 2008; Valente, 2012; Williams, Kennedy, Philipp, & Whiteman, 2017). Acknowledging the interdependence within and among "systems, and exploring the relationship which these interconnections represent, is a learning pathway to a systems thinking perspective" (Stibbe, 2009, p. 88). Because interconnections are the most important aspect of sustainability management, systems thinking provides a potential method for their understanding (Barile et al., 2018).

The complexity of sustainability and the necessity for a systems thinking approach to sustainability are increasingly acknowledged and considered essential for overcoming the prevailing reductionist methods (Barile et al., 2018). Systems thinking has been proposed as a management approach to the uncertain sustainability context, to visualize and execute the integration of the economic, social, and environmental aspects of sustainability to enable communities to foster both human and ecological well-being (Smith, 2011). From a systems thinking context, sustainability has been defined as "the ability of systems to persist, adapt, transform or transition in the face of constantly changing conditions" (Williams et al., 2017, p. 13). Ben-Eli (2018) offered the following systems-based definition of sustainability:

> A dynamic equilibrium in the process of interaction between a population and the carrying capacity of its environment such that the population develops to express its full potential without producing irreversible adverse effects on the carrying capacity of the environment upon which it depends.
> (p. 1340)

Sustainability cannot be understood absent a systems approach, because understanding sustainability requires basic understanding of general system behavior and specific understanding of human and environmental systems (Clayton & Radcliffe, 1996).

Porter and Cordoba (2009) categorized systems thinking worldviews into three general classifications: functionalist, interpretative, and complex adaptive.

These perspectives differ based on the complexity of the situation and represent the range and development of systems thinking approaches relevant to sustainability. Functionalist systems find basis in the natural sciences (Porter & Cordoba, 2009) and are linear and mechanistic (Sawyer, 2005). Interpretative systems are interdependent, integrated, and transformative in structure (Hammond, 2003; Rabinow & Sullivan, 1979), and complex adaptive systems are able to self-organize, learn from experience, and adjust to changes in the external environment (Ashton, 2009; Rotmans & Loorbach, 2009). The interpretative and complex adaptive categories of system perspectives are most relevant to sustainability because the environmental, economic, and social systems consist of large numbers of independent, interactive, and self-interested actors, while demonstrating interdependent, holistic, evolutionary attributes. Wang et al. (2014) proposed an interpretative approach to systems thinking for sustainability, situating sustainability as a dynamic learning process. Anticipatory planning and related operations are necessary to reverse unsustainable practices and establish resilience (Wang et al., 2014). Interpretive approaches are beneficial for situations with contradictory priorities, which may occur with different interpretations of sustainability, because systems thinking requires an "ongoing process of examination, learning, reframing and action, based on a mutually agreed definition of sustainability within a particular context" (Porter & Cordoba, 2009, p. 337).

While von Bertalanffy (1968a, 1968b) is frequently cited regarding general systems theory, the contribution of cybernetics is the result of the work of Beer (Beer, 1972a, 1972b, 1985). Systems thinking and cybernetics provide a two-fold contribution in examining complex system behavior and relationships, such as those that generally characterize sustainability issues (Barile et al., 2018). First, systems thinking can help identify sustainability issues that are firmly entrenched in our societal structures and culture. Second, systems thinking can help identify the recurring conditions of possibility of the crisis. Both contributions are essential for understanding the deep dynamics of unsustainability (Barile et al., 2018).

Sustainability leaders must balance the relative autonomy and survival propensity of organizations, with acknowledging their roles and responsibilities within broader systems (van Marrewijk, 2003). A sustainable community is one whose forward-thinking actions are resilient against social and environmental events, while not limiting the social benefits and ecological health of future generations (Siebert, 2018). Systems thinking is an appropriate tool for achieving sustainable communities (Siebert, 2018), and system leaders possess the systemic understanding necessary to influence the necessary sustainability action.

Williams et al. (2017) identified several essential theoretical concepts useful in understanding sustainability from a systems thinking approach: interconnections, feedback loops, adaptive capacity, emergence, and self-organization. However, these concepts should not be considered or applied independently because they are interrelated. System components are interconnected through feedback loops (Kunz et al., 2013), and understanding these components and corresponding interconnections enables understanding of the total system dynamics (Merali & Allen, 2011). Self-organization stimulates advanced emergent structures and processes (Dougherty & Dunn, 2011; Rotmans & Loorbach, 2009), with macro-level system adaptation regulated by local-level self-organization and emergence operations (Merali & Allen, 2011). When you investigate the source of sustainability behaviors and actions, you find a level of relationship-based perspectives and experiences, behind which lies the origin: the journey to an increased sense of connectedness (Laszlo et al., 2012).

Understanding system interconnections is essential for organizational leadership and the complex system management for sustainability (Metcalf & Benn, 2013), because the interconnected system components regulate entire system behavior (Merali & Allen, 2011). Feedback loops are the secondary effects resulting from a primary effect of one component on another, influencing the degree of that effect. Feedback loops produce system interconnections (Kunz et al., 2013), and the consequences of those feedbacks loops must be fully understood to prevent unpredictable system behavior (Allenby, 2009). The adaptive capacity of a system describes the ability of system participants to sustain basic structure and manage resilience (Ehrenfeld, 2007; Holling, 2001; Walker & Salt, 2006; Whiteman et al., 2004). Resilience describes the extent of change a system can handle while maintaining the same purpose, structure, and feedbacks (Walker & Salt, 2006). Adaptive capacity enables managers and complex systems to continuously learn from experience (Ferreira, Lopes, & Morais, 2006; Sterman, 2001; Valente, 2010), resulting in increased competitiveness, endurance, and resilience (Valente, 2010). Emergence appears in complex systems when unique, advanced networks and patterns emerge from interaction among systems variables (Rotmans & Loorbach, 2009), and it occurs when systems continually adapt to complex feedback loops and co-evolve with their environments (Batten, 2009; Dougherty & Dunne, 2011; Porter, 2006; Rotmans & Loorbach, 2009; Sterman, 2001). Self-organization describes "the ability of a system to structure itself, to create new structure, to learn, or diversify" (Meadows, 2009, p. 188), and it occurs when dynamics, patterns, and structures emerge inside the system absent any external influence (Batten, 2009; Rotmans & Loorbach, 2009; Sterman, 2001).

## Systems thinking as a foundation for system leadership

The systems thinking approach helps simplify the complexity and dynamism of the environment, providing a foundation for constructing ideas (Ramosaj & Berisha, 2014). As previously noted, systems thinking involves an "ongoing process of examination, learning, reframing and action, based on a mutually agreed definition of sustainability within a particular context" (Porter & Cordoba, 2009, p. 337). Systems thinking provides the mechanism to systemically understand situations that may be complicated, enabling users to see the big picture, and identify and address multiple leverage points to support beneficial change (Learning for Sustainability, 2019).

The systems thinking approach is essential for understanding and interpreting systems, a key requirement for system leadership. The application of systems thinking strengthens a holistic decision-making framework, by stimulating a comprehensive evaluation of goals and objectives, and the fundamental relationships among inputs, throughputs, outputs, processes, feedback, and review (Davidson & Venning, 2011). Moreover, systems thinking ensures that all essential system components are included in the framework (Wang, Van Wart, & Lebredo, 2014). This is significant because system components are understood in the context of contributions made to the entire system outcomes (van Krieken et al., 2006).

The iceberg model provides an excellent mechanism for understanding situations systemically to solve complex problems (Ambler, 2013). The iceberg model offers the following benefits: shifting focus from actions and symptoms to structures, thinking, and beliefs; assisting in development of mental models among organizational and team members to enhance consistent and appropriate action; and enhancing understanding of system leverage points (Ambler, 2013). This model is appropriate for systems thinking because, similar to approximately two-thirds of an iceberg being located below the surface, much of the structure and thinking of the systems with which we interact on a daily basis are not readily visible (Ambler, 2013). Seeing and understanding the entire system, including components and activities that are not readily visible, is essential to maneuvering and changing complex systems.

Examining the layers of the iceberg reveals several components: events, trends and patterns, structure, and a mental model (Ambler, 2013). Events occur on the surface level of the iceberg and answer the question, "what happened?" Linear thinking limits our understanding and our ability to create change, because it causes us to view the world as a series of events, superficially attributing cause and effect assumptions. The iceberg model provides a deeper level of understanding by collectively examining series of events to identify trends and patterns, which can then be examined to identify the dynamics causing the trend. Systemic structures are usually influenced by the beliefs, thinking, or perspectives of leaders, which may impact interpersonal dynamics, such as conflict, leadership, or change management approaches. If one can modify organizational thinking, beliefs, and perspectives, organizational-level behavior and outcomes will correspondingly change (Ambler, 2013).

An essential step in understanding and diagnosing systems is the art of asking questions (Ambler, 2013). By using the iceberg model, system leaders can ask discerning questions at all levels of the iceberg (Ambler, 2013). The primary objective of the iceberg model is to identify and influence system leverage points. This process is both art and science, requiring shifts in thinking from events to structures to beliefs, formulating better questions, and developing theories about the structure and underlying beliefs influencing the structure. This process enables leaders to experiment with alternative methods of system change and make additional adjustments based on feedback (Ambler, 2013).

The appropriateness of systems thinking for both system leadership and sustainability have been demonstrated. In the following section, we will explore how system leadership is an appropriate method for achieving sustainability, based on the systems theory, systems thinking, and system leadership foundations established in previous sections.

## System leadership for sustainability

According to Timmins (2015), system change is achieved by beginning with a coalition of the willing and building an evidence base outwards; involving all stakeholders; having constancy of purpose with a degree of flexibility; and possessing leadership stability. System leaders within the healthcare industry demonstrated that leaders can achieve significant success provided credit is not taken for organizational achievements (Timmins, 2015). System leaders are not heroic individuals who accomplish difficult achievements through seemingly impossible means (Timmins, 2015). Instead, they acknowledge the need to collaborate and build alliances by encouraging colleagues and stakeholders to collaborate toward a better future. System leaders lead through influence and persuasion, acknowledging that achieving sustainable progress takes time, and are resilient in the face of obstacles, maintaining steadfast purpose despite resistance. According to one of the leaders interviewed by Timmins, system leaders succeed by "being comfortable with chaos" (p. 4).

There is increasing recognition that no single organization can facilitate the scale of environmental, social, and economic change necessary to address the significant challenges currently faced by humankind (Confino, 2012). There is also increasing recognition that the interdependency of contemporary globalized society will require coordination across every system component that requires change (Confino, 2012). Scalability of sustainability efforts and initiatives across every organization, industry, and sector is essential to achieve significant impact. While countless individuals and organizations are acting to achieve a sustainable future, these efforts will be more successful with collaboration, communication, and cooperation. Leaders will be required who can cross boundaries to influence collective, scalable sustainability impact. These leaders must understand and appreciate systems, because the influence and change needed is systemic in nature.

To achieve sustainability, social, economic, and environmental systems must be influenced and changed. Systemic influence and change requires leaders capable of thinking systemically. While these leaders exist, many more leaders with systems thinking ability are required to achieve the necessary scale and impact. Many previous and current sustainability actors are exhibiting system leadership absent any knowledge that such a concept exists or that they are leading in this manner. Several of these system leaders are introduced or interviewed in subsequent chapters. While this section summarized the suitability of system leadership for sustainability, Chapter 2 describes in greater detail why system leadership is appropriate for achieving sustainability.

## System leadership from a global perspective

Sustainability is a global issue, requiring global leadership and action. Several factors have influenced the current period of globalization, with technology and communication the most prominent catalysts. Advances in technology, combined with instant communication, have made global trade and migration easier and more common. While these advances have benefited humankind, they have likewise influenced the unsustainable nature of contemporary globalization. The internal combustion engine, powered by fossil fuel consumption, has been the primary technological driver for the previous few centuries of globalization and subsequent economic growth. While this technology has significantly increased in efficiency, fossil fuel consumption has increased exponentially, adversely impacting air and water quality and surface and ocean temperatures, and has contributed to military conflict.

Future economic growth and globalization are unsustainable using existing models and technology. Innovative technologies exist and are being developed for reducing humankind's environmental impact. However, these technologies are not being implemented consistently across the planet. Moreover, the resources necessary to develop and implement alternative technologies and economic models are primarily controlled by wealthier developed nations. Equitable proliferation of sustainable technology and economic models will require leaders who can influence entire economic and social systems. These leaders must not only understand and be able to influence systems, they must also be capable of appreciating and respecting numerous cultural, political, and sociological perspectives. System leaders are needed globally, who are capable of understanding and influencing systems at local, regional, and global levels.

## Barriers to system leadership implementation

Timmins (2015) identified the barriers to effective system leadership to be money, training, incentives, and the existing system architecture including regulation. Fiscal, regulatory, and organizational pressures continue to influence individuals and organizations to focus on short-term survival, instead of long-term changes that may modify or even enhance organizational activity. Frequently, existing systems get in the way of system change and system leadership (Timmins, 2015). Several barriers to implementing system leadership with the context of sustainability are legal, economic, cultural, organizational, and philosophical in nature. These barriers and challenges are examined in greater detail in Chapter 4, within the specific sectors examined in Chapters 5 through 8, and at the individual level in Chapter 9. The problems with implementing such an approach are considered, especially in organizations and economies with short-term political and economic pressures that inhibit large-scale systems approach and long-term aims. To achieve effective, large-scale, long-term sustainability success, these barriers will need to be addressed, especially within the context of current and anticipated economic, social, and political climates nationally and globally.

## Conclusion

This chapter introduced the concepts of system leadership, systems theory, and systems thinking. Systems thinking was described as a foundation for both system leadership and sustainability. System leadership was introduced as an appropriate method for achieving sustainability, based on the systems theory, systems thinking, and system leadership foundations established in previous sections. The focus of the systems approach to leadership is not on leader behavior or conduct, but on the leader's determination to include the external environment and corresponding relationships in the leadership process (Ramosaj & Berisha, 2014). System leadership was examined from a global perspective, and the barriers to system leadership effectiveness and implementation were summarized. The chapters that follow examine in greater detail why system leadership is appropriate for sustainability; the core competencies, skills, and characteristics of system leadership; and the development of system leadership. Subsequent chapters examine system leadership among specific sectors and at the individual level. The final chapter will summarize system leadership for sustainability and include future recommendations, research, and trends.

## Chapter reflection questions

1 System leadership has been successfully applied to achieve sustainable improvements within the educational sector, and on a more limited basis within the healthcare industry. However, system leadership has not been applied in a broader, cross-boundary manner as proposed in this chapter and text. How can system leadership be applied on a broader scale across multiple organizations, industries, sectors, and nations?
2 While system leadership has been proposed as a method of accelerating progress against major societal problems (Senge et al., 2015), existing literature has not examined system leadership as appropriate for addressing sustainability. How can a relatively new leadership model be applied in a field in which this model has not been previously examined?
3 How would you employ system leadership to address an issue as critical and urgent as sustainability?

## References

Allenby, B. (2009). The industrial ecology of emerging technologies: Complexity and the reconstruction of the world. *Journal of Industrial Ecology*, *13*(2), 168–183. doi:10.1111/j.1530-9290.2009.00114.x

Ambler, G. (2013). *Systems thinking as a leadership practice*. Johannesburg, South Africa: Author.

Ashton, W. S. (2009). The structure, function, and evolution of a regional industrial ecosystem. *Journal of Industrial Ecology*, *13*(2), 228–246. doi:10.1111/j.1530-9290.2009.00111.x

Barile, S. (2000). *Contributi sul pensiero sistemico in economia d'impresa* [Contributions on systemic thinking in business economics]. Salerno, Italy: Arnia.

Barile, S. (2009). *Management sistemico vitale* [Vital systemic management] (Vol. 1). Torino, Italy: Giappichelli.

Barile, S., Orecchini, F., Saviano, M., & Farioli, F. (2018). People, technology, and governance for sustainability: The contribution of systems and cyber-systemic thinking. *Sustainability Science, 13*(5), 1197–1208. doi:10.1007/s11625-018-0621-y

Barile, S., Pels, J., Polese, F., & Saviano, M. (2012a). An introduction to the viable systems approach and its contribution to marketing. *Journal of Business Market Management, 5*(2), 54–78. Retrieved from https://ssrn.com/abstract=2239812

Barile, S., & Saviano, M. (2011). Foundations of systems thinking: The structure-system paradigm. *Various Authors, Contributions to Theoretical and Practical Advances in Management: A Viable Systems Approach (VSA): ASVSA, Associazione per la Ricerca sui Sistemi Vitali: International Printing*, 1–24. Retrieved from https://ssrn.com/abstract=2044579

Barile, S., & Saviano, M. (2018). Complexity and sustainability in management: Insights from a systems perspective. In *Social dynamics in a systems perspective* (pp. 39–63). Cham, Switzerland: Springer.

Barile, S., Saviano, M., Polese, F., & Di Nauta, P. (2012b). Reflections on service systems boundaries: A viable systems perspective: The case of the London Borough of Sutton. *European Management Journal, 30*(5), 451–465. doi:10.1016/j.emj.2012.05.004

Batten, D. F. (2009). Fostering industrial symbiosis with agent-based simulation and participatory modeling. *Journal of Industrial Ecology, 13*(2), 197–213. doi:10.1111/j.1530-9290.2009.00115.x

Beer, S. (1972a). *Brain of the firm*. London, England: Penguin Group.

Beer, S. (1972b). *Brain of the firm*. Harmondsworth, England: Allen Lane and Penguin Group.

Beer, S. (1985). *Diagnosing the system for organizations*. London, England: John Wiley & Sons.

Ben-Eli, M. U. (2018). Sustainability: Definition and five core principles, a systems perspective. *Sustainability Science, 13*, 1337–1343. doi:10.1007/s11625-018-0564-3

Clayton, A. M., & Radcliffe, N. J. (1996). *Sustainability: A systems approach*. London, England: Earthscan.

Confino, J. (2012, October 15). *The art of systems thinking in driving sustainable transformation*. Retrieved from www.theguardian.com/sustainable-business/systems-thinking-sustainable-transformation

Davidson, K. M., & Venning, J. (2011). Sustainability decision-making frameworks and the application of systems thinking: An urban context. *Local Environment, 16*(3), 213–228. doi:10.1080/13549839.2011.565464

Dougherty, D., & Dunne, D. D. (2011). Organizing ecologies of complex innovation. *Organization Science, 22*(5), 1214–1223. doi:10.1287/orsc.1100.0605

Ehrenfeld, J. R. (2007). Would industrial ecology exist without sustainability in the background? *Journal of Industrial Ecology, 11*(1), 73–84. doi:10.1162/jiec.2007.1177

Ehrenfeld, J. R. (2012). Beyond the brave new world: Business for sustainability. In P. Bansal & A. J. Hoffman (Eds.), *Oxford handbook of business and the natural environment* (pp. 611–619). Oxford, England: Oxford University Press.

Ferreira, A. J. D., Lopes, M. A. R., & Morais, J. P. F. (2006). Environmental management and audit schemes implementation as an educational tool for sustainability. *Journal of Cleaner Production, 14*(9–11), 973–982. doi:10.1016/j.jclepro.2006.01.003

Fullan, M. (2004). *Systems thinkers in action: Moving beyond the standards plateau*. London and Nottingham, England: DfES Innovation Unit and NCSL.

Fullan, M. (2005). *Leadership and sustainability: System thinkers in action*. London, England: Sage Publications.

Gaziulusoy, A. İ., Boyle, C., & McDowall, R. (2013). System innovation for sustainability: A systemic double-flow scenario method for companies. *Journal of Cleaner Production, 45*, 104–116. doi:10.1016/j.jclepro.2012.05.013

Gladwin, T. N., Kennelly, J. J., & Krause, T. S. (1995). Shifting paradigms for sustainable development: Implications for management theory and research. *Academy of Management Review, 20*(4), 874–907. doi:10.5465/amr.1995.9512280024

Golinelli, G. M. (2010). *Viable systems approach (VSA): Governing business dynamics*. Alphen aan den Rijn, Netherlands: Cedam Kluwer.

Hadid, W., Mansouri, S. A., & Gallear, D. (2016). Is Lean service promising? A socio-technical perspective. *International Journal of Operations & Production Management, 36*, 618–642. doi:10.1108/IJOPM-01-2015-0008

Hammond, D. (2003). *The science of synthesis: Exploring the social implications of general systems theory*. Boulder, CO: University Press of Colorado.

Holling, C. S. (2001). Understanding the complexity of economic, ecological, and social systems. *Ecosystems, 4*(5), 390–405. doi:10.1007/s10021-001-0101-5

Hopkins, D., & Higham, R. (2007). System leadership: Mapping the landscape. *School Leadership and Management, 27*(2), 147–166. doi:10.1080/13632430701237289

Kaine, G., & Cowan, L. (2011). Using general systems theory to understand how farmers manage variability. *Systems Research and Behavioral Science, 28*(3), 231–244. doi:10.1002/sres.1073

Kim, D. (2018). *Palette of systems thinking tools*. Boston, MA: Leverage Networks. Retrieved from https://thesystemsthinker.com/palette-of-systems-thinking-tools/

Kunz, N. C., Moran, C. J., & Kastelle, T. (2013). Conceptualising "coupling" for sustainability implementation in the industrial sector: A review of the field and projection of future research opportunities. *Journal of Cleaner Production, 53*, 69–80. doi:10.1016/j.jclepro.2013.03.040

Laszlo, C., Brown, J. S., Sherman, D., Barros, I., Boland, B., Ehrenfeld, J., . . . Werder, P. (2012). Flourishing: A vision for business and the world. *Journal of Corporate Citizenship, 46*(2012), 31–51. Retrieved from www.jstor.org/stable/jcorpciti.46.31

Learning for Sustainability. (2019). *Systems thinking*. Canterbury, New Zealand: Will Allen & Associates. Retrieved from http://learningforsustainability.net/systems-thinking/

Lozano, R. (2008). Envisioning sustainability three-dimensionally. *Journal of Cleaner Production, 16*, 1838–1846. doi:10.1016/j.jclepro.2008.02.008

Marcus, J., Kurucz, E. C., & Colbert, B. A. (2010). Conceptions of the business-society-nature interface: Implications for management scholarship. *Business & Society, 49*(3), 402–438. doi:10.1177/0007650310368827

McNamara, C. (2006). *Field guide to consulting and organizational development: A collaborative and systems approach to performance, change and learning*. Minneapolis, MN: Authenticity Consulting.

Meadows, D. (2009). *Thinking in systems: A primer* (1st ed.). Hartford, VT: Chelsea Green Publishing.

Merali, Y., & Allen, P. (2011). Complexity and systems thinking. In P. Allen, S. Maguire, & B. McKelvey (Eds.), *The SAGE handbook of complexity and management* (pp. 31–52). Thousand Oaks, CA: Sage Publications.

Metcalf, L., & Benn, S. (2013). Leadership for sustainability: An evolution of leadership ability. *Journal of Business Ethics, 112*(3), 369–384. doi:10.1007/s10551-012-1278-6

Mingers, J., & White, L. (2010). A review of the recent contribution of systems thinking to operational research and management science. *European Journal of Operational Research, 207*(3), 1147–1161. doi:10.1016/j.ejor.2009.12.019

Northouse, P. G. (2018). *Leadership: Theory and practice* (8th ed.). Thousand Oaks, CA: Sage Publications.

Pels, J., Barile, S., Saviano, M., Polese, F., & Carrubbo, L. (2014). The contribution of VSA and SDL perspectives to strategic thinking in emerging economies. *Managing Service Quality, 24*(6), 565–591. doi:10.1108/MSQ-09-2013-0199

Porter, T. B. (2006). Coevolution as a research framework for organizations and the natural environment. *Organization & Environment, 19*(4), 479–504. doi:10.1177/1086026606294958

Porter, T. B., & Cordoba, J. (2009). Three views of systems theories and their implications for sustainability education. *Journal of Management Education, 33*(3), 323–347. doi:10.1177/1052562908323192

Rabinow, P., & Sullivan, W. (1979). The interpretive turn: Emergence of an approach. In P. Rabinow & W. Sullivan (Eds.), *Interpretative social science* (pp. 1–21). Los Angeles, CA: University of California Press.

Ramosaj, B., & Berisha, G. (2014). Systems theory and systems approach to leadership. *Iliria International Review, 1*, 59–76. Retrieved from http://iliriapublications.org/index.php/iir/article/download/53/48

Robèrt, K. H., Broman, G., Waldron, D., Ny, H., Byggeth, S., Cook, D., . . . Haraldsson, H. V. (2004). *Strategic leadership towards sustainability*. Karlskrona, Sweden: Blekinge Institute of Technology.

Robertson, M. (2014). *Sustainability principles and practice*. Abingdon, England: Routledge.

Rockström, J., Steffen, W., Noone, K., Persson, Å., Chapin III, F. S., Lambin, E. F., . . . Nykvist, B. (2009). A safe operating space for humanity. *Nature, 461*(7263), 472–475. doi:10.1038/461472a

Roome, N. (2011). Looking back, thinking forward: Distinguishing between weak and strong sustainability. In P. Bansal & A. J. Hoffman (Eds.), *The Oxford handbook of business and the natural environment* (pp. 620–629). Oxford, England: Oxford University Press.

Rotmans, J., & Loorbach, D. (2009). Complexity and transition management. *Journal of Industrial Ecology, 13*(2), 184–196. doi:10.1111/j.1530-9290.2009.00116.x

Sawyer, R. (2005). *Social emergence: Societies as complex systems*. Cambridge, England: Cambridge University Press.

Senge, P. M. (1990). *The fifth discipline: The art & practice of the learning organization*. New York, NY: Doubleday and Currency.

Senge, P. M., Hamilton, H., & Kania, J. (2015). The dawn of system leadership. *Stanford Social Innovation Review, 13*(1), 27–33. Retrieved from https://ssir.org/articles/entry/the_dawn_of_system_leadership

Siebert, M. (2018). *Systems thinking and how it can help build a sustainable world*. Corvallis, OR: Post Carbon Institute. Retrieved from www.resilience.org/stories/2018-07-11/systems-thinking-and-how-it-can-help-build-a-sustainable-world/

Smith, T. (2011). Using critical systems thinking to foster an integrated approach to sustainability: A proposal for development practitioners. *Environmental Development & Sustainability, 13*(1), 1–17. doi:10.1007/s10668-010-9243-y

Starik, M., & Rands, G. P. (1995). Weaving an integrated web: Multilevel and multisystem perspectives of ecologically sustainable organizations. *Academy of Management Review, 20*(4), 908–935. doi:10.5465/amr.1995.9512280025

Steffen, W., Richardson, K., Rockström, J., Cornell, S. E., Fetzer, I., Bennett, E. M., . . . Folke, C. (2015). Planetary boundaries: Guiding human development on a changing planet. *Science, 347*(6223), 1259855. doi:10.1126/science.1259855

Sterman, J. D. (2001). System dynamics modeling: Tools for learning in a complex world. *California Management Review, 43*(4), 8–25. doi:10.2307/41166098

Stibbe, A. E. (2009). *The handbook of sustainability literacy: Skills for a changing world*. Cambridge, England: Green Books.

Tarrant, S. P., & Thiele, L. P. (2016). Practice makes pedagogy: John Dewey and skills-based sustainability education. *International Journal of Sustainability in Higher Education, 17*(1), 54–67. doi:10.1108/IJSHE-09-2014-0127

Timmins, N. (2015). *The practice of system leadership: Being comfortable with chaos*. London, England: The King's Fund. Retrieved from www.kingsfund.org.uk/sites/default/files/field/field_publication_file/System-leadership-Kings-Fund-May-2015.pdf

Valente, M. (2010). Demystifying the struggles of private sector paradigmatic change: Business as an agent in a complex adaptive system. *Business & Society, 49*(3), 439–476. doi:10.1177/0007650310369376

Valente, M. (2012). Theorizing firm adoption of sustaincentrism. *Organization Studies, 33*(4), 563–591. doi:10.1177/0170840612443455

van Krieken, R., Habibis, D., Smith, P., Hutchins, B., Haralambos, M., & Holden, R. (2006). *Sociology: Themes and perspectives*. Sydney, Australia: Pearson Education.

van Marrewijk, M. (2003). Concepts and definitions of CSR and corporate sustainability: Between agency and communion. *Journal of Business Ethics, 44*(2/3), 95–105. doi:10.1023/A:1023331212247

von Bertalanffy, L. (1968a). *General system theory: Foundations, development, applications* (Revised ed.). New York, NY: George Braziller.

von Bertalanffy, L. (1968b). General system theory: A critical review. In W. Buckley (Ed.), *Modern systems research for the behavioral scientist* (pp. 11–30). Chicago, IL: Aldine.

Walker, B., & Salt, D. (2006). *Resilience thinking*. Washington, DC: Island Press.

Wang, X., Van Wart, M., & Lebredo, N. (2014). Sustainability leadership in a local government context. *Public Performance & Management Review, 37*, 339–364. doi:10.2753/PMR1530-9576370301

Whiteman, G., Forbes, B. C., Niemelä, J., & Chapin III, F. S. (2004). Bringing feedback and resilience of high-latitude ecosystems into the corporate boardroom. *AMBIO: A Journal of the Human Environment, 33*(6), 371–376. doi:10.1579/0044-7447-33.6.371

Whiteman, G., Walker, B., & Perego, P. (2013). Planetary boundaries: Ecological foundations for corporate sustainability. *Journal of Management Studies, 50*(2), 307–336. doi:10.1111/j.1467-6486.2012.01073.x

Williams, A., Kennedy, S., Philipp, F., & Whiteman, G. (2017). Systems thinking: A review of sustainability management research. *Journal of Cleaner Production, 148*, 866–881. doi:10.1016/j.jclepro.2017.02.002

World Commission on Environment and Development. (1987). *Our common future*. Oxford, England: Oxford University Press.

# 2 Why system leadership is appropriate for sustainability

## Introduction

The earth exists within a vast solar system, existing within a vast galaxy of stars, which is a small, somewhat insignificant member of the greater universe. Numerous systems operate within and upon the earth, each consisting of multiple subsystems. Some of the systems are naturally occurring, while others are human made – economic, social, and geopolitical systems. These natural and human-made systems do not operate independently, but are interdependent, with the human-made systems unable to survive for long absent the natural systems (although the natural systems are quite capable of survival absent human-made systems). Economic activity would cease if the atmospheric systems ceased functioning, geopolitical systems would revert to anarchy if the ecosystem collapsed, and social systems cannot survive long absent the stability of all global systems. Few secondary school students would question the existence of, and relationships between and among, the countless systems within which humankind exists. Yet, while most contemporary leaders and followers acknowledge and accept the systemic interconnection and interdependence of the world we inhabit, these systems are still frequently treated as mechanistic processes, influenced by Newtonian and Industrial Age thinking. Therefore, as a result of this machine-like view, most of the natural and human-made systems on earth are strained, misaligned, and improperly managed.

When an automobile does not operate properly, a mechanic performs a diagnosis, followed by a tune-up or other repair designed to return the automobile to optimal performance. Similar responses, such as restructuring, lay-offs, additional investment, facility closures, and other mechanistic actions, are applied when businesses and organizations are not performing optimally. However, achieving a sustainable future requires more than mechanical adjustments – entire systems must be adjusted and properly maintained. The actions required to achieve a sustainable future must be initiated and influenced by system leaders, who are able to understand the interconnectedness and interdependence of all systems, subsystems, and entities and lead collective action to identify and solve problems.

Sustainability leadership is defined as taking responsibility for understanding and responding to sustainability challenges, regardless of whether the person holds a formal leadership position (Ferdig, 2007). This definition challenges common assumptions about who qualifies as a leader, further suggesting sustainability leaders lead *with* rather than *over* others, while considering the long-term feasibility of complex, interconnected living systems (Ferdig, 2007). The Sustainability Leadership Institute defines sustainability leaders as "individuals who are compelled to make a difference by deepening their awareness of themselves in relation to the world around them. In doing so, they adopt new ways of seeing, thinking and interacting that result in innovative, sustainable solutions" (n.d.). Addressing and managing sustainability issues require systemic change and competent change management agents. The degree of change required to ensure a sustainable future is significant and will undoubtedly be characterized by disagreement and conflict. Sustainability leaders acknowledge that participation in change, and the resulting conflict, stimulates new perspectives, discoveries, and innovations (Ferdig, 2007; Iftakhar & Bahauddin, 2018) that can reinvigorate organizations, communities, and the planet (Ferdig, 2007). Addressing sustainability issues frequently involves stakeholder disagreement, uncertainty, and associated problems, supporting the need for an interdisciplinary leadership approach that is aligned with sustainability (Shriberg & MacDonald, 2013). System leadership provides the model for such a leadership theory and practice.

Achieving a sustainable future will require innovation at all levels, beginning at the organizational level and extending across boundaries through industries, sectors, and systems. Effective sustainability decision-making requires a comprehensive systems approach because economic, social, and ecological systems are highly interconnected (Fiksel, 2006). However, the current collection of steady-state sustainability models are oversimplified, necessitating a better understanding of the dynamic, adaptive behavior and resilience of complex systems (Fiksel, 2006). Without this understanding, there is a risk of unintended consequences, such as the adoption of an innovative sustainable technology having an adverse effect on another technology or industry (Fiksel, 2006).

To cultivate innovative organizational sustainability, it is essential for sustainability leaders to accept and explain complexity, appreciate history and experience, share leadership and encourage innovation, collaborate across boundaries, demonstrate critical thinking, behave in an ethical and just manner, and reflect constantly (Stillman, 2015). Sustainability leaders are capable of interpreting, synthesizing, and translating complex issues; mitigating risk, uncertainty, and crises; identifying and acting on opportunities; solving problems; and resolving conflicts (Visser & Courtice, 2011). They understand how complex systems, such as organizations and markets, operate and the range of alternatives for making beneficial improvements within those systems (Visser & Courtice, 2011). Innovative leadership is critical, because organizations in all sectors must integrate sustainability into strategic plans and operational activities in order for the 2030 sustainability target to be met (Iftakhar & Bahauddin, 2018). The creation of a sustainable future requires leaders capable of navigating the complexities of the anthropocentric era and influencing across visible and invisible boundaries.

In Chapter 1, we examined system leadership, defined as "seeking to achieve change across organizations where people do not have direct line management responsibility" (Timmins, 2015). Ghate (2015) defined system leadership with greater detail as "leadership across organisational and geopolitical boundaries, beyond individual professional disciplines, within diverse organisational and stakeholder cultures, often without direct managerial control. . . . [i]n order to effect change for positive social benefit across multiple and intersecting systems" (p. 2). A system leader was defined as a unique individual capable of seeing and comprehending the larger system and catalyzing collective leadership to proactively co-create the future (Senge, Hamilton, & Kania, 2015). In this chapter, we examine system leadership as a suitable method for addressing the complex change required for a sustainable future, building upon the suggestion by Senge and colleagues that solving the complex social problems of the 21st century will require system leaders capable of activating collective leadership.

System leadership requires collective leadership across and between organizations, systems, and subsystems. The three core capabilities that produce collective leadership are the ability to see the overall system, cultivate reflection and more innovative conversations, and transform the collective attention away from reactive problem solving to co-creation of the future (Senge et al., 2015). The unsustainable nature of contemporary society is a result of the short-term thinking of business and policy leaders. Because system leadership balances short-term reactive problem solving with long-term value creation (Senge et al., 2015), system leadership is a promising and appropriate leadership style for sustainability.

In this chapter, the following propositions, each based on the common characteristics of sustainability and system leadership, are examined to demonstrate system leadership as an appropriate leadership style for sustainability.

1 Sustainability is a natural environmental concept, the promotion of which requires leadership approaches based upon the natural environment structure.
2 Sustainability is a boundaryless concept, the promotion of which requires system leadership capable of transcending boundaries and artificial barriers and engaging multiple stakeholders both vertically and horizontally.
3 Sustainability is a complex, global concept, requiring leadership capable of seeing the big picture and influencing the entire system.

Figure 2.1 illustrates the System Leadership for Sustainability model proposed in this text. The competencies, perspectives, and leadership styles discussed in this chapter and Chapter 3, when combined, may result in system leadership for sustainability.

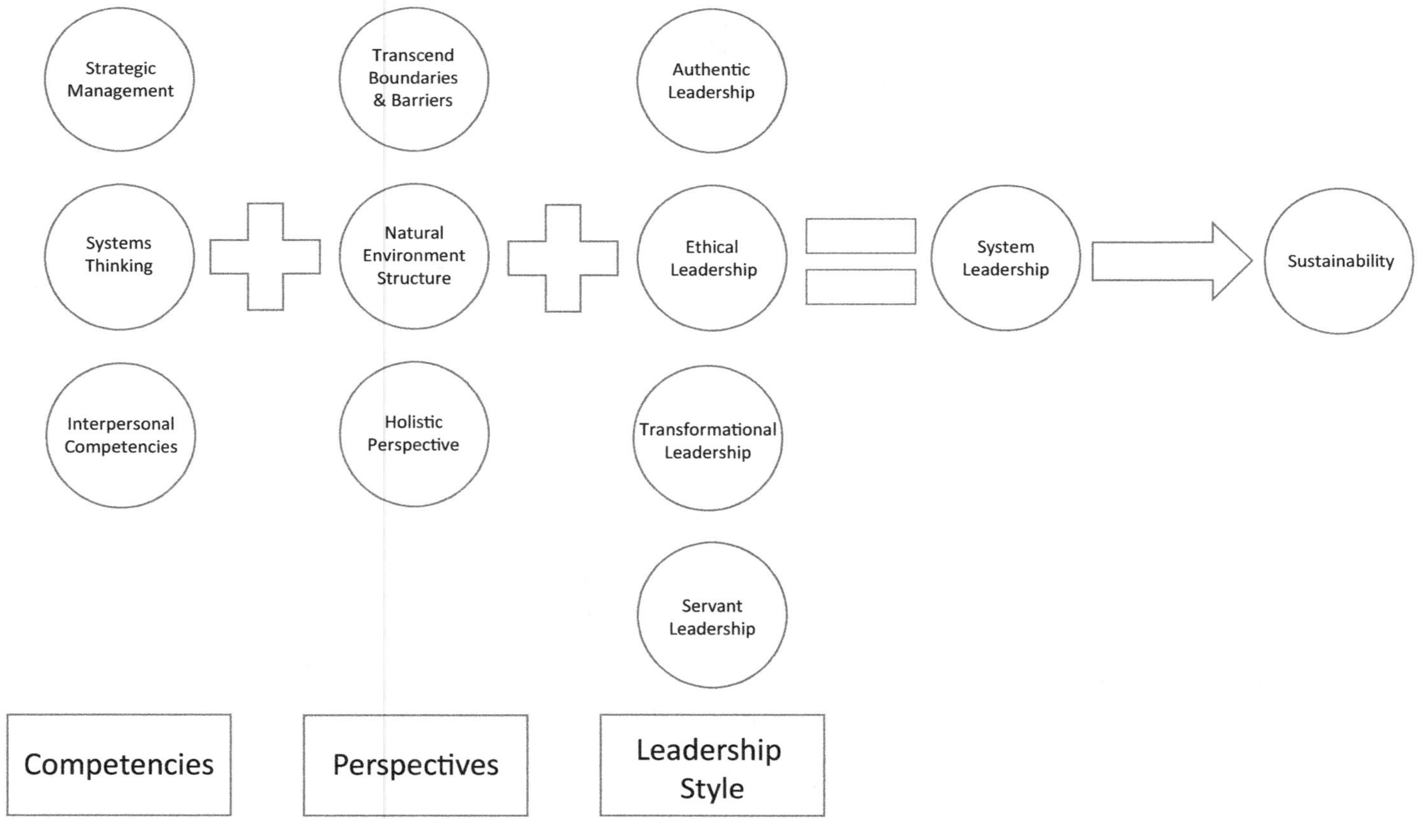


*Figure 2.1* System Leadership for Sustainability Model

## Sustainability leadership should be based on natural environmental structure

The first proposition to be considered in this chapter is: Sustainability is a natural environmental concept, the promotion of which requires leadership approaches based upon the natural environment structure. Existing leadership and environmental sustainability literature is anthropocentric, rooted in the mechanistic worldview of organizations and nature being managed by humans (MacGillivray, 2015). However, such mechanistic frameworks limit both the understanding and effectiveness of the development of sustainability strategies (MacGillivray, 2015). Sustainability leadership is based on a natural processes paradigm, instead of a mechanistic paradigm (Iftakhar & Bahauddin, 2018). Therefore, leaders who apply natural systems and processes in their sustainability worldviews enhance and authenticate their leadership abilities (MacGillivray, 2015). Moreover, it makes intuitive sense that the optimal way of solving problems that are essentially nature based is with approaches and solutions that are likewise nature based. An understanding of the interdependence between organizations and the natural environment is critical to a systemic sustainability leadership viewpoint, because organizations directly engage in feedback loops with the natural environment in the form of inputs and outputs (Starik & Kanashiro, 2013; Starik & Rands, 1995). This interdependent perspective of organizations and nature acknowledges systemic limits to growth within planetary boundaries, limited resources, and the interdependence of organizations, the economy, the environment, and society (Marcus, Kurucz, & Colbert, 2010; Rockström et al., 2009; Whiteman, Walker, & Perego, 2013; Winn & Pogutz, 2013).

Sustainability leadership is a complex role, requiring that leaders acknowledge and appreciate complexity. Iftakhar and Bahauddin (2018) suggest complexity is best understood by looking at nature as an example. Organizational and geopolitical systems and boundaries should be examined and understood in much the same way that we would analyze natural systems and boundaries. Moreover, these human-made systems and boundaries should be examined within the context of the interrelationship between human-made and natural systems and boundaries. According to Ostrom (2009), all natural resources are embedded in complex, social-ecological systems (SESs), consisting of various subsystems and variables within these subsystems at various levels similar to organisms which are composed of organs, which are composed of tissues, which are composed of cells, etc. (Pennisi, 2003). Understanding these systems, subsystems, and boundaries can lead to sustainable opportunities that are beneficial for multiple systems. For example, understanding the interrelationships among sustainable land uses demonstrates how sustainability actions in one area can complement, and even stimulate, sustainability actions in other areas, resulting in simultaneous, mutually beneficial outcomes (Daily & Ellison, 2002 – cited in Ferdig, 2007), such as environmental damage mitigation and job creation.

Complex natural processes and systems exhibit sustainable patterns and properties that offer important strategies for leadership (Iftakhar & Bahauddin, 2018). Leadership for sustainability is established on a natural systems worldview, instead of a Newtonian mechanistic worldview (Burns, Diamond-Vaught, & Bauman, 2015), because complex living systems exhibit sustainable characteristics and patterns, offering essential strategies for leadership (Barlow & Stone, 2011). The qualities of natural processes and systems that provide examples for leadership include resiliency, flexibility, awareness, creativity, and relationship (Wheatley, 2006). Because our planet is complicated, with multiple coexisting realities, living beings must be able to organize and adapt according to their environments. Therefore, sustainability leaders should possess qualities that are only found in natural, living systems, such as resiliency, flexibility, willingness to learn, and ability to self-renew (Iftakhar & Bahauddin, 2018).

Nature-based thinking is not isolated to sustainability leadership. Numerous innovators recognize and mimic naturally occurring processes in designing products, structures, and systems using biomimicry, which is "an approach to innovation that seeks sustainable solutions to human challenges by emulating nature's time-tested patterns and strategies" (Biomimicry Institute, 2018a). Innovators as early as Leonardo da Vinci in the 16th century observed and patterned inventions after natural processes and behavior (Romei, 2008). Contemporary examples of biomimicry include the Eastgate Building in Harare, Zimbabwe, with an internal climate control system patterned after termite mounds, and the Shinkansen bullet train, with a front-end design similar to a kingfisher beak, resulting in a quieter, faster, more energy-efficient high-speed train (Biomimicry Institute, 2018b).

Sustainability leadership is based upon natural systems thinking, which requires application of natural systems principles to facilitate outcomes consistent with dynamic, sustainable ecosystems (MacGillivray, 2015). Because systems thinking mirrors the processes and relationships witnessed in natural systems (Bateson, 2002), system leadership is, therefore, an appropriate process to influence and manage sustainability. While systems thinking has been successfully applied in various fields and disciplines (Nguyen & Bosch, 2013), including environmental conflict management (Elias, 2008), natural resource management (Ison, Maiteny, & Carr, 1997), business (Bashiri & Tabrizi, 2010), and decision-making (Maani & Maharraj, 2004), literature about systems thinking application in leadership has been primarily limited to the field of education (Fullan, 2004, 2005; Hill, 2006). However, systems thinking has the capacity to facilitate integrative thinking within the field of sustainability (Smith, 2011). Integrative thinking is necessary to resolve the decision-making paradoxes which result from economic considerations that contradict what is optimal from a social, ethical, or environmental viewpoint (Peterlin, Pearse, & Dimovski, 2015).

One example of the similarity between natural and social systems is the environmental boundaries occurring in natural systems, such as estuaries, that provide healthy, interactive, and productive ecological communities. MacGillivray

(2015) coined the term *intellectual estuary* to describe the diversity, richness, and potential productivity of boundaryless organizational environments, which mirrors the richness of estuaries in nature. Leadership between and among these intellectual estuaries provides the foundation for the second proposition about sustainability leadership.

## Sustainability leadership requires transcending boundaries and barriers

The second proposition to be considered in this chapter is: Sustainability is a boundaryless concept, the promotion of which requires system leadership capable of transcending boundaries and artificial barriers, engaging multiple stakeholders both vertically and horizontally. Peterlin et al. (2015) suggested a sustainable leadership perspective contributes to comprehensive strategic decision-making, by considering the long-term impact of decisions on multiple stakeholders. Much of the global sustainability movement has been influenced by the United Nations Sustainable Development Goals (SDG), also known as the 2030 Agenda, because the intent is for the SDGs to be accomplished by 2030. According to Iftakhar and Bahauddin (2018), achieving the SDGs will require the combined efforts of the public and private sectors, society, and individual citizens. Therefore, nurturing collaborative sustainability efforts will require leaders capable of understanding, managing, and, when necessary, eliminating boundaries.

The term boundary describes a broad range of concepts, including silo, barrier, or border, with boundaries serving a vital purpose within complex systems (MacGillivray, 2015). Boundaries are considered a fundamental concept of system sciences, with systems theorists considering the boundary creation an important, ethical process within social systems (MacGillivray, 2015). The boundary concept could be a conduit to understanding the nature of sustainability leadership in complex systems (MacGillivray, 2015). While traditional managers and leaders are accustomed to leading within single or multiple boundaries, sustainability leaders must be capable of transcending organizational and system boundaries.

As noted in the previous section, naturally occurring environmental boundaries, such as estuaries, provide healthy, interactive, productive ecological communities (MacGillivray, 2015). While organizational boundaries provide a point of separation between unrelated and related entities, they also provide an intersection for entities to connect and interact. Many organizations recognize the limitations that boundaries place on organizational effectiveness, choosing to abandon the traditional organizational structure for a matrix structure. The matrix structure is an example of a partially boundaryless system, in which organizational members frequently cross boundaries to report to multiple supervisors in separate functions or departments.

Achieving sustainability requires the expansion of boundaries and the examination of larger system implications (Stillman, 2015), because "[s]ustainability is a systems problem requiring collaborative solutions" (Fiksel, 2006, p. 20). A paradigm shift is occurring from a perspective that leadership is predominantly accomplished by one leader to a perspective in which leadership is accomplished by a collective (McCauley, Van Velsor, & Ruderman, 2010). Some sustainability leaders expand their actions and outcomes by expending their effort in horizontal, boundary-spanning situations (MacGillivray, 2015). However, it is crucial for sustainability leaders to collaborate across boundaries because "[c]hanging how unsustainable systems work cannot be separated from changing how we work" (Senge et al., 2008, p. 44). Although collaboration is essential for achieving sustainability objectives, systems thinking has not been fully utilized as a model for understanding sustainability (Lozano, 2008). This essential boundaryless collaboration requires relationships of cooperation and trust among individuals and organizations with little history of either (Senge et al., 2008).

As organizations and systems become increasingly complex, researchers and scholars are reevaluating beliefs and conclusions about leadership and complexity (Kotter, 2013; MacGillivray, 2015), in particular, within the context of boundaries (MacGillivray, 2015). Kiron et al. (2015) suggested that as sustainability concerns become increasingly complex, global, and essential to success, organizations are recognizing that they cannot achieve the necessary impact alone. To achieve sustainability, leadership at multiple levels must embrace leadership styles that promote shared responsibility toward achieving sustainability, with a long-term focus, to establish systems that promote current and future fulfillment of sustainability goals (Iftakhar & Bahauddin, 2018). Achieving sustainability requires strong leadership, a well-articulated implementation plan, and engagement of a diverse group of stakeholders at multiple levels (Iftakhar & Bahauddin, 2018).

Leaders desiring to expand management boundaries and anticipate restraints intended to create a desirable future outcome will be required to challenge the existing, established worldviews (Senge et al., 2008). Organizations whose leaders fail to develop these boundary-transcending competencies typically respond to growing problems with temporary solutions that are within their direct control (Senge et al., 2008). MacGillivray (2015) noted participants in her sustainability leadership studies did not consciously think about boundaries. Moreover, the boundaryless approach, requiring leaders to address deeper problems, also presents leaders with totally new opportunities (Senge et al., 2008). In writing about Mandela's leadership style, Kalungu-Banda (2006) noted, "great leaders affect people across the artificial boundaries of their place in society" (p. 28).

Achieving the boundaryless leadership necessary for sustainability requires development and implementation of strategies capable of encouraging cooperation and collaboration both within and outside the organization. Two strategies for enhancement of sustainable organizational practices through cross-boundary collaboration are educate the vertical and enhance permeability (MacGillivray, 2015). Suggested techniques for educating the vertical include over-exaggerating the linear and sequential properties of objects, tying conversations to organizational priorities, using vertical thinking when communicating with vertical thinkers, and engaging credible outsiders with those in the hierarchy. It is essential to make primary and secondary boundaries more permeable, because the predominance of hierarchies, and the ever-increasing complexity and global nature of sustainability issues, necessitates a high level of knowledge, effort, and innovation transfer across boundaries (MacGillivray, 2015). The complexity and global nature of sustainability, combined with the need to collaborate and lead across multiple boundaries, provide the foundation for the third, and final, proposition about sustainability leadership.

## Sustainability leadership requires a holistic perspective

The third proposition to be considered in this chapter (which is related to and builds upon the second proposition) is: Sustainability is a complex, global concept, requiring holistic leadership capable of seeing the big picture and influencing the entire system. Building upon the previous proposition about the boundaryless nature of sustainability, sustainability leaders must be capable not only of influencing across boundaries, but also of understanding and influencing the entire system to collaborate and cooperate toward a common goal. Complex sustainability issues such as climate change or social injustice present dynamic challenges that can occur across several systems (Daloz Parks, 2005; Heifetz & Laurie, 2001). System leadership provides the framework for leading sustainability initiatives across multiple systems.

Individuals and organizations must recognize that their well-being is dependent upon the well-being of the entire system. Because system leaders encourage people to recognize that individual and organizational success is dependent upon creation of well-being within the larger systems in which they function (Senge et al., 2015), system leadership is appropriate for sustainability. Seeing the big picture provides leaders with the insight necessary to develop strategies enabling them to design products, infrastructures, organizations, and policies that promote system health, rather than short-term solutions that often exacerbate the existing problem (Senge et al., 2008). This holistic aspect of leadership for sustainability suggests that leaders view individuals and society as elements of a broader interconnected system into which they must integrate (Maak & Pless, 2006).

As stated earlier, sustainable activity is generally complex, with a limited number of linear cause and effect relationships (MacGillivray, 2015). Sustainable activity occurs within complex systems, previously defined by Richardson (2001) as interconnected systems consisting of multiple entities within nonlinear connections, resulting in diverse behavior, and self-organizing abilities. Moreover, complex systems are characterized as learning organizations (McElroy, 2000). The ability to see systems and creative processes are natural and essential complements to one another (Senge et al., 2008). Absent this ability, individuals develop fragmented views of the problem, therefore resorting to superficial quick fixes (Senge et al., 2008). Seeing the present systematically is crucial to creating the future (Senge et al., 2008). Sustainability leaders consider the complex relationships among individuals, organizations, markets, and ecosystems, with the objective of achieving organizational welfare and prosperity by respecting societal values, making value-based strategic decisions, and preserving the natural environment in which we all integrally participate (Peterlin et al., 2015).

The ability to view and understand the big picture requires an understanding of two interrelated domains: complexity theory and complex adaptive systems. Complexity theory and complex adaptive systems (CAS) promote an alternative understanding of physical and social systems when compared with linear and reductionist approaches (Dodder & Dare, 2000), and therefore provide lenses through which to see and understand the complex nature of sustainability. While a detailed explanation of complexity theory and CAS is beyond the scope of this text, the key concepts and characteristics of the two domains are summarized in the following paragraphs.

Originating in systems theory, complexity theory is an interdisciplinary approach, influenced by natural science research examining uncertainty and non-linearity (Grobman, 2005), wherein scientists from diverse fields recognized they were examining similar phenomena from different perspectives (MacGillivray, 2015). The focus of complexity theory is with interactions and corresponding feedback loops that continually change systems. While complexity theorists suggest systems are unpredictable, systems are also constricted by order-generating principles (Burnes, 2005). Complexity theory has been proven useful in understanding how organizations or systems adapt to their environments and manage uncertainty.

Complex systems are interconnected systems consisting of multiple entities within nonlinear connections, resulting in diverse behavior, and self-organizing abilities (Richardson, 2001). The process of self-organization was originally proposed by Ashby (1947, 1962) as an involuntary process in which some system of broad order results from local interactions between components of a previously disorganized system. During self-organization, dynamic, deterministic systems automatically transition towards a state of balance and stability described as an attractor in a basin of surrounding environments (Ashby, 1947, 1962). Once the system becomes self-organized, further system evolution is limited to occurrence within the attractor, implying symbiosis or coordination between subsystem components. The self-organization process does not need control or intervention by any external agent and is frequently triggered by random internal changes and further augmented by positive feedback. The resulting system or organization is completely decentralized, dispersed across all system members, adaptive, and capable of self-repair and survival. Each of the subsystems has adapted to the conditions that created all of the other subsystems (Ashby, 1947). Proponents of chaos theory describe self-organization "in terms of islands of predictability in a sea of chaotic unpredictability" (Kisak, 2016). Heinz von Foerster (1960) introduced the principle of "order from noise", suggesting that the self-organization process is assisted by random disturbances, or noise, allowing the system to explore a variety of states and increasing the likelihood that the system will identify and enter a "strong" or "deep" attractor.

CAS are complex systems consisting of multiple components and actors, and in which understanding one of the components or actors does not guarantee an understanding of the entire system. The six critical components of a complex adaptive system are self-organization, emergence, relationships, feedback, adaptability, and non-linearity (Andrus, 2005). CAS exist on the border between order and anarchy and are composed of a system of multiple interconnected members gathering information, learning and operating in parallel in an environment produced by the competition and cooperation of its members (Dodder & Dare, 2000). CAS exist in a state of perpetual novelty in which order is not predetermined but is an ongoing process, always unfolding, always in transition and co-evolving with its environment (Dodder & Dare, 2000). CAS typically reside in multiple organizational levels operating in a manner in which actors at one level frequently influence actors and actions at subsequent levels, and by nature, have a convoluted, unpredictable future (Dodder & Dare, 2000). This macro-level condition, characterized by a complex structure of interactions, may inhibit observer ability to explain and describe collective system behavior in terms of system components (Gupta & Anish, 2009).

In contrast with organized systems, wherein member behavior is inhibited by system rules, chaotic systems are characterized by the lack of behavior-inhibiting rules. However, in a CAS, the system moderately inhibits member behavior, while simultaneously allowing members to modify the system through self-organizing systemic interactions. This self-organizing ability is an important CAS quality, enabling CAS to learn to adapt, differentiating each CAS from other self-organizing systems (Gupta & Anish, 2009).

Cells are an example of a CAS in that organisms consist of cells, and ecosystems consist of organisms. Real-life examples of CAS include complex macroeconomic systems, stock markets, multinational corporations, political parties, geopolitical organizations, and global terrorist networks (Andrus, 2005). Within the context of sustainability leadership, CAS may include industries (composed of businesses, regulatory bodies, customers, shareholders, and other stakeholders) and regions (composed of businesses, ecosystems, governmental institutions, and communities).

Because organizations are CAS functioning within broader CAS, the determination of how to drive sustainability places incredible demand on organizational leaders (Metcalf & Benn, 2013). Therefore, sustainability leadership requires leaders capable of predicting and managing through complexity, solving complex problems, engaging stakeholders in dynamic adaptive change, and possessing emotional intelligence. Sustainability leaders are critical agents in influencing how organizational sustainability connects with the broad CAS in which the organization exists, and completing that connection requires exceptional leadership (Metcalf & Benn, 2013).

In this section, sustainability has been described as a natural, environmental, boundaryless, complex, and global concept. The characteristics of sustainability require system leadership using approaches based upon the natural environment structure, capable of transcending boundaries and artificial barriers, engaging multiple stakeholders both vertically and horizontally, capable of seeing the big picture, and influencing the entire system. Moreover, according to Berger and Luckman (1966), individuals are an outcome of social and cultural systems, and vice versa. Therefore, it is appropriate that any response to a social and cultural problem, such as sustainability, be systems based. The following section includes a general discussion of the characteristics of system leadership within the context of the three previously discussed propositions, and how those characteristics may be cultivated.

## Discussion

While a common assumption about leadership is that leaders are more effective if they exhibit certain behaviors, possess certain traits, and influence others through linear cause and effect relationships, sustainability leadership is complicated, containing a limited number of linear cause and effect relationships (MacGillivray, 2015). Sustainability leadership requires a paradigm shift from the Newtonian, mechanistic worldview, in which phenomena are reduced to logical, manageable components, to a complexity science worldview, in which all objects and entities are interdependent, unpredictable, and nonlinear (Ferdig, 2007). Sustainability is a complex, complicated problem that requires innovative solutions and is often polarized by economic and political actors.

Leadership for sustainability implies a broad, contemporary appreciation of leadership characterized by actions influenced by sustainability values, leading from a natural systems perspective and developing an inclusive, collaborative, and contemplative leadership process (Burns et al., 2015). Moreover, leadership for sustainability builds communities, promotes stakeholder collaboration, and enhances long-term value (Avery & Bergsteiner, 2011). System leadership is a process of persuasion demanding an evidence base for change, because evidence is the optimal method of persuading the skeptical (Timmins, 2015). Many of the sustainability issues humankind currently faces appear to be overwhelming, inexplicable, and beyond resolution. Because system leaders perceive situations characterized by polarization and problems considered to be unsolvable to be opportunities for innovation (Senge et al., 2015), system leadership is an appropriate approach for achieving sustainability.

Sustainability leadership must occur within and across multiple levels, with one of the most important levels being the organizational level. At the organizational level, sustainability leaders must engage and distribute power and authority among all organizational members, while creating sustainable governance systems that steadily move the organization to provide socioeconomic well-being while simultaneously preserving the environment (Doppelt, 2010). Sustainability-focused organizational leaders may expand their spheres of influence beyond their immediate departments and organizations and into related industries, fields, and sectors. More specifically, business leaders may contribute significantly to sustainability, being able to respond more quickly and nimbly than public or nonprofit organizations and being motivated by increasing market demand for sustainability and corporate social responsibility. Because strong organizational sustainability is based on systems thinking combined with organizational and social innovation (Abdelkafi & Tauscher, 2015), achieving business-level sustainability will require systems-thinking-based sustainability leadership. Moreover, ensuring the sustainable management of natural systems will require the development and implementation of innovative technologies (Holliday, Schmidheiny, & Watts, 2017), further supporting the role of business as an incubator of sustainability leadership.

According to Ferdig (2007), three outcomes should be considered by sustainability leaders when taking any individual or collective action. The first consideration should be with how the action affects the *ecosystem, subsystems, and super systems* upon which everyone depends to sustain life. The second consideration should be with how the action affects global *social well-being*. The final consideration should be with how the action affects global *economic stability and growth potential*. Ferdig concluded that leaders cannot effectively function outside the integrated interconnections existing among and between social and natural systems.

Sustainability leaders act consciously, individually, and collectively, resulting in beneficial outcomes for vibrant economic, environmental, and social systems (Ferdig, 2007). Their actions are based upon an understanding that everyone and everything is interconnected and exists in a dynamic system, and that nothing happens in isolation (Ferdig, 2007). Sustainability leaders must possess the ability to comprehend the interconnectedness and interdependency of the entire system, at all levels, and to understand how changes in system components and members impact the entire system (Visser & Courtice, 2011). Moreover, the economic, environmental, and social systems influenced by sustainability leaders often overlap, with sustainability actions frequently impacting multiple systems. An example of a sustainability action impacting multiple systems would be an economic development initiative simultaneously creating jobs by reclaiming a contaminated brownfield site for construction of a new facility benefiting the community (Ferdig, 2007).

In addition to bringing followers together and stimulating creative participation, sustainability leaders should encourage them to embrace a relationship with uncertainty, chaos, and emergence. However, even when values and ideals are shared, collaborative problem solving can still be difficult. Sustainability leaders influence reasonable direction within an integrated structure, while recognizing their limited ability to maintain control with any level of confidence. As such, sustainability leaders embrace continuous change as inevitable, while maintaining sufficient flexibility to allow for unexpected adjustments (Ferdig, 2007). System leadership provides a method for sustainability leaders to galvanize stakeholders to embrace the uncertainty, chaos, and emergence to achieve collaborative problem solving for sustainability.

Scharmer and Kaufer (2013) suggest that to transform systems, the mind, heart, and will of system members must be opened. Opening the mind requires leaders to challenge assumptions, opening the heart requires accessible leaders who genuinely listen to others, and opening the will requires leaders to approach system transformation absent pre-established goals and agendas (Senge et al., 2015). The lack of opening mind, heart, and will coincides with the failures of most change initiatives, which are often premised on stringent assumptions and agendas, failing to recognize that system transformation is about relationship transformation among system members. Sustainability leaders are open to alternative worldviews and ideologies, both locally and across broad geographic, cultural, and political boundaries, and are able to properly integrate those views and beliefs (Visser & Courtice, 2011). Well-intentioned change initiatives often fail because leaders are unable or unwilling to espouse this concept (Senge et al., 2015).

The boundaryless leadership method requires the ability to influence the adoption of sustainability practices and initiatives at and across multiple organizational, industry, and system levels. Stillman (2015) identified four categories of values, practices, and processes common among individuals working to adopt worthwhile sustainability practices at all organizational levels. The four categories included embedding the mission, living the mission, balancing ideals and practices, and knowing that relationships matter. The *relationships matter* category further contained five themes: "melting boundaries, engaging stakeholders, partnering across the supply chain, working like family, and valuing customers" (Stillman, 2015, p. 39). The first two themes support the proposition that sustainability is boundaryless, requiring system leaders capable of transcending boundaries and artificial barriers and engaging multiple stakeholders. The melting boundaries theme consisted of four subthemes: organizing partnerships, working the system, navigating complex systems, and sustaining relationships (Stillman, 2015), all of which support the premises of both the boundaryless and the holistic propositions introduced in this chapter.

In their review of the literature on leadership for sustainability, Williams, Kennedy, Philipp, and Whiteman (2017) identified several characteristics of sustainability leaders that supported a systems thinking approach to leadership for sustainability. Sustainability leaders must possess extraordinary potential and a holistic worldview on the complexities of embedded organizations (Lozano, 2012; Metcalf & Benn, 2012, 2013; Painter-Morland, 2008). Assuming a holistic worldview requires management and analysis of complex information for effective decision-making (Metcalf & Benn, 2012). These leaders must maintain a long-term focus (Boiral, Baron, & Gunnlaugson, 2014) and incorporate different viewpoints to allow for decentralized decision-making (Wong, Ormiston, & Tetlock, 2011). Moreover, leaders within complex systems must be capable of integrating and accommodating multiple contradictory goals (Boiral et al., 2014).

A systems-based leadership approach implies shared responsibility among all participants and a leadership goal of building value-driven organizations

(Painter-Morland, 2008). From a holistic perspective, leadership activities influence organizational functions such as operations, strategy, and communication, thereby impacting the sustainability dimensions of the organization (Boiral et al., 2014; Lozano & Huisingh, 2011). Moreover, the complex interactions between individuals and groups shape common organizational systems (Painter-Morland, 2008). Achieving sustainability will require leaders who can predict complex systems dynamics and respond quickly to facilitate organizational change (Metcalf & Benn, 2012, 2013). Support clearly exists for the argument that system leadership is an appropriate framework and model for achieving sustainability.

System-based sustainability leadership does not happen by chance. Individuals reach a holistic, systems approach to sustainability as a result of a primary interest in one of three broad and often overlapping categories: (1) appreciation, concern, and possibly activism for the environment; (2) social awareness and social service action; and (3) interest in responsible business and economic development (Ferdig, 2007). The two most common attractors described by participants for demonstrating sustainable leadership were response to a crisis, problem, or opportunity and cross-boundary learning and action (MacGillivray, 2015).

Sustainability leadership necessitates a departure from a mechanistic, anthropocentric worldview to a complex, boundaryless, nature-based systems worldview. Leadership that is based on integrity and grounded in a living systems worldview calls for a dynamic leadership process (Burns et al., 2015). Transitioning organizations, industries, and entire systems will require systems-based, boundaryless, holistic leadership. The path toward a sustainable future presents complicated, interconnected challenges, which will require collective action (Iftakhar & Bahauddin, 2018). Therefore, rather than giving direction and providing solutions, leaders should create opportunities for others to develop their own solutions through collaboration (Ferdig, 2007; Iftakhar & Bahauddin, 2018). Sustainability leaders are devoted change agents, participating in work that demonstrates a developing demeanor rooted in interdependence, relationships, and mindfulness (Burns et al., 2015).

Sustainability leaders must see, think, and act both within and beyond their present spheres of influence, building collaborative coalitions capable of bringing about significant and lasting change. Seeking balance among multiple, often competing, demands for economically, socially, and environmentally sustainable outcomes can be a meaningful leadership path (Ferdig, 2007). Acknowledging our fundamental interdependence with the planet and all living creatures and developing legitimate relationships are essential to healing the planet and society (Burns et al., 2015). Sustainability leaders recognize the necessity, meaningfulness, and rewards inherent in influencing change for the betterment of society and the planet.

## Conclusion

Senge et al. (2015) questioned whether a sufficient accumulation of system leaders would develop in time to address the systemic challenges facing our planet and society. However, in the same article, the authors cite two reasons for optimism. First, as the interconnectedness of key societal challenges continues to become manifest, an increasing number of people are recognizing and embracing a systemic orientation. While the current population of system leaders is limited, an emerging foundation of practical knowledge is contributing to the development of leaders who recognize the importance and affinity of the systemic approach and collective leadership. Second, over the last three decades, a significant number of tools have been developed to assist system leaders, a few of which have been discussed in Chapter 1 of this text. Application of the proper tool, at the proper time, and with an open-minded attitude can dramatically shift the ability to achieve collective stakeholder success (Senge et al., 2015).

Visser and Courtice (2011) simplistically described a sustainability leader as "someone who inspires and supports action towards a better world" (p. 3). According to Ferdig (2007), any person who accepts responsibility for understanding and responding to sustainability issues is acting as a sustainability leader, regardless of whether that person holds a formal leadership position. These informal leaders influence with rather than over others in a manner that supports long-term survival of complex, interdependent living systems. Sustainability leadership is the manifestation of a growing movement of individuals determined to live their lives and lead their organizations in a manner that minimizes impact on the planet and society, while enhancing the health of local and global economies (Ferdig, 2007).

As leaders begin to properly shift their focus, collaborative networks emerge that are appropriate for the complexity of the problem, making previously unmanageable circumstances capable of being managed (Senge et al., 2015). Moreover, there is an extensive, not well-articulated hunger for meaningful change, driven by increasing cynicism that the methods being used to solve critical societal problems are too superficial to address the root cause of those problems. While this cynicism can lead to resignation that our environmental and societal systems will continue to decay, it can also motivate people to become open-minded about new directions and opportunities. Systemic change has succeeded because of increased awareness that the inner and outer aspects of change are related. As our awareness continues to grow, an increasing number of system leaders who mobilize collective leadership will appear (Senge et al., 2015).

In this chapter, we examined three propositions, rooted in the common characteristics of sustainability and system leadership to demonstrate that system leadership is an appropriate leadership style for sustainability. Sustainability is a natural environmental concept, boundaryless, complex, and global in nature. Therefore, sustainability leadership requires leadership that is based upon the natural environment structure, capable of transcending boundaries and barriers, engaging multiple stakeholders both vertically and horizontally, and of seeing the big picture and influencing the entire system. System leadership is clearly the ethos of sustainability leadership.

## Chapter reflection questions

1 System leadership has been presented as a model for achievement of a sustainable future. Do you believe system leadership would be appropriate in all organizational settings? Why or why not?

2 In this chapter, three propositions were examined: sustainability is a natural environmental concept that requires leadership approaches based upon the natural environment structure; sustainability is a boundaryless concept that requires system leadership capable of transcending boundaries and artificial barriers, engaging multiple stakeholders both vertically and horizontally; and sustainability is a complex, global concept, requiring leadership capable of seeing the big picture and influencing the entire system. Of these three propositions, which do you believe is the most important, and why?

3 In this chapter, it was suggested that sustainability leadership necessitates a departure from a mechanistic, anthropocentric worldview to a complex, boundaryless, nature-based systems worldview. In this modern, technology-focused world, how can we transition from a mechanistic, anthropocentric worldview to a complex, boundaryless, nature-based systems worldview? How can system leadership facilitate this transition?

## References

Abdelkafi, N., & Tauscher, K. (2015). Business models for sustainability from a system dynamics perspective. *Organization & Environment*, *29*(1), 74–96. doi:10.1177/1086026615592930

Andrus, D. C. (2005). The wiki and the blog: Toward a complex adaptive intelligence community. *Studies in Intelligence*, *49*(3), 1–30. Retrieved from https://ssrn.com/abstract=755904

Ashby, W. R. (1947). Principles of the self-organizing dynamic system. *The Journal of General Psychology*, *37*(2), 125–128. doi:10.1080/00221309.1947.9918144

Ashby, W. R. (1962). Principles of the self-organizing system. In H. von Foerster & G. W. Zopf, Jr. (Eds.), *Principles of self-organization* (pp. 255–278). Arlington, VA: U.S. Office of Naval Research.

Avery, G. C., & Bergsteiner, H. (2011). How BMW successfully practices sustainable leadership principles. *Strategy & Leadership*, *39*(6), 11–18. doi:10.1108/10878571111176583

Barlow, Z., & Stone, M. K. (2011). Living systems and leadership: Cultivating conditions for institutional change. *Journal of Sustainability Education*, *2*, 1–23. Retrieved from www.susted.org/

Bashiri, M., & Tabrizi, M. M. (2010). Supply chain design: A holistic approach. *Expert Systems with Applications*, *37*(1), 688–693. doi:10.1016/j.eswa.2009.06.006

Bateson, G. (2002). *Mind and nature: A necessary unity*. Cresskill, NJ: Hampton Press.

Berger, P. L., & Luckman, T. (1966). *The social construction of reality: A treatise in the sociology of knowledge*. New York, NY: Anchor Books.

Biomimicry Institute. (2018a). *What is biomimicry?* Missoula, MO: Author. Retrieved from https://biomimicry.org/what-is-biomimicry/

Biomimicry Institute. (2018b). *Biomimicry examples*. Missoula, MO: Author. Retrieved from https://biomimicry.org/biomimicry-examples/

Boiral, O., Baron, C., & Gunnlaugson, O. (2014). Environmental leadership and consciousness development: A case study among Canadian SMEs. *Journal of Business Ethics, 123*(3), 363–383. doi:10.1007/s10551-013-1845-5

Burnes, B. (2005). Complexity theories and organizational change. *International Journal of Management Reviews*, 7(2), 73–90. doi:10.1111/j.1468-2370.2005.00107.x

Burns, H., Diamond-Vaught, H., & Bauman, C. (2015). Leadership for sustainability: Theoretical foundations and pedagogical practices that foster change. *International Journal of Leadership Studies, 9*(1), 88–100. Retrieved from http://citeseerx.ist.psu.edu

Daily, G. C., & Ellison, K. (2002). *The new economy of nature: The quest to make conservation profitable*. Washington, DC: Island Press.

Daloz Parks, S. (2005). *Leadership can be taught*. Boston, MA: Harvard Business School Publishing.

Dodder, R., & Dare, R. (2000, October). Complex adaptive systems and complexity theory: Inter-related knowledge domains. In *ESD, 83: Research seminar in engineering systems*. Retrieved from www.researchgate.net/publication/268426778_Complex_Adaptive_Systems_and_Complexity_Theory_Inter-related_Knowledge_Domains

Doppelt, B. (2010). *Leading change toward sustainability: A change-management guide for business, government and civil society* (2nd ed.). Sheffield, England: Greenleaf Publishing.

Elias, A. A. (2008). Towards a shared systems model of stakeholders in environmental conflict. *International Transactions in Operational Research, 15*(2), 239–253. doi:10.1111/j.1475-3995.2008.00631.x

Ferdig, M. A. (2007). Sustainability leadership: Co-creating a sustainable future. *Journal of Change Management*, 7(1), 25–35. doi:10.1080/14697010701233809

Fiksel, J. (2006). Sustainability and resilience: Toward a systems approach. *Sustainability: Science, Practice, and Policy, 2*(2), 14–21. doi:10.1080/15487733.2006.11907980

Fullan, M. (2004). *Systems thinkers in action: Moving beyond the standards plateau*. London, England: Department for Education and Skills.

Fullan, M. (2005). *Leadership and sustainability: System thinkers in action*. London, England: Sage Publications.

Ghate, D. (2015). *System leadership: Expanding understanding of leadership drivers in whole systems*. London, England: The Colebrooke Centre for Evidence and Implementation. Retrieved from www.cevi.org.uk

Grobman, G. M. (2005). Complexity theory: A new way to look at organizational change. *Public Administration Quarterly, 29*, 350–382. Retrieved from www.jstor.org/stable/41288239

Gupta, A., & Anish, S. (2009). Insights from complexity theory: Understanding organizations better. *IIMB Management Review*. Retrieved from http://spidi2.iimb.ernet.in/~tejas/articles/12.php

Heifetz, R., & Laurie, D. (2001). The work of leadership. *Harvard Business Review*. Retrieved from http://hbr.org/2001/12/the-work-of-leadership/ar/1

Hill, R. (2006). *Leadership that lasts: Sustainable school leadership in the 21st Century*. Leicester, England: Association of School and College Leaders.

Holliday, C. O., Schmidheiny, S., & Watts, P. (2017). *Walking the talk: The business case for sustainable development*. New York, NY: Routledge.

Iftakhar, N., & Bahauddin, K. M. (2018, January 10). *Why leadership is essential for achieving Sustainable Development Goals*. Seoul, South Korea: International Policy Digest. Retrieved from https://intpolicydigest.org/2018/01/10/why-leadership-is-essential-for-achieving-sustainable-development-goals/

Ison, R. L., Maiteny, P. T., & Carr, S. (1997). Systems methodologies for sustainable natural resources research and development. *Agricultural Systems, 55*(2), 257–272. doi:10.1016/S0308-521X(97)00010-3

Kalungu-Banda, M. (2006). *Leading like Madiba: Leadership lessons from Nelson Mandela*. Lansdowne, South Africa: Double Storey Books.

Kiron, D., Kruschwitz, N., Haanaes, K., Reeves, M., Fuisz-Kehrbach, S. K., & Kell, G. (2015). Joining forces: Collaboration and leadership for sustainability. *MIT Sloan Management Review, 56*(3), 1–31. Retrieved from https://sloanreview.mit.edu

Kisak, P. F. (2016). *The self organization of disordered systems: Examples of self-organization in nature*. Scotts Valley, CA: CreateSpace Independent Publishing Platform.

Kotter, J. P. (2013). Management is (still) not leadership. *Harvard Business Review, 9*. Retrieved from https://hbr.org

Lozano, R. (2008). Envisioning sustainability three-dimensionally. *Journal of Cleaner Production, 16*, 1838–1846. doi:10.1016/j.jclepro.2008.02.008

Lozano, R. (2012). Towards better embedding sustainability into companies' systems: An analysis of voluntary corporate initiatives. *Journal of Cleaner Production, 25*, 14–26. doi:10.1016/j.jclepro.2011.11.060

Lozano, R., & Huisingh, D. (2011). Inter-linking issues and dimensions in sustainability reporting. *Journal of Cleaner Production, 19*, 99–107. doi:10.1016/j.jclepro.2010.01.004

Maak, T., & Pless, N. M. (2006). Responsible leadership in a stakeholder society: A relational perspective. *Journal of Business Ethics, 66*(1), 99–115. doi:10.1007/s10551-006-9047-z

Maani, K., & Maharraj, V. (2004). Links between systems thinking and complex decision-making. *System Dynamics Review, 20*(1), 21–48. doi:10.1002/sdr.281

MacGillivray, A. E. (2015). Leadership, boundaries, and sustainability. In D. B. Willis, F. Steier, & P. Stillman (Eds.), *Sustainability leadership: Integrating values, meaning, and action* (pp. 277–307). Santa Barbara, CA: Fielding Graduate University.

Marcus, J., Kurucz, E. C., & Colbert, B. A. (2010). Conceptions of the business-society-nature interface: Implications for management scholarship. *Business & Society, 49*(3), 402–438. doi:10.1177/0007650310368827

McCauley, C. D., Van Velsor, E., & Ruderman, M. N. (2010). Introduction: Our view of leadership development. In E. Van Velsor, C. D. McCauley, & M. N. Ruderman (Eds.), *The center for creative leadership handbook of leadership development* (3rd ed., pp. 1–26). San Francisco, CA: Jossey-Bass.

McElroy, M. W. (2000). Integrating complexity theory, knowledge management and organizational learning. *Journal of Knowledge Management, 4*(3), 195–203. doi:10.1108/13673270010377652

Metcalf, L., & Benn, S. (2012). The corporation is ailing social technology: Creating a "fit for purpose" design for sustainability. *Journal of Business Ethics, 111*(2), 195–210. doi:10.1007/s10551-012-1201-1

Metcalf, L., & Benn, S. (2013). Leadership for sustainability: An evolution of leadership ability. *Journal of Business Ethics, 112*, 369–384. doi:10.1007/s10551-012-1278-6

Nguyen, N. C., & Bosch, O. J. (2013). A systems thinking approach to identify leverage points for sustainability: A case study in the Cat Ba Biosphere Reserve, Vietnam. *Systems Research and Behavioral Science, 30*(2), 104–115. doi:10.1002/sres

Ostrom, E. (2009). A general framework for analyzing sustainability of social-ecological systems. *Science, 325*(5939), 419–422. doi:10.1126/science.1172133

Painter-Morland, M. (2008). Systemic leadership and the emergence of ethical responsiveness. *Journal of Business Ethics, 82*(2), 509–524. doi:10.1007/s10551-008-9900-3

Pennisi, E. (2003). Tracing life's circuitry. *Science, 302*(5651), 1646–1649. doi:10.1126/science.302.5651.1646

Peterlin, J., Pearse, N. J., & Dimovski, V. (2015). Strategic decision making for organizational sustainability: The implications of servant leadership and sustainable leadership approaches. *Economic & Business Review, 17*(3), 273–290. doi:10.15458/85451.4

Richardson, K. A. (2001, November). On the status of natural boundaries: A complex systems perspective. *Proceedings of the Systems in Management 7th Annual ANZSYS Conference 2001* (pp. 229–238), Churchlands, Australia: Edith Cowan University. doi:10.1207/S15327000EM0304_3

Rockström, J., Steffen, W., Noone, K., Persson, Å., Chapin III, F. S., Lambin, E. F., . . . Nykvist, B. (2009). A safe operating space for humanity. *Nature, 461*(7263), 472–475. doi:10.1038/461472a

Romei, F. (2008). *Leonardo Da Vinci*. Minneapolis, MN: The Oliver Press.

Scharmer, O., & Kaufer, K. (2013). *Leading from the emerging future: From ego-system to eco-system economies*. Oakland, CA: Berrett-Koehler Publishers.

Senge, P., Smith, B., Kruschwitz, N., Laur, J., & Schley, S. (2008). *The necessary revolution: How individuals and organizations are working together to create a sustainable world*. New York, NY: Doubleday.

Senge, P., Hamilton, H., & Kania, J. (2015). The dawn of system leadership. *Stanford Social Innovation Review, 13*(1), 27–33. Retrieved from https://ssir.org/articles/entry/the_dawn_of_system_leadership

Shriberg, M., & MacDonald, L. (2013). Sustainability leadership programs: Emerging goals, methods & best practices. *Journal of Sustainability Education, 5*, 1–21. Retrieved from www.susted.org/

Smith, T. (2011). Using critical systems thinking to foster an integrated approach to sustainability: A proposal for development practitioners. *Environment, Development and Sustainability, 13*(1), 1–17. doi:10.1007/s10668-010-9243-y

Starik, M., & Kanashiro, P. (2013). Toward a theory of sustainability management: Uncovering and integrating the nearly obvious. *Organization & Environment, 26*(1), 7–30. doi:10.1177/1086026612474958

Starik, M., & Rands, G. P. (1995). Weaving an integrated web: Multilevel and multisystem perspectives of ecologically sustainable organizations. *Academy of Management Review, 20*(4), 908–935. doi:10.5465/amr.1995.9512280025

Stillman, P. (2015). Sustainability as organizational culture: Uncovering values, practices, and processes. In D. B. Willis, F. Steier, & P. Stillman (Eds.), *Sustainability leadership: Integrating values, meaning, and action* (pp. 13–51). Santa Barbara, CA: Fielding Graduate University.

Sustainability Leadership Institute. (n.d.). *Leadership*. Omaha, NE: Author. Retrieved from www.sustainabilityleadershipinstitute.org/leadership.php

Timmins, N. (2015). *The practice of system leadership: Being comfortable with chaos*. London, England: The King's Fund. Retrieved from www.kingsfund.org.uk/sites/default/files/field/field_publication_file/System-leadership-Kings-Fund-May-2015.pdf

Visser, W., & Courtice, P. (2011). *Sustainability leadership: Linking theory and practice*. Cambridge, England: Cambridge Institute for Sustainability Leadership. doi:10.2139/ssrn.1947221

Von Foerster, H. (1960). On self-organizing systems and their environments. In M. C. Yovits & S. Cameron (Eds.), *Self-organizing systems* (pp. 31–50). London, England: Pergamon Press.

Wheatley, M. J. (2006). *Leadership and the new science: Discovering order in a chaotic world.* San Francisco, CA: Berrett-Koehler Publishers.

Whiteman, G., Walker, B., & Perego, P. (2013). Planetary boundaries: Ecological foundations for corporate sustainability. *Journal of Management Studies, 50*(2), 307–336. doi:10.1111/j.1467-6486.2012.01073.x

Williams, A., Kennedy, S., Philipp, F., & Whiteman, G. (2017). Systems thinking: A review of sustainability management research. *Journal of Cleaner Production, 148*, 866–881. doi:10.1016/j.jclepro.2017.02.002

Winn, M. I., & Pogutz, S. (2013). Business, ecosystems, and biodiversity: New horizons for management research. *Organization & Environment, 26*(2), 203–229. doi:10.1177/1086026613490173

Wong, E. M., Ormiston, M. E., & Tetlock, P. E. (2011). The effects of top management team integrative complexity and decentralized decision making on corporate social performance. *Academy of Management Journal, 54*(6), 1207–1228. doi:10.5465/amj.2008.0762

# 3 System leadership characteristics and competencies

## Introduction

Leaders are a critical element in the sustainability process, and leading sustainability change efforts requires new leadership competencies (Haney, Pope, & Arden, 2018). System leaders possess characteristics and core competencies that uniquely prepare them to influence across boundaries and organizations. In this section, we will examine the characteristics, skills, elements, and core competencies of both sustainability and system leaders. The leadership styles most appropriate for system leadership will also be explored.

In Chapter 2, three propositions were made concerning the appropriateness of system leadership for sustainability:

1 Sustainability is a natural environmental concept, the promotion of which requires leadership approaches based upon the natural environment structure.
2 Sustainability is a boundaryless concept, the promotion of which requires system leadership capable of transcending boundaries and artificial barriers, engaging multiple stakeholders both vertically and horizontally.
3 Sustainability is a complex, global concept, requiring leadership capable of seeing the big picture and influencing the entire system.

These three propositions will frame our discussion in this chapter about system leadership core competencies based on the identified characteristics and skills of both sustainability and system leaders.

## Sustainability leadership characteristics and traits

Because organizations are complex adaptive systems that function within broader complex adaptive systems, understanding how to create a sustainable organization places unprecedented demand on organizational leaders (Metcalf & Benn, 2013). Therefore, leadership for sustainability requires individuals with exceptional capabilities and competencies, who can navigate complexity, solve complex problems, engage stakeholders in productive organizational change, and possess emotional intelligence. Sustainability leaders must be able to promote the relationship of the organization and stakeholders with the broader system, a task that requires unique leaders and leadership systems (Metcalf & Benn, 2013).

Researchers with the Cambridge Institute for Sustainability Leadership identified the seven essential characteristics of individuals engaged in sustainability issues, incorporating them into a leadership for sustainability model (Visser & Courtice, 2011). The seven characteristics are "systemic, interdisciplinary understanding; emotional intelligence; values orientation; compelling vision; inclusive style; innovative approach; and long-term perspective" (Peirce, 2011, p. 7). Moreover, Dalati, Raudeliūnienė, and Davidavičienė (2017) identified the following list of sustainability leadership characteristics:

- Developing organizational vision with a sense of purpose and values shared by leaders and followers.
- Capable of effective communication and persuasive approaches in demonstrating clear goals and objectives.
- Competent in building trust and surpassing self-interest for the benefit of the group or organization.
- Advocating personal integrity and sensitivity to concerns, interests, and property of stakeholders and broader society.
- Demonstrated capacity and skills for building teams and instilling social collective identity.
- Capable of inspiring followers and building a motivated workforce by demonstrating exceptional levels of effort and energy.

Further, Šimanskienė and Župerkienė (2014) compiled a comprehensive list of sustainable leadership characteristics. The following are a few essential characteristics that are related to system leadership:

- have a clear, sustainability-oriented business vision;
- pursue goals that are oriented towards long-term progress;
- take responsibility for individuals, groups, organizations, and society;
- possess a high degree of trust and goodwill;
- are collaborative; and
- encourage training and learning.

Visser and Courtice (2011) developed a sustainability leadership model based on leadership theory and the sustainability practice of leaders. The model components are the internal and external leadership context; the individual leader's traits, styles, skills, and knowledge; and leadership actions. Although none of these components are unique to sustainability leaders, when combined, they summarize a unique collection of characteristics and actions for reacting to sustainability challenges (Visser & Courtice, 2011). They also identified and included several traits possessed by sustainability leaders that are strongly correlated with leadership for sustainability: being caring and morally driven; systemic/holistic thinking; having an inquiring, open mind; demonstrating self-awareness and empathy; and being both visionary and courageous (Visser & Courtice, 2011).

Several other prominent traits in the model are high levels of emotional intelligence, sincerity, humility, and reflexiveness, which is the ability of a person to recognize their own position in and influence situations (Visser & Courtice, 2011). Scharmer (2008) observed that the immense demands faced by business or government leaders necessitates a deeper space of reflection as one of the anchor points for these leaders to remain effective. For many leaders, the most essential trait is that sustainability leaders possess enthusiasm, creativity, optimism, and courage, are results oriented, and can balance dedication and idealism with ambition and pragmatism. Collins (2001) suggested that leaders must maintain absolute confidence that they can and will succeed, regardless of the obstacles, while simultaneously confronting the most serious aspects of their current circumstances (Visser & Courtice, 2011).

## System leadership skills

Having examined the characteristics of sustainability leaders, we will shift attention to the skills and elements of system leaders. It should be noted that there are several instances in which the skills and characteristics of both sustainability and system leadership overlap. In a subsequent section, we will find further overlap between the core competencies of sustainability leaders and the core capabilities of system leaders. These areas will provide support for the propositions that system leadership is appropriate for achieving sustainability.

Leaders are essential to the organizational change process necessary for organizations to achieve sustainability improvements (Eccles, Perkins, & Serafeim, 2012). However, leaders engaging in the necessary, complicated sustainability challenges must develop a new set of leadership skills and traits (Osagie, Wesselink, Blok, Lans, & Mulder, 2016; Ploum, Blok, Lans, & Omta, 2018). Leaders who develop system leadership skills may be able to engage and empower across organizational boundaries to effect the change necessary to achieve significant sustainability results.

System leadership skills include the ability to achieve significant accomplishments without taking credit for those accomplishments, emotional intelligence, and recognition that whistle-blowers can be powerful change agents (Timmins, 2015). These leaders acknowledge that individuals, not individual efforts, stimulate the success agents of competitive organizations (Kaliannan & Adjovu, 2015). Brown (2011) discussed post-conventional development skills that may promote effective sustainability management, including the ability to integrate ideas, develop long-term visions with profound purposes, a systems perspective of reality, and develop collaborative relationships. Moreover, Boiral, Baron, and Gunnlaugson (2014) theorized that the skills common to both sustainability leadership and the upper stages of consciousness development "include a broader and systemic perspective, long-range focus, integration of conflicting goals, collaboration with stakeholders, complexity management, collaborative learning" (p. 363).

## System leadership elements

Fullan (2005) described the eight elements of system leadership within the context of education as public service with a moral purpose; commitment to changing context at all levels; lateral capacity building through networks; new vertical relationships that are co-dependent, encompassing both capacity building and accountability; deep learning; dual commitment to short-term and long-term results; cyclical energizing; and the long lever of leadership. While intended for the education sector, these elements support a model for system leadership in other sectors and deserve some attention in this chapter. Fullan (2003b) described how moral purpose must transcend the individual to become an organizational and system quality in which all participants are committed to adopting moral purpose in all essential activities. Moreover, public officials must maintain moral purpose if they desire to achieve and maintain long-term success (Fullan, 2005). System change begins with a commitment to change context, which provides individuals with new experiences, capabilities, and insights into the actions that can be accomplished through application of the remaining six elements (Fullan, 2005). System leaders must be able to reframe the sustainability discussion, both within and outside their organizations.

There are several benefits from lateral capacity-building network strategies (Fullan, 2005). First, people learn best from more experienced peers, provided sufficient opportunity exists for ongoing, meaningful exchange. Second, the system is structured to encourage, develop, and disseminate effective, innovative practices with respect to Heifetz's (1994) adaptive challenges. Third, leadership is developed and implemented in multiple areas. Fourth, inspiration and control at the local level are enhanced, which is essential for maintenance of effort and commitment. The weaknesses of these network strategies are that too many networks may inhibit organizational focus, network members may share beliefs and opinions rather than useful expertise, and networks often operate outside of organizational control, inhibiting potential ideas from moving out of the networks and into implementation (Fullan, 2005).

Sustainable societies must obtain local ownership and capacity, as well as external accountability to achieve system-wide change within the whole system (Fullan, 2005), because sustainability problems must ultimately be addressed locally. The challenge is with motivating individuals to seek favorable outcomes and holding individuals and organizations accountable for their actions, which is accomplished with a combination of intelligent accountability (Miliband, 2004) and collaboration and networks (Fullan, 2005). With intelligent accountability, communities collaborate in solving problems and develop better practices, mutual commitment, and peer accountability. However, achieving results with collaborative cultures is challenging, because the process is peer-based and constantly interactive (Fullan, 2005). Sustainability requires deep learning by leaders and their constituents, which requires collaborative cultures of inquiry to shift organizations from a dysfunctional learning culture toward the continuous development of an adaptive problem-solving culture (Fullan, 2005).

System leadership requires commitment to both short-term and long-term results. Governments and organizations must demonstrate progress in relation to both short-term and long-term priorities, because stakeholders and constituents require short-term measurable results in addition to long-term organizational or societal benefits. However, long-term progress should not be compromised to achieve short-term success. Fullan (2005) emphasized the need for establishing targets, taking immediate action, and intervening when poor performance makes intervention necessary. As the system gradually becomes stronger, major problems occur less frequently because corrective action is more likely to occur at an earlier stage (Fullan, 2005).

Sustainability is cyclical for two important reasons: energy, and the occasions when additional time and talent are necessary to achieve the next adaptive improvement (Fullan, 2005). Loehr and Schwartz (2003) stated that energy is the primary source of high performance, classifying the four sources of energy as physical, emotional, mental, and spiritual. The collection of strategies that pioneered initial sustainability success is not necessarily capable of achieving the next level of sustainability. Cyclical energizing requires learning organizations that explore, learn, analyze, and develop improved solutions. While a precise model of cyclical energizing does not yet exist, the concept should be an essential element of sustainability strategy (Fullan, 2005). The long lever of leadership is an essential element of sustainability because the transition toward sustainability requires leadership at all levels, with the primary work of leaders being the introduction of the other seven elements, which simultaneously enhance each other. Accomplishing this requires a system populated with leaders capable of thinking in bigger terms and acting in a manner that impacts broader portions of the whole system (Fullan, 2005). These leaders must reach beyond immediate organizations and systems, demonstrating far-reaching leadership throughout entire systems.

## Sustainability leadership core competencies

Core competencies describe the defining capabilities or advantages that distinguish an organization or individual from other organizations or individuals. Although the objective of a competency is connected with a specific task or problem (Haney et al., 2018), a thorough understanding of competency must include attitudes, intentions, values, and ethics, in addition to cognitive and practical elements such as knowledge and abilities (Barth & Michelsen, 2013; Hesselbarth & Schaltegger, 2014; Osagie et al., 2016; Ploum et al., 2018; Visser & Crane, 2010; Wesselink, Blok, van Leur, Lans, & Dentoni, 2015). Achieving competence in sustainability requires both cognitive and practical development to manage increasing complexity, learn values, and continually reflect on the competency process (Barth & Michelsen, 2013; Haney et al., 2018; Savage, Tapics, Evarts, Wilson, & Tirone, 2015).

Several scholars have produced lists of leadership for sustainability core competencies. Regardless of conceptual or empirical approach, the lists are quite similar with considerable overlap. Moreover, the lists include both sustainability and management attributes, with many of the competencies similar to the competencies identified by Martin and Ernst (2005) for leadership under circumstances of paradox and complexity (Haney et al., 2018). These competencies do not replace but expand and enhance traditional competencies, and when combined, represent a shift in organizational perspective from being an isolated entity to a component of a value network or extensive economic ecosystem (Weinreb, 2015). These competencies support a perspective change from a shareholder focus to a social purpose and stakeholder focus, encouraging organizational members to integrate their personal ethical and altruistic values with their careers (Weinreb, 2015).

The leadership for sustainability core competencies include systems thinking, external collaboration, social innovation, sustainability literacy, active values, forward thinking, normative thinking, strategic thinking, and interpersonal abilities (Haney et al., 2018; Hesselbarth & Schaltegger, 2014; Lans, Blok, & Wesselink, 2014; Osagie et al., 2016; Ploum et al., 2018; Strandberg, 2015; Wesselink et al., 2015; Wiek, Withycombe, & Redman, 2011). However, Ploum et al. noted the competencies common to multiple studies were strategic thinking, systems thinking, and interpersonal competence. As discussed in Chapter 1, system leaders develop three core capabilities that produce collective leadership (Senge, Hamilton, & Kania, 2015). These include the ability to see the overall system, cultivate reflection and more innovative conversations, and transform the collective attention away from reactive problem solving to co-creation of the future. In the following sections, the common sustainability competencies (Ploum et al., 2018) and the three core capabilities of system leadership (Senge et al., 2015) are examined within the context of the three propositions identified in Chapter 2 and restated earlier in this chapter.

## System leadership is based upon natural environment structure

The first proposition advancing system leadership for sustainability is that sustainability is a natural environmental concept, the promotion of which requires leadership approaches based upon the natural environment structure. The core capability of being able to see the larger system (Senge et al., 2015) and the sustainability competency of systems thinking (Ploum et al., 2018) support this proposition because understanding the natural environment requires a systems thinking perspective. In Chapter 2, sustainability leadership was described as being based upon natural systems thinking, which requires application of natural systems principles to facilitate outcomes consistent with dynamic, sustainable ecosystems (MacGillivray, 2015). Sustainability leadership requires that leaders acknowledge and appreciate complexity, with Iftakhar and Bahauddin (2018) suggesting complexity is best understood through examination of the model offered by nature.

In complex situations, individuals normally focus on the system components most visible from their personal vantage point, which often results in disagreement about which person has the correct perspective (Senge et al., 2015). Assisting individuals with seeing the broader system is essential for building a shared understanding of complex problems, resulting in collaboration for joint development of solutions that were not visible to any of them individually. This collaborative problem-solving approach produces collective action toward whole system health, instead of symptomatic responses to individual problems (Senge et al., 2015). Systems thinking and the ability to see the entire system enable system leaders to appreciate that considerable activity occurs beyond the immediate view of the observer, much like the iceberg model mentioned in Chapter 1 (Ambler, 2013).

Systems thinker(s) frequently have multidisciplinary qualifications that integrate technical and creative experience, and they may also have expertise in systems management concepts such as resilience and managing change (Weinreb, 2015). Systems thinker(s) are connected, holistic thinkers who understand the circumstances surrounding a problem or situation and its connection to broader trends (Weinreb, 2015). Moreover, sustainable leaders are skilled systems thinker(s) and constantly aware of the broader context of problems and situations beyond the immediate organizational boundaries (Russell Reynolds Associates, 2015). Weinreb suggested systems thinking and teamwork are essential elements of successful leadership for sustainability.

Systems thinking is effective for the following reasons:

- Increases awareness of how an individual or organization might be unknowingly contributing to the problems being solved.
- Empowers individuals to focus effort on the point of greatest impact by reflecting on and modifying motives, perspectives, and behavior.
- Organizes diverse stakeholders to take actions to improve long-term whole system effectiveness, instead of satisfying short-term self-interests.
- Supports forecast and mitigation of negative long-term consequences of well-intentioned actions.
- Recognizes high-impact interventions to concentrate limited resources for maximum, long-term, system-wide improvement.
- Motivates and enhances continuous learning.

(Stroh, 2015)

System thinkers demonstrate systems intelligence, defined as intelligent behavior in the context of complex systems containing interaction and feedback (Summers, 2011). An individual demonstrating systems intelligence effectively engages with whole system feedback mechanisms, perceiving self as part of the whole and recognizing the influence of the individual on the whole system, and the influence of the whole on the individual (Summers, 2011). Additional information on systems thinking is located in Chapter 1, and analysis of methods and tools for development of systems thinking is located in Chapter 4.

## System leadership requires transcending boundaries and barriers

The second proposition advancing system leadership for sustainability is that sustainability is a boundaryless concept, the promotion of which requires system leadership capable of transcending boundaries and artificial barriers, engaging multiple stakeholders both vertically and horizontally. The core capabilities of promoting reflection and more innovative conversation and transforming the collective focus from reactive problem solving to proactive co-creation of the future (Senge et al., 2015), combined with the sustainability competency of interpersonal competence (Ploum et al., 2018), support this proposition, because transcending social boundaries and barriers requires interpersonal abilities. System leaders must possess interpersonal competencies to cross boundaries and engage diverse stakeholders in collaborative activity. Wiek et al. (2011) defined the interpersonal competency as "the ability to motivate, enable, and facilitate collaborative and participatory sustainability research and problem solving" (p. 211).

Sustainability leaders must be willing to collaborate with external stakeholders, because significant environmental impact may occur upstream or downstream of organizational operations, suggesting collaboration with suppliers and customers; even collaboration with competitors may be necessary (Weinreb, 2015). Collaboration assists organizations with developing social capital development, exploring new markets, and altering the contexts in which organizations operate (Weinreb, 2015). Moreover, 87% of global CEOs surveyed identified cross-sector collaboration and cooperation as the essential method to expedite progress toward Agenda 2030 and the United Nations (UN) Sustainable Development Goals (Accenture, 2016).

Reflection requires that leaders consider their thinking, review assumptions that influence conversations, and appreciate the limitations created by accepted mental models (Senge et al., 2015). Deep, mutual reflection is an essential step in empowering groups and organizations to acknowledge another perspective and reality, which is necessary for replacing mistrust with trust and for nurturing collective creativity (Senge et al., 2015). A leader demonstrating active values is self-aware of emotions and motivations and is sensitive to the emotions and motivations of other individuals (Weinreb, 2015). Self-aware leaders view themselves and their efforts as part of a greater purpose, inspiring them to mobilize their organizations to benefit society. Strandberg (2015) suggested that emotional intelligence encourages resiliency, confidence, and reciprocity among colleagues and stakeholders.

## System leadership requires big picture perspective to influence entire systems

The third proposition advancing system leadership for sustainability is that sustainability is a complex, global concept, requiring leadership capable of seeing the big picture and influencing the entire system. There are two manners in which the core capabilities of being able to see the larger system and transforming the collective attention away from reactive problem solving to co-creation of the future (Senge et al., 2015) and the sustainability competencies of strategic thinking and interpersonal competence (Ploum et al., 2018) support this proposition. First, using a big picture perspective to influence entire systems requires strategic thinking and interpersonal abilities. Second, seeing the big picture and influencing entire systems requires a systems thinking perspective. Seeing the big picture and acknowledging details are two essential systems thinking abilities (Russell Reynolds Associates, 2015). System thinkers are capable of anticipating potential changes and deviations, thinking beyond their functional role and thinking long-term when making decisions. Because systems thinking and interpersonal competencies were described in earlier sections, the remainder of this section is devoted to strategic thinking and management.

Within the context of sustainability, the term strategic is defined as "the ability to collectively design and implement interventions, transitions, and transformative governance strategies toward sustainability" (Wiek et al., 2011, p. 210). Strategic management is defined as the formulation, implementation, and evaluation of managerial actions and processes that increase the value of an organization (Teece, 1990), concentrating on issues faced by managers of entire organizations or multifunctional departments (Frederickson, 1990). The focus of strategic management is with key goals and objectives of senior management, based on analysis of available resources and evaluation of existing internal and external environments. Strategic management requires assessment of the organization, and the environment in which it operates, to determine the long-term objectives necessary to adapt and adjust to that environment through opportunity and risk reduction (Alkhafaji & Nelson, 2013). Development of strategic management requires the expansion of timelines from days, weeks, and months to years, decades, and centuries. While much of the literature on strategic management is focused on senior management within organizations, strategic management can be developed and implemented by individuals not occupying senior management positions.

One of the challenges of any form of management or leadership is separating strategic management and activities from tactical ones. Strategic plans are focused on achieving overall goals and objectives, while business planning focuses on specific task or project implementation (Davidson & Venning, 2011). When functioning in professional or supervisory roles, individuals often perform tactical activities, which are short-term actions for achieving specific goals or objectives. Strategy describes the long-term, overarching goals and objectives of an organization and dictates short-term tactical activity. A sustainability leader will likely be required to perform tactical activities in addition to planning, implementing, and managing strategy. However, development and implementation of longer-term strategic action is necessary for successful progress within and across organizations and systems.

While the strategic management process is essential for organizational strategies, it is equally important for the strategic management of sustainability initiatives that may span multiple organizations, sectors, or systems. System leaders must be able to apply the previous six steps while considering the diverse and often conflicting missions, goals, and strategies of multiple stakeholders. Likewise, performing analyses, formulating and implementing strategies, and evaluating the outcomes become complicated when the goal is to manage strategy across multiple boundaries.

Senior managers are ultimately responsible for every decision and action of every organizational member. One important role top managers serve is that of strategic leader. Organizational researchers study leadership in relation to strategic management because an organization's top managers must provide effective strategic leadership (Robbins & Coulter, 2012). Strategic leadership describes the ability to anticipate, visualize, maintain flexibility, think strategically, and collaborate within the organization to facilitate necessary changes to create a beneficial organizational future (Barndt & Carvey, 1982). There are eight dimensions of strategic leadership: determining organizational purpose or vision; preserving and capitalizing on organizational core competencies; developing organizational human capital; developing and maintaining a strong organizational culture; building and managing organizational relationships; challenging and changing existing organizational perspectives; stressing the need for ethical decision-making and behavior; and implementing uniform, equitable organizational controls (Adam & Ebert, 1992).

## Leadership styles for system leadership

Leadership is the process of influencing other people to work toward a common objective (Northouse, 2018). Successful leaders unify individuals in a creative coalition, empowering them to actively participate in a relationship with chaos, uncertainty, and change (Wheatley, 2006). Effective leadership requires self-reflection, development of self-awareness, and recognition of the leader's relationship with the world, which collectively enables leaders to influence change in others (Heifetz, Grashow, & Linsky, 2009).

System leadership is not a style, but may serve as a compatible model to enhance and describe existing leadership styles. Three leadership styles have been examined as directly or indirectly relevant to organizational sustainability and corporate social responsibility (CSR): authentic, ethical, and transformational (Metcalf & Benn, 2013). Although these leadership styles share common attributes, each has unique characteristics (Metcalf & Benn, 2013). Moreover, leadership for sustainability shares common characteristics with other leadership styles, while maintaining unique attributes (Peterlin, Pearse, & Dimovski, 2015). Servant leadership has also been examined within the context of sustainability (Beehner, in press). While limited research exists examining collective leadership within the context of sustainability, this collaborative leadership style may also be appropriate for system leadership for sustainability. The authentic, ethical, transformational, collective, spiritual, and servant leadership styles are examined in this section, to better understand the appropriateness of these styles for system leadership for sustainability.

Authentic leadership is concerned with the authenticity, or genuineness, of the leader (Northouse, 2018), characterized by behavior patterns generated by the positive psychological features and strong ethics of the leader (Walumbwa, Avolio, Gardner, Wernsing, & Peterson, 2008). Authentic leadership behavior is frequently initiated by a critical life event and is distinguished by self-awareness, a personal moral perspective, balanced processing, and relative transparency (Northouse, 2018). Cavagnaro and Curiel (2012) suggested that authentic leadership is appropriate for sustainability because this style includes the necessity for self-leadership. Authentic leaders use authority to motivate followers to overcome major challenges, thereby assisting followers to manage change and personal growth (Heifetz, 1994).

Ethical leadership is grounded in ethical theory, providing leaders with a foundation of principles to enhance decision-making (Northouse, 2018). Ethical leaders are honest, treat others with respect, place the interests of others above self-interest, base all decision-making on equity and integrity, and are dedicated to community building (Northouse, 2018). Because leadership is an act of influence, it implies an ethical obligation to the individuals being influenced. While leadership for sustainability is grounded in ethical leadership (Brown & Treviño, 2006), it also extends the ethical purview by considering the requirements of multiple stakeholders, future generations, and the natural environment (Peterlin et al., 2015). Sustainability is fundamentally a values-driven idea (Barth & Michelsen, 2013; Frisk & Larson, 2011). Because the challenges presented by unsustainability are moral and ethical in nature, sustainability requires a leadership style established on moral and ethical behavior.

Transformational leadership is a process by which both leaders and followers are transformed and changed (Burns, 1978). Transformational leadership is the opposite of transactional leadership, which is characterized as a sequence of transactions between leaders and followers (Bass, 1990). Transformational leaders create connections with followers, empowering them to exceed expectations and motivating them by considering feelings, beliefs, values, and long-term goals. While followers may be attracted to transformational leaders who advocate for a cause with a compelling vision for the future, the potential for abuse exists, because leaders may motivate followers to embrace a new vision that may be contradictory to expressed values and not in their best interests to pursue (Northouse, 2018).

Transformational and sustainability leadership share four similar attributes: dedication to holistic understanding, intellectual stimulation of stakeholders, providing motivation by inspiring action, and an individualized approach to stakeholders (Avolio, Bass, & Jung, 1999; Bass, Avolio, Jung, & Berson, 2003). However, the focus of the two leadership styles differs, with transformational leaders using personal charisma to influence existing followers (House, Spangler, & Woycke, 1991) and sustainability leaders ensuring the ability of future generations to experience an equitable existence (Peterlin et al., 2015).

Collective leadership is the process of multiple individuals taking responsibility for organizational and system success, characterized by an understanding that all organizational members, at all levels, are accountable for leadership (Timmins, 2015). Collective leadership empowers individuals to cultivate organizations capable of collaborative work that is beneficial for all stakeholders (Timmins, 2015). The focal point of collective leadership is not with an individual leader, but with the interaction of group members who lead through shared leadership responsibilities (Hiller, Day, & Vance, 2006). However, while collaboration may provide the optimal conditions for change scalability, collaboration is challenging and requires skills such as humility and awareness, which are frequently lacking in leaders of larger organizations (Confino, 2012). Although collaborative problem solving is challenging, even when consensus and common values exist, leaders acknowledge that the uncertainty and tension created by individual differences creates opportunities for developing innovative solutions (Ferdig, 2007).

Collective leadership, also described as distributed or shared leadership, began receiving significant attention in the early 21st century as scholars shifted focus beyond leadership traits, behaviors, and styles to consider the collective role of teams and groups. Shared leadership is defined "as a dynamic, interactive influence process among individuals in groups for which the objective is to lead one another to the achievement of group or organizational goals or both" (Pearce & Conger, 2002, p. 1). Collective leadership occurs when team members demonstrate leadership behaviors to guide the team and maximize team performance (Bergman, Rentsch, Small, Davenport, & Bergman, 2012), and it requires that influence be shared by team members (Northouse, 2018). Shared or collective leadership enables organizations to respond more quickly to complex contemporary issues and challenges (Morgeson, DeRue, & Karam, 2010; Pearce, Manz, & Sims, 2009; Solansky, 2008). Addressing sustainability issues may require system leaders capable of demonstrating collective leadership to scale the impact of their influence.

Spiritual leadership is a value-based, integrated leadership style focused on social interactions among leaders, followers, and colleagues to promote development of an organizational culture that improves organizational success (Fry & Nisiewicz, 2013). Fry and Egel (2017) proposed a spiritual leadership model that inserts sustainability into the triple bottom line (TBL), influenced by the emerging discipline of workplace spirituality. The model is based on the idea that the spiritual elements underlying dominant spiritual and religious traditions offer a foundation to develop the necessary abilities to foster a sustainability perspective by pursuing higher degrees of consciousness, self-awareness, and other-centeredness. While the focus of religion is with theological systems of beliefs, rituals, and ceremonies, spirituality implies establishing a personal relationship with a divine being (Fry & Egel, 2017). In the spiritual leadership context, the focus of spirituality is with the intangible aspects of the human spirit, which is the energizing life principle that encourages us to seek the broadest measure of human experience (Fry & Egel, 2017).

Spiritual values and practices have been demonstrated to be consistent with leadership effectiveness, with the spiritual values of integrity, honesty, and humility having a positive influence on leadership success (Fry & Egel, 2017). Therefore, fulfilling spiritual needs in the workplace positively enhances health and well-being, establishing the foundation for spiritual leadership. Spiritual leadership is considered essential for developing uniformity of vision and value across individual, team, and organizational levels and is applicable to both religious and secular organizations (Fry, 2003). Spiritual leadership motivates and inspires followers through acceptance of a transcendent vision and an organizational culture based on humanitarian values to fulfill common desires for spiritual well-being through calling and membership, and eventually, triple bottom line maximization (Fry & Egel, 2017). Essential features of spiritual leadership are creating a vision in which leaders and followers develop a sense of calling resulting in feelings of meaning, purpose, and making a difference and creating an organizational culture based on the principles of altruistic love, in which individuals experience feelings of membership, acceptance, and appreciation (Fry & Egel, 2017).

There are several reasons why embedding sustainability in the triple bottom line is difficult, with many leaders lacking the capacity to perceive or accomplish this (Fry & Egel, 2017). First, leadership for sustainability demonstrates a developing consensus for leaders to live and lead in a manner that accounts for their impact on the environment, society, and the economy. Second, this demands leaders with exceptional capabilities, because sustainability requires organizations to function within intricate, interdependent, and dynamic systems that necessitate responsible decision-making and complex problem solving. Third, leaders must undertake a personal pilgrimage in which inherent human selfishness evolves or becomes focused on empathy, compassion, and awareness of self, colleagues, organizations, communities, and the environment, and how these elements are related (Fry & Egel, 2017). The spiritual leadership style may be useful for system leaders to influence sustainability by appealing on a level that transcends individual or organizational material needs.

Greenleaf (1970) introduced servant leadership as a style wherein the leader begins with an innate desire to serve others, resulting in a conscious decision to lead. Greenleaf suggested individuals often do not intentionally desire to become servant leaders, but they acquire the role while serving others. Servant leaders place follower needs first, seeking to help their followers develop, and become more likely to serve others, whereas non-servant leaders place self or organizational needs first, with service to others an afterthought and only if useful in achieving objectives. Like transformational leaders, servant leaders attempt to empower and cultivate followers, culminating in a level of awareness in which individuals go beyond personal self-interests for the good of others. Greenleaf (1977) suggested servant leaders must possess the ability to communicate a vision of hope. The ultimate measure of servant leadership is whether followers grow as individuals and eventually become servant leaders themselves (Greenleaf, 1977).

Leaders acknowledge that no organizational member, function, or component is unimportant (Zohar, 1997). Servant leadership emanates from a level of intentional, revolutionary vision (McCann & Holt, 2010), with servant leaders transforming organizations, envisioning new paradigms, and influencing new ideas and innovations, all accomplished through "being" rather than "doing" (Zohar, 1997). In serving others, servant leaders acknowledge the needs of followers, empowering them to accept responsibility for the betterment of society, characteristics that are synonymous with and complementary of an altruistic concept such as sustainability.

Leadership for sustainability requires leadership for both meaningful and necessary change (van Dierendonck & Sousa, 2016). Servant leaders may provide the positive influence necessary to ensure successful organizational change efforts, because they can develop meaningful, harmonious work environments, which are essential for organizational change (van Dierendonck & Sousa, 2016). Servant leaders strengthen a sense of purpose in their organizations through a combination of personal attention and the capacity to demonstrate that change is a higher purpose that transcends the organization (van Dierendonck & Sousa, 2016). Because there is often no legal obligation to conserve resources, sustainability is a voluntary, ethical action. Servant leadership is an ethical leadership style, encouraging leaders to behave "in ways that serve the greater good of the organization, community, and society at large" (Northouse, 2018, p. 219). Because servant leaders place others first, that benevolence extends to and benefits individuals beyond the influence of the leader. In addition to considering the needs of followers, servant leaders are interested in the disadvantaged, desiring to eliminate inequality and social injustices (Northouse, 2018), all of which are important to sustainability. The sustainable and servant leadership styles expand the view of change as evolving in concentric circles of unified thought, where the leader involves others in the process of cultivating community and sustainability (Peterlin et al., 2015).

## Conclusion

This chapter described the characteristics, skills, elements, and core competencies of system leaders. The core competencies were examined within the context of the three propositions introduced in Chapter 2, advocating that sustainability requires leadership approaches based upon the natural environment structure, leadership capable of transcending boundaries and artificial barriers, and leadership capable of seeing the big picture and influencing the entire system. We then considered several leadership styles that are compatible with system leadership for achievement of sustainability. Whatever leadership style is chosen, system leadership provides a promising framework for leading sustainability efforts in the challenging conditions faced by humankind in the 21st century. Because leadership is not an inherited trait but can be developed, system leadership can likewise be developed, which is the subject of the following chapter.

## Chapter reflection questions

1. Several characteristics and core competencies of system leadership have been described in this chapter. Which one do you think will have the greatest impact, and why?
2. Several leadership styles have been examined. Which leadership style do you think is most compatible with system leadership and sustainability efforts, and why?
3. Which of the characteristics and core competencies do you believe that you possess? How would you apply those in exercising system leadership within your organization?
4. Which of the characteristic and core competencies do you believe would be the easiest to teach and learn, and why? Which ones would be the most difficult, and why?

## References


Accenture. (2016). *The UN global compact: Accenture strategy CEO study*. Retrieved from www.accenture.com/us-en/insight-un-global-compact-ceo-study

Adam, E. E., & Ebert, R. J. (1992). *Production and operations management* (5th ed.). Upper Saddle River, NJ: Prentice Hall.

Alkhafaji, A., & Nelson, R. A. (2013). *Strategic management: Formulation, implementation, and control in a dynamic environment*. Abingdon, England: Routledge.

Ambler, G. (2013). *Systems thinking as a leadership practice*. Johannesburg, South Africa: Author.

Avolio, B. J., Bass, B. M., & Jung, D. (1999). Re-examining the components of transformational and transactional leadership using the Multifactor Leadership Questionnaire. *Journal of Occupational and Organizational Psychology*, 7, 441–462. doi:10.1348/096317999166789

Barndt, S. E., & Carvey, D. W. (1982). *Essentials of operations management*. Upper Saddle River, NJ: Prentice Hall.

Barth, M., & Michelsen, G. (2013). Learning for change: An educational contribution to sustainability science. *Sustainability Science*, *8*(1), 103–119. doi:10.1007/s11625-012-0181-5

Bass, B. M. (1990). From transactional to transformational leadership: Learning to share the vision. *Organizational Dynamics*, *18*(3), 19–31. doi:10.1016/0090-2616(90)90061-S

Bass, B. M., Avolio, B. J., Jung, D. I., & Berson, Y. (2003). Predicting unit performance by assessing transformational and transactional leadership. *Journal of Applied Psychology*, *88*(2), 207–218. doi:10.1037/0021-9010.88.2.207

Beehner, C. G. (in press). Servant leadership as a pathway to a sustainable future. In S. Dhiman (Ed.), *Positive leadership and change: A practical guide for workplace transformation*. Heidelberg, Germany: Springer Nature.

Bergman, J. Z., Rentsch, J. R., Small, E. E., Davenport, S. W., & Bergman, S. M. (2012). The shared leadership process in decision-making teams. *The Journal of Social Psychology*, *152*(1), 17–42. doi:10.1080/00224545.2010.538763

Boiral, O., Baron, C., & Gunnlaugson, O. (2014). Environmental leadership and consciousness development: A case study among Canadian SMEs. *Journal of Business Ethics, 123*(3), 363–383. doi:10.1007/s10551-013-1845-5

Brown, B. C. (2011). *Conscious leadership for sustainability: A study of how leaders and change agents with postconventional consciousness design and engage in complex change initiatives* (doctoral dissertation). Fielding Graduate University, Santa Barbara, CA.

Brown, M. E., & Treviño, L. K. (2006). Ethical leadership: A review and future directions. *The Leadership Quarterly, 17*(6), 595–616. doi:10.1016/j.leaqua.2006.10.004

Burns, J. M. (1978). *Leadership*. New York, NY: Harper & Row.

Cavagnaro, E., & Curiel, G. H. (2012). *The three levels of sustainability*. Sheffield, England: Greenleaf Publishing.

Collins, J. (2001). *Good to great: Why some companies make the leap . . . and others don't*. New York, NY: Harper Business.

Confino, J. (2012, October 15). *The art of systems thinking in driving sustainable transformation*. Retrieved from www.theguardian.com/sustainable-business/systems-thinking-sustainable-transformation

Dalati, S., Raudeliūnienė, J., & Davidavičienė, V. (2017). Sustainable leadership, organizational trust on job satisfaction: Empirical evidence from higher education institutions in Syria. *Business, Management and Education, 15*(1), 14–27. doi:10.3846/bme.2017.360

Davidson, K. M., & Venning, J. (2011). Sustainability decision-making frameworks and the application of systems thinking: An urban context. *Local Environment, 16*(3), 213–228. doi:10.1080/13549839.2011.565464

Eccles, R. G., Perkins, K. M., & Serafeim, G. (2012). How to become a sustainable company. *MIT Sloan Management Review, 53*(4), 43. Retrieved from www.hbs.edu

Ferdig, M. A. (2007). Sustainability leadership: Co-creating a sustainable future. *Journal of Change Management*, 7(1), 25–35. doi:10.1080/14697010701233809

Frederickson, J. W. (1990). Introduction: The need for perspectives. In J. W. Frederickson (Ed.), *Perspectives on strategic management* (pp. 1–8). New York, NY: Harper Business.

Frisk, E., & Larson, K. L. (2011). Educating for sustainability: Competencies & practices for transformative action. *Journal of Sustainability Education, 2*(1), 1–20. Retrieved from www.jsedimensions.org/wordpress/wp-content/uploads/2011/03/FriskLarson2011.pdf

Fry, L. (2003). Toward a theory of spiritual leadership. *The Leadership Quarterly, 14*, 693–727. doi:10.1016/j.leaqua.2003.09.001

Fry, L., & Egel, E. (2017). Spiritual leadership: Embedding sustainability in the Triple Bottom Line. *The Graziadio Business Review, 20*(3), 39–40. Retrieved from www.researchgate.net

Fry, L. W., & Nisiewicz, M. S. (2013). *Maximizing the triple bottom line through spiritual leadership*. Stanford, CA: Stanford University Press.

Fullan, M. (2003a). *Change forces with a vengeance*. London, England: Routledge Falmer.

Fullan, M. (2003b). *The moral imperative of school leadership*. Thousand Oaks, CA: Corwin Press and Toronto: Ontario Principals Council.

Fullan, M. (2005). *Leadership and sustainability*. Thousand Oaks, CA: Corwin Press and Toronto: Ontario Principals Council.

Greenleaf, R. K. (1970). *The servant as leader*. Indianapolis, IN: The Robert K. Greenleaf Center.

Greenleaf, R. K. (1977). *Servant leadership: A journey into the nature of legitimate power and greatness*. New York, NY: Paulist Press.

Haney, A. B., Pope, J., & Arden, Z. (2018). Making it personal: Developing sustainability leaders in business. *Organization & Environment*. doi:10.1177/1086026618806201

Heifetz, R. (1994). *Leadership without easy answers*. Cambridge, MA: Harvard University Press.

Heifetz, R., Grashow, A., & Linsky, M. (2009). *The practice of adaptive leadership*. Boston, MA: Harvard Business School Publishing.

Hesselbarth, C., & Schaltegger, S. (2014). Educating change agents for sustainability: Learnings from the first sustainability management master of business administration. *Journal of Cleaner Production*, *62*, 24–36. doi:10.1016/j.jclepro.2013.03.042

Hiller, N. J., Day, D. V., & Vance, R. J. (2006). Collective enactment of leadership roles and team effectiveness: A field study. *The Leadership Quarterly*, *17*(4), 387–397. doi:10.1016/j.leaqua.2006.04.004

House, R. J., Spangler, W. D., & Woycke, J. (1991). Personality and charisma in the U.S. presidency: A psychological theory of leader effectiveness. *Administrative Science Quarterly*, *36*(3), 364–396. doi:10.2307/2393201

Iftakhar, N., & Bahauddin, K. M. (2018, January 10). *Why leadership is essential for achieving sustainable development goals*. Seoul, South Korea: International Policy Digest. Retrieved from https://intpolicydigest.org/2018/01/10/why-leadership-is-essential-for-achieving-sustainable-development-goals/

Kaliannan, M., & Adjovu, S. N. (2015). Effective employee engagement and organizational success: A case study. *Procedia Social and Behavioral Sciences*, *172*, 161–168. doi:10.1016/j.sbpro.2015.01.350

Lans, T., Blok, V., & Wesselink, R. (2014). Learning apart and together: Towards an integrated competence framework for sustainable entrepreneurship in higher education. *Journal of Cleaner Production*, *62*, 37–47. doi:10.1016/j.jclepro.2013.03.036

Loehr, J., & Schwartz, T. (2003). *The power of full engagement*. New York, NY: Free Press.

MacGillivray, A. E. (2015). Leadership, boundaries, and sustainability. In D. B. Willis, F. Steier, & P. Stillman (Eds.), *Sustainability leadership: Integrating values, meaning, and action* (pp. 277–307). Santa Barbara, CA: Fielding Graduate University.

Martin, A., & Ernst, C. (2005). Exploring leadership in times of paradox and complexity. *Corporate Governance: The International Journal of Business in Society*, *5*(3), 82–94. doi:10.1108/14720700510604724

McCann, J. T., & Holt, R. A. (2010). Servant and sustainable leadership: An analysis in the manufacturing environment. *International Journal of Management Practice*, *4*(2), 134–148. doi:10.1504/IJMP.2010.033691

Metcalf, L., & Benn, S. (2013). Leadership for sustainability: An evolution of leadership ability. *Journal of Business Ethics*, *112*(3), 369–384. doi:10.1007/s10551-012-1278-6

Miliband, D. (2004). *Personalized learning: Building new relationships with schools*. Speech presented to the North of England Education Conference, Belfast, Northern Ireland, 8 January.

Morgeson, F. P., DeRue, D. S., & Karam, E. P. (2010). Leadership in teams: A functional approach to understanding leadership structures and processes. *Journal of Management*, *36*(1), 5–39. doi:10.1177/0149206309347376

Northouse, P. G. (2018). *Leadership: Theory and practice* (8th ed.). Thousand Oaks, CA: Sage Publications.

Osagie, E. R., Wesselink, R., Blok, V., Lans, T., & Mulder, M. (2016). Individual competencies for corporate social responsibility: A literature and practice perspective. *Journal of Business Ethics*, *135*(2), 233–252. doi:10.1007/s10551-014-2469-0

Pearce, C. L., & Conger, J. A. (2002). *Shared leadership: Reframing the hows and whys of leadership*. Thousand Oaks, CA: Sage Publications.

Pearce, C. L., Manz, C. C., & Sims, H. P. (2009). Where do we go from here? Is shared leadership the key to team success? *Organizational Dynamics*, *38*(3), 234–238. doi:10.1016/j.orgdyn.2009.04.008

Peirce, M. (2011). Introduction. In *A journey of a thousand miles: The state of sustainability leadership 2011* (pp. 11–20). Cambridge, England: Cambridge Institute for Sustainability Leadership.

Peterlin, J., Pearse, N. J., & Dimovski, V. (2015). Strategic decision making for organizational sustainability: The implications of servant leadership and sustainable leadership approaches. *Economic & Business Review, 17*(3), 273–290. doi:10.15458/85451.4

Ploum, L., Blok, V., Lans, T., & Omta, O. (2018). Toward a validated competence framework for sustainable entrepreneurship. *Organization & Environment, 31*(2), 113–132. doi:10.1177/1086026617697039

Robbins, S. P., & Coulter, M. (2012). *Management* (11th ed.). Upper Saddle River, NJ: Pearson Prentice Hall.

Russell Reynolds Associates. (2015). *Sustainable leadership: Talent requirements for sustainable enterprises.* New York, NY: Author. Retrieved from www.russellreynolds.com/en/Insights/thought-leadership/Documents/russell_reynolds_sustainable_leadership.pdf

Savage, E., Tapics, T., Evarts, J., Wilson, J., & Tirone, S. (2015). Experiential learning for sustainability leadership in higher education. *International Journal of Sustainability in Higher Education, 16*(5), 692–705. doi:10.1108/IJSHE-10-2013-0132

Scharmer, O. (2008). *CISL sustainability leadership research interview.* Cambridge, England: Cambridge Institute for Sustainability Leadership.

Senge, P., Hamilton, H., & Kania, J. (2015). The dawn of system leadership. *Stanford Social Innovation Review, 13*(1), 27–33. Retrieved from https://ssir.org/articles/entry/the_dawn_of_system_leadership

Šimanskienė, L., & Župerkienė, E. (2014). Sustainable leadership: The new challenge for organizations. *Forum Scientiae Oeconomia, 2*(1), 81–93. Retrieved from www.researchgate.net

Solansky, S. T. (2008). Leadership style and team processes in self-managed teams. *Journal of Leadership and Organizational Studies, 14*(4), 332–341. doi:10.1177/1548051808315549

Strandberg, C. (2015, May 2019). *Building resilient organizations.* Burnaby, BC, Canada: Strandberg Consulting. Retrieved from https://corostrandberg.com/building-resilient-organizations/

Stroh, D. P. (2015). *Systems thinking for social change: A practical guide to solving complex problems, avoiding unintended consequences, and achieving lasting results.* White River Junction, VT: Chelsea Green Publishing.

Summers, P. (2011). Systems thinking in local government. *Systemist, 33*, 88–111. Retrieved from www.researchgate.net/publication/262414621_Systems_thinking_in_local_government

Teece, D. J. (1990). Contributions and impediments of economic analysis to the study of strategic management. In J. W. Frederickson (Ed.), *Perspectives on strategic management* (pp. 39–80). New York, NY: Harper Business.

Timmins, N. (2015). *The practice of system leadership: Being comfortable with chaos.* London, England: The King's Fund. Retrieved from www.kingsfund.org.uk/sites/default/files/field/field_publication_file/System-leadership-Kings-Fund-May-2015.pdf

van Dierendonck, D., & Sousa, M. (2016). Finding meaning in highly uncertain situations: Servant leadership during change. In *Leadership lessons from compelling contexts* (pp. 403–424). Bingley, England: Emerald Group.

Visser, W., & Courtice, P. (2011). *Sustainability leadership: Linking theory and practice.* Available at SSRN 1947221. Cambridge, England: Cambridge Institute for Sustainability Leadership.

Visser, W., & Crane, A. (2010). *Corporate sustainability and the individual: Understanding what drives sustainability professionals as change agents.* doi:10.2139/ssrn.1559087

Walumbwa, F. O., Avolio, B. J., Gardner, W. L., Wernsing, T. S., & Peterson, S. J. (2008). Authentic leadership: Development and validation of a theory-based measure. *Journal of Management, 34*(1), 89–126. doi:10.1177/0149206307308913

Weinreb, E. (2015). *5 core competencies of sustainability leadership*. Retrieved from www.greenbiz.com/article/5-core-competencies-sustainability-leadership

Wesselink, R., Blok, V., van Leur, S., Lans, T., & Dentoni, D. (2015). Individual competencies for managers engaged in corporate sustainable management practices. *Journal of Cleaner Production, 106*(Supplement C), 497–506. doi:10.1016/j.jclepro.2014.10.093

Wheatley, M. J. (2006). *Leadership and the new science: Discovering order in a chaotic world*. San Francisco, CA: Berrett-Koehler Publishers.

Wiek, A., Withycombe, L., & Redman, C. L. (2011). Key competencies in sustainability: A reference framework for academic program development. *Sustainability Science, 6*(2), 203–218. doi:10.1007/s11625-011-0132-6

Zohar, D. (1997). *Rewiring the corporate brain: Using the new science to rethink how we structure and lead organizations*. San Francisco, CA: Berrett-Koehler Publishers.

# 4 Development of system leadership for sustainability

## Introduction

The previous chapters established a foundation of system leadership, examined the characteristics, skills, and core competencies of system leadership, and explored why this model is appropriate for sustainability. The focus of this chapter is on how to develop sustainability system leadership, within the context of the three propositions introduced in Chapter 2: sustainability requires leadership approaches based upon the natural environment structure, sustainability requires system leadership capable of transcending boundaries and artificial barriers, and sustainability requires leadership capable of seeing the big picture and influencing the entire system. As previously stated, system leadership enhances, rather than replaces, existing leadership styles. System leadership informs how a given leadership style is best implemented and is applicable to multiple leadership styles.

Cultivating sustainability leaders requires development of new ways of thinking, a fundamental desire to act, and acquisition of new knowledge and skills (Haney, Pope, & Arden, 2018). These leaders will be required to develop cognitive, functional, and values-oriented competencies to successfully address sustainability issues (Haney et al., 2018). Because sustainability is an issue without boundaries, these leaders must be able to apply these competencies across boundaries, influencing entire systems. System leadership provides the framework for new ways of thinking and for influencing across multiple boundaries and systems. Moreover, system leadership requires collective leadership, because no single leader or entity possesses all the information and resources necessary to achieve sustainability (Confino, 2012). However, there has been insufficient effort for the development of system leaders (Timmins, 2015). This chapter may be useful in filling the apparent void in system leadership development.

## Development of leadership based upon the natural environment structure

The first proposition advancing system leadership for sustainability is that sustainability is a natural environmental concept, the promotion of which requires leadership approaches based upon the natural environment structure. The core capability of being able to see the larger system (Senge, Hamilton, & Kania, 2015) and the sustainability competency of systems thinking (Ploum, Blok, Lans, & Omta, 2018) support this proposition, because understanding the natural environment requires a systems thinking perspective. Natural systems consist of numerous entities and processes that are interconnected and interdependent. Leaders who understand natural, environmental systems are able to understand and influence social and economic systems, because all three are based on systems thinking.

The application of systems thinking in system leadership provides a foundation for a sustainable worldview. In this section, methods of applying and developing systems thinking toward sustainability are examined. Systems thinking is a way of viewing the world that one does not necessarily learn, but develops over time, much like any other practice. From a systems perspective, sustainability describes the ability of systems to endure, adapt, evolve, or transition in a dynamic environment (Williams, Kennedy, Philipp, & Whiteman, 2017). Systems thinking is a beneficial tool for understanding change across multiple scales (Williams et al., 2017). A scale is defined as "the spatial, temporal, quantitative, or analytical dimensions used to measure and study any phenomenon" (Cash et al., 2006, p. 2). A holistic understanding of sustainability, including the spatial and temporal scales, is essential for achieving sustainability objectives and avoiding arrangements that produce unintended consequences (Metson, Aggarwal, & Childers, 2012).

Siebert (2018) has identified some basic habits to incorporate systems thinking into sustainability: be a critical thinker; be a badger; expand the time horizons of your thinking; expand the special horizons of your thinking; see the connections; and consider multiple perspectives. Being a critical thinker requires thinking beyond ideas embraced by social groups, political parties, news media, or other mainstream forces, questioning the motives of any individual or group claiming authoritative knowledge (Siebert, 2018). Being a badger requires curiosity about the world and how it functions – politically, socially, economically, culturally, ideologically, and environmentally. Badgers are recognized for their expert analytical skills, asking probing questions, and unearthing obscure information and knowledge (Siebert, 2018).

Expanding the time horizons of thinking requires examining human history to better understand our current trajectory and way of life (Siebert, 2018). This retrospective analysis provides a better perspective by highlighting several aspects of humankind: the current human existence differs from any in human history, characterized by the rapid expansion of the fossil-fuel based economy; the possibilities of a post-fossil fuel future; and, the connection to our ancestors and their collective consciousness. The development of sustainable habitats requires a long-term perspective that considers the impact of our actions on current and future generations (Siebert, 2018). Expanding the spatial horizons of thinking requires expansion of an individual's sphere of concern and influence beyond existing boundaries. An unfortunate consequence of the Industrial Revolution and the expansion of Western civilization is the expansion of individualist versus collectivist thinking. A systems perspective requires an understanding of small and large spatial scales and acknowledgment of the far-reaching consequences of our individual and collective actions in terms of human and ecological health (Siebert, 2018).

Seeing the connections involves critical thinking with broader spatial and temporal perspectives, because nothing exists in isolation, and these connections define the essential actions for achieving sustainability (Siebert, 2018). Understanding the interconnections of observed phenomena is essential for understanding the nature of and finding solutions for the sustainability issues faced by humankind, and systems thinking assists with identifying and comprehending the relevance and importance of observed interconnections (Stibbe, 2009). Finally, considering multiple perspectives involves expanding awareness and determines how we define problems and influence systems (Siebert, 2018). Across the globe, various perspectives exist, and the modern industrial perspective is not the only one possible or necessarily the most beneficial.

Siebert (2018) suggested leaders embrace systems thinking practices, combining their expertise and passions to take immediate action toward construction of a sustainable future. "People's good intentions to improve social systems are often undermined when they apply conventional thinking to chronic, complex problems" (Stroh, 2015, p. 18). Therefore, to understand social system behavior, we must examine the interactions of the system and components, with the broader system in which they exist (Ackoff, 1994). Systems thinking provides a foundation for the interpretative approach required for recognition of the interconnectedness of the forces of observed phenomenon (Barile, Orecchini, Saviano, & Farioli, 2018). As a result of these interconnections, complex recursive structures emerge that represent how the observed reality appears to be organized. Acknowledging these recursive structures is essential for managing the emerging complexity, such as occurs with sustainability issues (Barile et al., 2018). Recursion is a popular idea in cybernetics and other areas of systems thinking and is the foundation of the Viable Systems Model (VSM; Beer, 1972) that is significant in application of cybernetics to management (Barile et al., 2018).

Understanding and applying systems thinking requires support at both methodological and practical levels. Cybernetics has been identified as a practical tool that is helpful in integrating the contribution of systems thinking (Barile et al., 2018). While systems thinking is helpful for seeing the whole system and preventing dysfunctional fragmentation (Espejo, 2018), cybernetics is helpful for discerning how to manage stability in the interactions between individuals, organizations, and systems (Barile et al., 2018). Therefore, cybernetics provides the practical tools that support the methodological tools of systems thinking, enabling management of complexity. The systems approach provides an appropriate model for understanding sustainability, appreciating its inherent systemic attributes, and when combined with cybernetics offers a tool to address sustainability management (Barile et al., 2018).

Development of comprehensive systems thinking requires individuals and organizations to understand several key characteristics of systems: the role and function of inputs and outputs; making energy requires energy; making materials requires energy; sustaining life requires sustained healthy habitats; and politics matters (Siebert, 2018). Products are not created out of nothing, and there is no "away" to which we can throw our products after use. The energy and resource inputs necessary to maintain life and lifestyle must be sustainably managed and the impacts of their extraction and consumption fully understood and respected. Human life is dependent on the health and vitality of our natural environment, and the transition to a sustainable world will require evaluation of our impacts on the natural environment. Evaluating and understanding our impact on the earth is both objective and subjective, requiring an understanding of systems thinking to be effective. Finally, politics is defined as the complex relationships between individuals living in society and managing those relationships through modification of rules, regulations, and government systems. Therefore, politics provides the structural conditions that will either support or inhibit the shift to a sustainable world (Siebert, 2018).

The following recommendations may enhance the broad adoption of a systems approach to sustainability:

- Encourage interdisciplinary research collaboration by creating incentives for interdepartmental cooperation on essential societal issues.
- Enhance communications to educators, government officials, the media, and the general public to express the urgency of sustainability issues.
- Develop policy-development methods that acknowledge the complex, interconnected characteristics of ecological and socioeconomic systems, including conceptualization methods and corresponding metrics.
- Explore methods for introducing environmental awareness into business, such as developing integrated energy management services and sustainable architectural systems.
- Develop instruments for integrated conversation among business, government, and academia, transitioning from an antagonistic approach to a cooperative approach.

(Fiksel, 2006)

While systems thinking is a mental model, reliance on only the mental dimension provides an incomplete perspective (Stroh, 2015). The development of systems thinking requires the integration of the mental, emotional, physical, and spiritual dimensions (Stroh, 2015). By embracing the emotional dimension, systems thinker(s) learn to identify emotional attachment to beliefs and assumptions and how those attachments limit our perspective. "Systems thinking is a team sport" (Stroh, 2015, p. 207), because stakeholders with diverse viewpoints can work together to develop a common agenda for coordinated action. While there may be emotional or mental dimensions involved, this coordinated action occurs in the physical dimension. Finally, systems thinking is a spiritual practice, because it encourages recognition of how everything is interconnected, that we can make positive or negative choices, and making proper choices requires development of specific behaviors and traits (Stroh, 2015). Developing system thinkers is an adaptive challenge, requiring leaders be enabled to experience and become more effective at leading organizations toward sustainability (Fullan, 2005). While technical problems have a known answer, adaptive challenges have solutions existing outside the knowledge base (Heifetz, 2003).

## Development of leadership for transcending boundaries and artificial barriers

The second proposition advancing system leadership for sustainability is that sustainability is a boundaryless concept, the promotion of which requires system leadership capable of transcending boundaries and artificial barriers, engaging multiple stakeholders both vertically and horizontally. The core capabilities of promoting reflection and more innovative conversation and transforming the collective focus from reactive problem solving to proactive co-creation of the future (Senge et al., 2015), combined with the sustainability competency of interpersonal competence (Ploum et al., 2018), support this proposition, because transcending boundaries and barriers requires interpersonal abilities.

The third core capability of system leadership is the ability to cultivate reflection and more innovative conversations (Senge et al., 2015). While reflection is an internal attribute and innovative conversations are external, both are relevant interpersonal competencies, because inner conditions influence external relationships. Successful leaders take time to "get on the balcony" (Heifetz & Laurie, 2001, p. 6) to objectively evaluate their actions by stepping outside of their role and comfort zone and objectively look at how their actions impact the organization and individual members. This requires interpersonal competencies and the specific core competencies of external collaboration and active values. A leader demonstrating active values is self-aware of emotions and motivations and sensitive to the emotions and motivations of other individuals (Weinreb, 2015). Systemically, these attributes are interconnected because active values will influence a desire for reflection, and external collaboration will influence innovative conversations. Therefore, development of these attributes and competencies is complemented by systems thinking, further supporting the system leadership model.

Sustainability leaders must be willing to collaborate with entities outside of their organization, because environmental impacts extend beyond organizational boundaries (Weinreb, 2015). Collaboration assists organizations with acquiring social capital, expanding into new markets, and changing the conditions in which they operate (Weinreb, 2015). While business leaders have been embracing sustainability collaboration, efforts have been limited to partnerships with individual nongovernmental organizations (NGOs) or pre-competitive industry alliances. However, the confidence acquired during collaboration has prepared the framework for further collaboration (Confino, 2012). Education is an essential component for a multiple stakeholder collaborative framework, and social learning is a crucial technique for achieving the cultural change necessary to progress toward sustainability (Goekler, 2003; Saviano, Di Nauta, Montella, & Sciarelli, 2018a, 2018b; Wiek, Farioli, Fukushi, & Yarime, 2012).

Emotional intelligence (EI) is an important leadership ability in which leaders understand and manage their own emotions, as well as understand and influence the emotions of those with whom they interact. As noted in Chapter 3, EI was repeatedly identified as an essential system leadership characteristic and skill (Metcalf & Benn, 2013; Peirce, 2011; Strandberg, 2015; Timmins, 2015; Visser & Courtice, 2011). Goleman (1995) identified five dimensions of EI:

- Self-awareness: individual awareness of the emotions being experienced.
- Self-management: the ability to manage one's emotions and impulses.
- Self-motivation: the ability to persist despite obstacles and failures.
- Empathy: the ability to perceive what other individuals are feeling.
- Social skills: the ability to manage other individuals' emotions.

EI can be learned through being personally motivated, practicing extensively what is learned, accepting feedback, and using feedback and learning to reinforce new skills (Serrat, 2017). The development of emotional intelligence enhances the ability of sustainability leaders to influence across boundaries and systems. Moreover, successful engagement requires leaders who can develop positive relationships and demonstrate significant intellectual and emotional intelligence (Baue & Wood, 2015).

Organizational speaker Preston Ni (2014) offered six keys to increasing emotional intelligence. First, reduce negative emotions by reducing negative personalization (jumping to negative conclusions when feeling adversely about an individual's behavior) and reducing fear of rejection by providing multiple options to ensure positive alternatives in difficult situations. Second, maintain the ability to remain calm and manage stress by avoiding caffeinated beverages and lowering body temperature when feeling nervous and anxious, and participating in aerobic exercise in response to feelings of nervousness or anxiety. Third, learn to be assertive and express difficult emotions when personal boundaries are crossed, without behaving in an accusatory manner. Fourth, be proactive rather than reactive when engaged with a difficult individual, by pausing prior to responding, being empathetic to the other individual's position, and learning to assert the potential consequences that may result from the encounter. Fifth, learn to "bounce back" from challenging situations by replacing frustration with optimism. Finally, learn to express intimate emotions when engaged in close, personal relationships in a nourishing, constructive manner (Ni, 2014).

The four dimensions of systems thinking were previously identified as mental, emotional, physical, and spiritual (Stroh, 2015). Acknowledging the spiritual dimension enables system leaders to cultivate character strengths, identified by Stroh as curiosity, respect, compassion, awareness, vision, courage, patience, and flexibility. While conversations about spirituality within the workforce and other organizational settings may seem awkward, a surge in interest in workplace spirituality and spiritual leadership supports such conversations when approached from a nondenominational, secular perspective. The spiritual leadership style, which was influenced by workplace spirituality, was examined within the context of sustainability in Chapter 3.

## Development of leadership for seeing the big picture and influencing entire systems

The third proposition advancing system leadership for sustainability is that sustainability is a complex, global concept, requiring leadership capable of seeing the big picture and influencing the entire system. The core capabilities of being able to see the larger system and transforming the collective attention away from reactive problem solving to co-creation of the future (Senge et al., 2015) and the sustainability competencies of strategic thinking and interpersonal competence (Ploum et al., 2018) support this proposition. Developing and maintaining a big picture perspective to influence entire systems requires strategic thinking and interpersonal abilities.

This leadership core competency can be developed through systems thinking, which was discussed in an earlier section, and strategic management. To embed sustainability into the organizational strategy, system leaders must develop the competency of strategic management. While entire texts and courses are devoted to the topic of strategic management, in this section strategic management is defined and methods for development of strategic management and strategic thinking are summarized.

Strategic management is developed through the expansion of spatial and temporal boundaries. When making strategic decisions, leaders must consider longer time periods than the week, month, fiscal quarter, or even year. Strategic thinkers consider the impacts of their individual and collective actions beyond their current and future roles and lifetimes. This requires the ability to look at the broader picture, including components and actors that may not be readily visible. Strategic managers develop the ability to see the broader picture and think strategically by asking probing questions concerning how and why an event occurred or a task is performed in a certain manner.

There are six stages to the strategic management process, and there are several tools available to assist with strategic management. The stages of strategic management are:

1 Identify the organization's current mission, goals, and strategies.
2 Perform an external analysis.
3 Perform an internal analysis.
4 Formulate strategies.

5 Implement strategies.
6 Evaluate results.

(Robbins & Coulter, 2012)

Two tools that are useful for the second and third stage are the SWOT analysis and the PESTEL framework. The SWOT analysis is used to identify the strengths, weaknesses, opportunities, and threats of a proposed strategy. The PESTEL framework is a marketing analysis tool used to examine the macro-environment, by identifying the political, economic, social, technological, environmental, and legal factors related to an action. The results of the analysis provide the threats and weaknesses for a SWOT analysis.

Forward thinking or anticipatory thinking is defined as "the ability to collectively analyze, evaluate, and craft rich 'pictures' of the future related to sustainability issues and sustainability problem-solving frameworks" (Wiek et al., 2011, pp. 207, 209). Sustainability leaders recognize that organizations must embrace forward-thinking attitudes to ensure resource access and continue their social license to operate (Weinreb, 2015). Although a detailed examination of strategic management development is beyond the scope of this text, the previous section provided a foundation on which system leaders can begin developing this ability. Having established a foundation for the development of the three system leadership competencies, the focus of the following section is with development of system leadership.

## Development of system leadership for sustainability

Most system leaders demonstrate system leadership with no specific knowledge that such a leadership model exists. Awareness of this leadership model may stimulate further interest among current and future sustainability leaders. Therefore, methods and techniques for development of system leadership are beneficial for individuals seeking to achieve positive systemic change and are examined in this section. Because this leadership model has received limited research attention to date, this section offers a foundation for system leadership development, based on existing systems thinking and sustainable leadership development models. The proposed methods of system leadership are by no means comprehensive. Further testing and development of these models and techniques should provide a more robust method of system leadership development.

The Australian Council for International Development (ACFID) developed an online course to assist with implementing the sustainable development goals, with a focus on systems thinking and collaboration. The learning objectives of the course are for participants to increase their:

- Understanding of systems thinking and collaboration as approaches to achieve large-scale impact.
- Skills and confidence to apply systems thinking by practicing using systems assessment tools.

- Skills and confidence to apply collaborative responses to achieve systems change through practical frameworks and tools to start, design, and sustain a strategic and structured collaborative response.

(ACFID, 2019)

ACFID focuses work on the SDGs around four elements that they consider essential for transformational change: thinking systemically, working collaboratively, reporting on impact, and going beyond business as usual (ACFID, 2019). These elements are supportive of system leadership; therefore, this online course may provide an excellent framework for development of system leadership for sustainability.

System leadership can be cultivated through development of the three previously identified core competencies of strategic management, comprehensive systems perspective, and interpersonal competencies. Developing expertise in only one of these competencies is insufficient. However, when all three competencies are developed, system leadership is possible. System leadership abilities are not acquired overnight but result from learning and practice. The best method for learning and practice is by working collaboratively with others who manifest system leadership. Practice can consist of mapping any simple problem, such as planning a vacation or understanding the steps that led up to a personal event. While this may seem mundane, development of maps and models enhances systems thinking, which further strengthens system leadership. Additional content concerning development of system leadership for sustainability at the individual level is included in Chapter 9.

## How to create systems change

Sustainability requires system-wide change at multiple levels. Changing entire systems requires changing the entire context within which individuals work (Fullan, 2005). Moreover, Fullan (2003) argued that changing systems requires increasing the volume of meaningful interaction between and among individuals, within and across levels and systems. While changing context requires time and cumulative effort, once in motion context change possesses a self-generating ability to continue (Fullan, 2005). Gladwell (2000) suggested context was an essential factor in change, suggesting that modifying group behavior requires creating a community around the group in which new beliefs can be communicated, practiced, and nurtured.

The systemic change required to build a sustainable future will require a new vision for individuals, organizations, and sectors. Sustainable leaders are capable of creating an inspiring vision for all stakeholders through seeing the bigger picture, understanding the details, exercising equitable decision-making, and keeping the vision simple (Russell Reynolds Associates, 2015). Sustainable leaders engineer a better organizational future through awareness of broader, more complex systems outside the organization and a profound understanding of how to manage the conflicting demands of multiple stakeholders

(Hind, Wilson, & Lenssen, 2009; Russell Reynolds Associates; Senge, 1990; Waddock, 2007).

Change often begins with unsatisfactory situations, but skillful system leaders assist with moving beyond reactive responses to crafting a positive outlook on the future (Senge et al., 2015). This change process occurs slowly as leaders assist others with articulating their profound passions and increasing confidence based on tangible collective success. The change process requires creating inspiring visions, along with accepting uncomfortable realities about current circumstances and learning how to apply the strain between vision and reality to develop new approaches (Senge et al., 2015).

Creating a sustainable future requires systemic change at multiple levels. Changing systems and assisting diverse stakeholders in developing and adopting a common vision require expertise and skill (Confino, 2012). An essential component of creating systemic change is the development of a positive vision of the future (Confino, 2012). Moreover, to create change, a leader must first realize that change internally, resulting in authentic leadership for change. Authenticity is the condition of being trustworthy and is based on character and competence (Cavagnaro & Curiel, 2012). The authentic leadership style was summarized in Chapter 3.

The essential ingredients in successful whole systems change are ensuring every stakeholder is equally represented from the beginning and throughout the change process, a clear map of system components and relationships, and a feeling of trust among stakeholders (Confino, 2012). It is essential that all stakeholders feel they are represented, valued, and can benefit from the change process and the proposed change. System change requires moving beyond what "should" be done and what is not being done to developing a positive future vision. This shift in focus is an important psychological learning component, because it immediately shifts individuals from narrow, short-term thinking to a longer-term perspective of the issues. Any change program requires support at all levels, and it is essential that cultural differences between collaborating organizations be acknowledged and respected if collaborative change is to be successful (Confino, 2012).

There are several reasons why systems thinking is suitable for overcoming the challenges of change:

- Individuals are motivated to change when they recognize their role exacerbates the problems they are trying to solve.
- Collaboration becomes mobilized because individuals learn how they collectively create the undesirable outcomes that they experience.
- Individuals become focused to work on important coordinated changes to achieve meaningful and sustainable system-wide outcomes.
- Continuous learning is stimulated, which is a crucial aspect of any meaningful systemic change.

(Stroh, 2015)

Altering the current trajectory of human activity requires a second order change and a comprehensive transformation of the entire system, instead of a few behavioral aspects (Ben-Eli, 2018). Five core principles form an integrated, systemic set, which should be acted on simultaneously to achieve whole system change:

- The *material domain*, which constitutes the basis for regulating the flow of materials and energy that underlie existence.
- The *economic domain*, which provides a guiding framework for defining, creating, and managing wealth.
- The *domain of life*, which provides the basis for appropriate behavior in the biosphere in relation to all other species.
- The *social domain*, which provides the basis for social interactions.
- And the *spiritual domain*, which identifies the necessary attitudinal, value orientation and provides the basis for a universal code of ethics.

(Ben-Eli, 2018, p. 1341)

The systemic aspect is representative of the interdependence of reality and requires simultaneous action on all five principles, because focusing on only one principle will likely yield limited results for the entire system. The emphasis on fundamental structures can assist us in transitioning from manipulating words and motives to proactive architecture of the structures and mechanisms required for achieving effective change and the associated desired outcomes (Ben-Eli, 2018).

## Global aspects of system leadership development

Globalization has increased exponentially since the end of World War II, resulting in increased interdependence among nations. The rapid advancement of globalization has created a demand for leaders who understand the impact of culture on leadership performance (Northouse, 2018). Globalization impacts system leadership in several significant forms: politically, geographically, socioeconomically, and culturally. Politics can impact system leaders trying to influence across boundaries, when those boundaries represent differing ideologies. This can happen both between nations and within a nation, especially when the political ideology is not supportive of issues such as climate change or environmental regulation. Geography impacts system leadership when leaders are influencing across distant boundaries. The effects of geography are partially mitigated by advancing technology, communication, and social media, which reduce the impact of time and distance. The socioeconomic dimension can impact system leadership when there is disparity between the leader and the individuals being influenced. Wealthy leaders may be mistrusted by poorer individuals and groups who believe the leader is acting with an ulterior motive, such as resource exploitation or political control. Likewise, poorer leaders may be perceived by wealthier individuals and groups as envious of their wealth. Cultural difference can have a significant impact on system leadership efforts and, therefore, is examined in greater detail in the following paragraphs.

One of the challenges of leadership is leading individuals and groups from cultures that differ from that of the leader. System leadership requires leaders to lead across cultural and national boundaries. In the traditional sense, the term culture refers to the customs, arts, institutions, and achievements of a nation, people, or other social group. However, organizations also have distinct cultures, which can differ significantly from other organizations, even within the same industry, sector, or geographic area. It is essential to acknowledge and respect the cultural differences between organizations engaged in collaborative efforts (Confino, 2012), as well as the broader cultural difference of all parties. Cultural training is needed to assist system leaders with understanding and responding appropriately in other cultural contexts.

Researchers have attempted to identify and describe the various elements and dimensions of culture (Hofstede, 1980, 2001; House, Hanges, Javidan, Dorfman, & Gupta, 2004). Within the context of culture and leadership, the studies by House et al. provide the most comprehensive collection of findings in their Global Leadership and Organizational Behavior Effectiveness (GLOBE) research program. The GLOBE research program, founded by House in 1991, conducts ongoing research to increase understanding of cross-cultural interactions and the effects of culture on leader effectiveness. GLOBE researchers analyzed the cultural dimensions of 62 nations in their effort to identify the cultural characteristics of citizens in those countries. GLOBE researchers have identified nine cultural dimensions: uncertainty avoidance, power distance, institutional collectivism, in-group collectivism, gender egalitarianism, assertiveness, future orientation, performance orientation, and humane orientation (Northouse, 2018). These cultural dimensions form the basis for understanding how individuals in different countries vary in leadership approach (Northouse, 2018), and are summarized in the following paragraphs.

Uncertainty avoidance describes the extent of reliance of a society, organization, or group on established social norms, rituals, and procedures to avoid uncertainty and how cultures use rules, structures, and law to manage predictability. Countries such as the United States are more likely to demonstrate an entrepreneurial nature, with individual risk taking and spontaneous decision-making encouraged. In contrast, in some Middle Eastern countries, risk taking and spontaneous actions are infrequent, with decisions typically made after considerable deliberation. In cultures with high uncertainty avoidance, agreements and negotiations take time and are established on a level of trust and reliability developed through long-term commitment (Northouse, 2018).

Power distance describes the degree to which members of a group expect and agree upon power sharing equality and determines cultural stratification, creating social levels based on power, authority, prestige, status, and wealth. India is an example of a high power distance country, because it operates under the caste system, in which societal members acknowledge power and authority as facts of life, recognizing that all citizens maintain their "rightful place". In sharp contrast, the United States is a low power distance culture, in which others are openly approached concerning disagreement on issues, regardless of social, political, or career position (Northouse, 2018).

Institutional collectivism describes the extent to which an organization or culture advocates institutional or societal collective action and whether groups identify more with overall collective interests or individual goals and achievements (Northouse, 2018). In-group collectivism refers to the degree to which individuals reveal pride, loyalty, unity, and devotion in their organizations or families. The nation of Iran demonstrates high in-group collectivism, where individuals respect family and religious affiliation above anything else (Northouse, 2018). Gender egalitarianism measures the extent to which an organization or culture limits gender role dissimilarities and encourages gender equality and how those societies minimize gender in determining individual, organizational, and community roles. Sweden is one of the highest ranked nations for gender egalitarianism, based on a strong belief that men and women should share equal power and influence. Nations with low gender egalitarianism, such as Afghanistan, do not allow girls to attend school and frequently allow girls to be killed for defying family wishes (Northouse, 2018).

Assertiveness describes the degree to which members of a culture demonstrate determination, confrontational behavior, and aggression in social relationships. The spectrum of assertiveness ranges from forcefulness, aggression, and toughness to timidity, submissiveness, and sympathy in social relationships. Germany and the United States are ranked high on the assertiveness dimension (Northouse, 2018). Future orientation refers to the extent to which individuals display future-oriented behaviors such as planning, investing, and gratification delay. Future orientation prioritizes preparation for the future instead of spontaneity and present enjoyment. Most Middle Eastern nations are past oriented, focusing on traditional values and customs and demonstrating conservative management approaches, and are reluctant to change established habits. In contrast, many Americans believe they can control the future and embrace change for the sole purpose of changing (Northouse, 2018).

Performance orientation describes the extent to which an organization or culture reinforces and rewards individuals for performance, measured by the extent to which individuals are rewarded for establishing and reaching difficult goals. One indicator of the performance orientation of a country is how schools are ranked as passing or failing based on standardized student test results (Northouse, 2018). The Anglo nations of Canada, the United States, England, Australia, and New Zealand score high on performance orientation. Humane orientation describes the extent a culture supports and rewards individuals for being equitable, altruistic, benevolent, and considerate to others and reinforces awareness of others, social support, and community values (Northouse, 2018). Further information about the cultural clusters, including which countries comprise each cluster and the specific characteristics of a country's culture, can be found at the GLOBE website (https://globeproject.com/).

In addition to cultural leadership dimensions, GLOBE researchers identified six global leadership behaviors: charismatic/value based, team oriented, participative, humane oriented, autonomous, and self-protective (House & Javidan, 2004). Charismatic/value-based leadership describes the ability to stimulate, motivate, and require high performance from followers based on firm core values. This leadership behavior encompasses being idealistic, inspirational, selfless, authentic, decisive, and outcome oriented. Team-oriented leadership encourages team building and a common purpose among team members, emphasizing collaboration, integration, diplomacy, non-malevolence, and administrative competence. Participative leadership describes the extent to which leaders involve followers in decision-making and implementation and requires non-autocratic behavior. Humane-oriented leadership prioritizes being supportive, considerate, respectful, and generous and demonstrating humility with and empathy to other individuals. Autonomous leadership describes being independent and individualistic. Self-protective leadership manifests behaviors that safeguard the safety and well-being of the leader and followers and is characterized by leadership that is structured, self-serving, conflict generating, and preserving of dignity (House & Javidan, 2004). Researchers have incorporated these global leadership behaviors in assessing the perspectives of various cultural clusters about leadership (Northouse, 2018). Understanding cultural-based leadership behavior is important for system leaders who desire to influence individuals, organizations, and groups in other cultures, in terms of understanding both what constitutes appropriate behavior and what behavior to expect from other leaders.

## Barriers and challenges to system leadership development

While system leadership may seem suitable for achieving sustainability, barriers and challenges will likely surface during system leadership development. One possible barrier to system leadership development is that individuals are resistant to change, and system leadership requires change. Individuals exhibiting system leadership must modify behavior and perspectives to successfully influence actors operating outside their traditional spheres of influence. Likewise, the individuals being influenced must be willing to modify existing behavior and actions. The behavioral and perspective changes required by system leadership are uncomfortable but necessary if sustainable outcomes are to be achieved.

System leadership represents a leadership model which does not fit comfortably within traditional, hierarchical, or bureaucratic leadership models. System leadership requires influencing beyond traditional boundaries, both upward and downward on the established hierarchy. Some individuals may feel uncomfortable trying to influence an individual or group from a higher career position or socioeconomic status. Moreover, the individuals being influenced may feel uncomfortable accepting influence and direction from individuals operating outside their traditional organizational system or structure. While business leaders may be accustomed to collaborating and cooperating with nonprofit, NGO, or governmental agencies, they may be reluctant to accept guidance from those sectors. Likewise, public and nonprofit leaders might be skeptical of the motives of a business leader seeking to influence their activities and behavior.

System leadership may be further complicated by cultural differences, especially among cultures that are high in power distance or individualism. Moreover, some individuals may feel uncomfortable being influenced by individuals from other cultures, sectors, or socioeconomic status. This can be especially difficult if a person from a collectivist culture is attempting to influence an individual from a predominantly individualist culture. Development of system leadership will require understanding and appreciation of the cultural differences described in the previous section. Developing this ability will take time – what is most important is for system leaders to respect these differences and transparently explain when they are not knowledgeable about how to respond to cultural differences. Respect and transparency are essential components of the interpersonal competence necessary for system leadership.

## Conclusion

While considerable literature exists concerning system leadership capabilities and corresponding development tools, few are aware of this research beyond those involved with collaborative systemic change endeavors (Senge et al., 2015). As the system leadership framework and benefits become more established, this leadership model should find greater acceptance and utilization among scholars and practitioners. System leadership development will require broader dissemination of existing tools and capabilities, along with additional research concerning the effectiveness of tools and capabilities. Moreover, system leadership will benefit from existing sustainability system leaders sharing best practices and mentoring colleagues.

Current and future leaders should understand the need to link sustainable leadership to the organizational bottom line and to utilize it as a tool to drive and create innovation, and to effectively promote forward thinking both within and outside the organization (McCann & Holt, 2010). Slankis (2006) identified 10 pillars of sustainable leadership:

1. Change orientation: a willingness to change an organization.
2. Broad systems thinking: the ability to connect the organization.
3. Social and environmental consciousness: viewing the role of the organization externally and its impact.
4. Business savvy and credibility: linking sustainability and stakeholder value.
5. Adaptability: manage, implement, and change.
6. Patience: commitment to the long-term.
7. Translational skills: thought into action.
8. Persuasiveness: communicating and building relationships.
9. Energy and passion: communicate vision and encourage innovation to drive innovation.
10. Mentoring and development: commitment to sound lasting leadership through development of people.

(pp. 2–3)

Several of these pillars resonate with the proposed model and framework of system leadership for sustainability. Increased focus on these pillars in organizations can link the gap between social values and organizational performance (McCann & Holt, 2010).

Stroh (2015) suggested that "[w]hen faced with a complex problem that persists despite their best efforts to solve it, people tend to blame limited resources as well as promote their own successes, downplay their failures, and view others in the system competitively" (p. 43). System leaders look beyond failure, blame, or competition, recognizing that systemic change is achieved through collective, collaborative effort. Moreover, the challenges of sustainability require a forward-looking, boundaryless approach, recognizing failures as learning and improvement opportunities. Development and exercise of system leadership is not easy, but it is essential to achieve sustainability. This chapter examined the development of system leadership by first examining the development of leadership competencies appropriate for the three propositions of system leadership for sustainability. This chapter does not represent the final authority for the development of system leadership. Rather, a foundation has been developed upon which future scholars and practitioners can examine and develop practical methods for development and implementation of system leadership for sustainability.

## Chapter reflection questions

1 One of the earlier debates within the field of leadership was whether leadership could be taught (are leaders born or made, or both?). Do you think system leadership can be taught? Do you think system leadership can be developed?

2 In this chapter we discussed the various dimensions of culture. In which cultural dimension(s) do you think system leadership might be more effective, and why? In which cultural dimension(s) do you think system leadership might be less effective, and why?

3 Which cultural dimension might be more conducive to development of system leadership, and why? Which cultural dimension might be more resistant to development of system leadership, and why?

## References

Ackoff, R. L. (1994). Systems thinking and thinking systems. *System Dynamics Review, 10*(2–3), 175–188. doi:10.1002/sdr.4260100206

Australian Council for International Development (ACFID). (2019). *Implementing the sustainable development goals: Applying systems thinking and collaborative responses.* Deakin, Australia: Author.

Barile, S., Orecchini, F., Saviano, M., & Farioli, F. (2018). People, technology, and governance for sustainability: The contribution of systems and cyber-systemic thinking. *Sustainability Science, 13*(5), 1197–1208. doi:10.1007/s11625-018-0621-y

Baue, B., & Wood, R. (2015, August–November). Leveraging integral leadership to shift sustainability mindsets into a thriveability paradigm. *Integral Leadership Review*, 279–284. Retrieved from http://integralleadershipreview.com/

Beer, S. (1972). *Brain of the firm*. London, England: Penguin Group.

Ben-Eli, M. U. (2018). Sustainability: Definition and five core principles, a systems perspective. *Sustainability Science, 13*, 1337–1343. doi:10.1007/s11625-018-0564-3

Cash, D., Adger, W. N., Berkes, F., Garden, P., Lebel, L., Olsson, P., . . . Young, O. (2006). Scale and cross-scale dynamics: Governance and information in a multilevel world. *Ecology and Society, 11*(2), 8. Retrieved from www.ecologyandsociety.org/vol11/iss2/art8/

Cavagnaro, E., & Curiel, G. H. (2012). *The three levels of sustainability*. Sheffield, England: Greenleaf Publishing.

Confino, J. (2012, October 15). *The art of systems thinking in driving sustainable transformation*. Retrieved from www.theguardian.com/sustainable-business/systems-thinking-sustainable-transformation

Espejo, R. (2018). Introduction. In S. Barile, R. Espejo, I. Perko, & M. Saviano (Eds.), *Cybernetics and systems: Social and business decisions*. London, England: Routledge-Giappichelli.

Fiksel, J. (2006). Sustainability and resilience: Toward a systems approach. *Sustainability: Science, Practice, & Policy, 2*(2) 14–21. Retrieved from http://ejournal.nbii.org

Fullan, M. (2003). *Change forces with a vengeance*. London, England: Routledge Falmer.

Fullan, M. (2005). *Leadership and sustainability: System thinkers in action*. London, England: Sage Publications.

Gladwell, M. (2000). *Tipping point*. Boston, MA: Little Brown.

Goekler, J. (2003). Teaching for the future: Systems thinking and sustainability. *Green Teacher*, (70), 8. Retrieved from www.proquest.com

Goleman, D. (1995). *Emotional intelligence*. New York, NY: Bantam Books.

Haney, A. B., Pope, J., & Arden, Z. (2018). Making it personal: Developing sustainability leaders in business. *Organization & Environment*. doi:10.1177/1086026618806201

Heifetz, R. (2003). Adaptive work. In T. Bentley & J. Wilsdon (Eds.), *The adaptive state* (pp. 68–78). London, England: Demos.

Heifetz, R., & Laurie, D. (2001). The work of leadership. *Harvard Business Review*. Retrieved from http://hbr.org/2001/12/the-work-of-leadership/ar/1

Hind, P., Wilson, A., & Lenssen, G. (2009). Developing leaders for sustainable business. *Corporate Governance: The International Journal of Business in Society, 9*(1), 7–20. doi:10.1108/14720700910936029

Hofstede, G. (1980). *Culture's consequences: International differences in work-related values*. Beverly Hills, CA: Sage Publications.

Hofstede, G. (2001). *Culture's consequences: Comparing values, behaviors, institutions, and organizations across nations*. Thousand Oaks, CA: Sage Publications.

House, R. J., Hanges, P. J., Javidan, M., Dorfman, P. W., & Gupta, V. (Eds.). (2004). *Culture, leadership, and organizations: The GLOBE study of 62 societies*. Thousand Oaks, CA: Sage Publications.

House, R. J., & Javidan, M. (2004). Overview of GLOBE. In R. J. House, P. J. Hanges, M. Javidan, P. W. Dorfman, V. Gupta, & Associates (Eds.), *Culture, leadership, and organizations: The GLOBE study of 62 societies* (pp. 9–28). Thousand Oaks, CA: Sage Publications.

McCann, J. T., & Holt, R. A. (2010). Servant and sustainable leadership: An analysis in the manufacturing environment. *International Journal of Management Practice, 4*(2), 134–148. doi:10.1504/IJMP.2010.033691

Metcalf, L., & Benn, S. (2013). Leadership for sustainability: An evolution of leadership ability. *Journal of Business Ethics, 112*(3), 369–384. doi:10.1007/s10551-012-1278-6

Metson, G., Aggarwal, R., & Childers, D. L. (2012). Efficiency through proximity. *Journal of Industrial Ecology, 16*(6), 914–927. doi:10.1111/j.1530-9290.2012.00554.x

Ni, P. (2014). *How to let go of negative thoughts & emotions: A practical guide*. San Francisco, CA: Preston Ni Communication Coaching.

Northouse, P. G. (2018). *Leadership: Theory and practice* (8th ed.). Thousand Oaks, CA: Sage Publications.

Peirce, M. (2011). Introduction. In *A journey of a thousand miles: The state of sustainability leadership 2011* (pp. 11–20). Cambridge, England: Cambridge Institute for Sustainability Leadership.

Ploum, L., Blok, V., Lans, T., & Omta, O. (2018). Toward a validated competence framework for sustainable entrepreneurship. *Organization & Environment*, *31*(2), 113–132. doi:10.1177/1086026617697039

Robbins, S. P., & Coulter, M. (2012). *Management* (11th ed.). Upper Saddle River, NJ: Pearson Prentice-Hall.

Russell Reynolds Associates. (2015). *Sustainable leadership: Talent requirements for sustainable enterprises*. New York, NY: Author. Retrieved from www.russellreynolds.com/en/Insights/thought-leadership/Documents/russell_reynolds_sustainable_leadership.pdf

Saviano, M., Di Nauta, P., Montella, M. M., & Sciarelli, F. (2018a). Managing protected areas as cultural landscapes: The case of the Alta Murgia National Park in Italy. *Land Use Policy*, *76*, 290–299. doi:10.1016/j.landusepol.2018.03.052

Saviano, M., Di Nauta, P., Montella, M. M., & Sciarelli, F. (2018b). The cultural value of protected areas as models of sustainable development. *Sustainability*, *10*(5), 1567. doi:10.3390/su10051567

Senge, P. (1990). *The fifth discipline: The art & practice of the learning organization*. New York, NY: Doubleday.

Senge, P., Hamilton, H., & Kania, J. (2015). The dawn of system leadership. *Stanford Social Innovation Review*, *13*(1), 27–33. Retrieved from https://ssir.org/articles/entry/the_dawn_of_system_leadership

Serrat, O. (2017). Understanding and developing emotional intelligence. In O. Serrat (Ed.), *Knowledge solutions: Tools, methods, and approaches to drive organizational performance* (pp. 329–333). Singapore: Springer.

Siebert, M. (2018). *Systems thinking and how it can help build a sustainable world*. Corvallis, OR: Post Carbon Institute. Retrieved from www.resilience.org/stories/2018-07-11/systems-thinking-and-how-it-can-help-build-a-sustainable-world/

Slankis, E. (2006). *Sustainable thinking, sustainable leadership-the new E.Q. Leadership*. Retrieved from www.rayberndtson.ca

Stibbe, A. E. (2009). *The handbook of sustainability literacy: Skills for a changing world*. Cambridge, England: Green Books.

Strandberg, C. (2015, May 2019). *Building resilient organizations*. Burnaby, BC, Canada: Strandberg Consulting. Retrieved from https://corostrandberg.com/building-resilient-organizations/

Stroh, D. P. (2015). *Systems thinking for social change*. White River Junction, VT: Chelsea Green Publishing.

Timmins, N. (2015). *The practice of system leadership: Being comfortable with chaos*. London, England: The King's Fund. Retrieved from www.kingsfund.org.uk/sites/default/files/field/field_publication_file/System-leadership-Kings-Fund-May-2015.pdf

Visser, W., & Courtice, P. (2011). *Sustainability leadership: Linking theory and practice*. Cambridge, England: Cambridge Institute for Sustainability Leadership. doi:10.2139/ssrn.1947221

Waddock, S. (2007). Leadership integrity in a fractured knowledge world. *Academy of Management Learning and Education*, *6*, 543–557. doi:10.5465/amle.2007.27694954

Weinreb, E. (2015). *5 core competencies of sustainability leadership*. Retrieved from www.greenbiz.com/article/5-core-competencies-sustainability-leadership

Wiek, A., Farioli, F., Fukushi, K., & Yarime, M. (2012). Sustainability science: Bridging the gap between science and society. *Sustainability Science*, 7(1), 1–4. doi:10.1007/s11625-011-0154-0

Wiek, A., Withycombe, L., & Redman, C. L. (2011). Key competencies in sustainability: A reference framework for academic program development. *Sustainability Science*, *6*(2), 203–218. doi:10.1007/s11625-011-0132-6

Williams, A., Kennedy, S., Philipp, F., & Whiteman, G. (2017). Systems thinking: A review of sustainability management research. *Journal of Cleaner Production*, *148*, 866–881. doi:10.1016/j.jclepro.2017.02.002

# 5 System leadership for sustainability in business

## Introduction

The dominant business model of the second half of the 20th century was at least partially influenced by Nobel Prize–winning economist Milton Friedman (1970), who argued the only responsibility of business was to generate profit for shareholders, who could then choose whether and to what extent to demonstrate social responsibility. However, the emerging sustainable business model considers an environmental perspective, proposing that a sustainable business produces goods and services of value to the present generation while ensuring necessary goods and services are available to future generations (Beehner, 2017). Harvey (2001) proposed, "chasing profits is peripheral; the real point of business is to serve as one of the institutions through which society develops and exercises the capacity for constructive action" (pp. 38–39). This argument is supported by Dean (2014), who suggested the overarching purpose of an economic system is to provide value to society, not simply accumulate capital. However, Dean contends that while capitalism may have produced our current environmental circumstances, capitalism is also a powerful method to create value while simultaneously correcting our adverse environmental conditions.

While business and commerce have been the cause of many of our planetary problems, businesses possess the human and financial resources to solve them. Businesses and business leaders represent a significant avenue for achieving a sustainable future due to their considerable influence, because more than two-thirds of the world's largest economies are businesses, not nations (Green, 2016). In this chapter, we explore the essential role of business in sustainability, and systems thinking and related tools are examined within a business sustainability context. The role of system leadership in driving business sustainability locally and globally is discussed, including within the field of project management. System leadership implementation methods and techniques are introduced, and barriers and challenges to system leadership for business sustainability are identified. The chapter concludes with a general discussion of system leadership for sustainability and a personal interview summary of a business sustainability system leader.

## Sustainability and business

Business leaders are constantly seeking ways to maintain a competitive advantage in the 21st-century global marketplace. Because of the complexity of the post-financial crisis economic climate, the challenges faced by leaders will continue to increase, resulting in a possible increase in business failures. To persevere under these conditions, businesses require leaders who can manage and overcome these challenges. Sustainability is both a challenge and an opportunity, which business is increasingly obligated to address. An increasing number of consumers are demanding sustainable products and services, and a broad range of stakeholders are demanding business accountability for environmental and social impacts. Moreover, technological advances are increasing pressure on businesses to become more sustainable. Business sustainability confronts business leaders with the challenge of addressing environmental and social goals, in addition to commercial goals (Goleman & Lueneburger, 2010). Moreover, sustainability management questions the underlying assumptions of the traditional capitalist economic framework, such as the maximization of consumer comfort and utility, both of which provide the basis for reasonable, predictable economic growth (Opdebeeck, 2014).

The present global ecological disaster is a result of human exploitation of natural resources in a capitalist, consumerist global economy dominated by a mechanistic worldview (van Schalkwyk, 2011). The root of our primary environmental problem is human arrogance, which places immediate personal welfare above long-term needs of present and future generations and the planet (Berry, 1999). Businesses are the largest consumers of natural resources, generating the largest cumulative impact on the environment. Moreover, because of the breadth and depth of labor and employment, the business sector influences the social architecture in most developed nations (Jones & Upward, 2014). Therefore, consideration of business actions separate from social-ecological systems overlooks the highly interconnected challenges of sustainability (Marcus, Kurucz, & Colbert, 2010; Starik & Kanashiro, 2013; Walker et al., 2009; Whiteman, Walker, & Perego, 2013). While sustainability and social benefits are rarely regarded to be business model elements (Jones & Upward, 2014), and the objective of traditional capitalism is generating profits, there is increasing concern both inside and outside industry about how those profits are generated (Soyka, 2012).

Business is often portrayed as profit-driven organizations providing limited social benefits, while consistently exploiting the natural environment (Beehner, 2019). Business leaders often categorize adverse environmental and social effects as a cost of doing business, with environmental responsibility typically consisting of superficial actions to become "less unsustainable" (Jones & Upward, 2014). Holthaus (2012) offers a gloomier scenario of capitalism as a system focused on exploitation of natural resources, racism, sexism, and military conflict, with military technology being the United States' largest commercial export. However, an increasing number of sustainability scholars and practitioners envision a transition from a linear economy to a circular economy, characterized by obtaining maximum value of natural resources through long-term retention, followed by recovery and regeneration of consumed products at end of product life (Andersen, 2007; Waste and Resources Action Programme, 2018).

Although business leaders increasingly acknowledge a responsibility for sustainability, many struggle with how to achieve sustainability within a capitalist business model. While sustainability was not on the corporate agenda for most businesses in the 1990s, an increasing number of 21st-century business leaders consider sustainability a strategic opportunity, with many considering sustainability a core competency (Goleman & Lueneburger, 2010). There is increasing acceptance that business sustainability is both the right thing and the smart thing to do (Soyka, 2012). Regardless of how genuine the motive, many business leaders acknowledge the increasing demand for sustainable products and services and the growing number of competitors assimilating sustainability into their business models (Beehner, 2017). Ninety-five percent of global CEOs recently surveyed acknowledged a personal responsibility to ensure their company has a core purpose and role in society (Accenture, 2016).

A business model is a shared blueprint that business leaders use to understand outcomes of business decisions, organizational changes, and relationships among businesses and stakeholders (Jones & Upward, 2014). The purpose of a business model is to describe the logic for the existence of the organization and how success is defined and measured (Jones & Upward, 2014). Although some have proposed modification of the existing capitalist business model to accommodate sustainability, others have suggested that entirely new models are needed (Blowfield & Murray, 2014).

Jones and Upward (2014) proposed an anticipatory business model wherein businesses are strongly sustainable, or "flourishing", enterprises. A strongly sustainable business is characterized by a network of stakeholders, such as customers, suppliers, distributors, and investors, who all have tangible effects on the natural environment and society. An anticipatory system is defined as a natural system containing an internal predictive model of both the system and its surroundings, enabling it to alter state or conditions in conformance with anticipated events or conditions (Jones & Upward, 2014). The anticipatory business model is similar to the living system model (Rosen, 1991), characterized as a biological process whereby the effects of an organism's actions in the natural environment can be anticipated by assumptions about relationships informed by the model. Unlike traditional systems, which are feedback-based, an anticipatory system contains feed-forward loops that assist participants with anticipating desirable future outcomes. This anticipatory model is proactive, instead of reactive, and is relevant for understanding business models. The anticipatory business model assumes that the business continually adjusts to its environment, encompassing all available resources and their origins, similar to a living system operating with awareness of its environment (Jones & Upward, 2014). The anticipatory model can be useful for reasoning about proposed changes to business operations, because the enterprise is depicted as a living system with leaders anticipating results from decisions that were based on this model (Jones & Upward, 2014).

In addition to the social benefits of sustainability, business leaders recognize the financial benefits accrued through sustainable practices. These financial benefits can be direct, measured by increased revenue and decreased cost, and indirect, which while more difficult to measure, nonetheless favorably impact business. Some of the business benefits of practicing sustainability are brand image improvement, increased competitive advantage, increased productivity, cost reduction, improved regulatory compliance capability, enhanced employee and investor attraction and retention, waste reduction, and shareholder satisfaction (Rogers, 2016).

It is essential that business leaders recognize the value created by sustainability. According to the value proposition, the primary purpose of business is creation and maximization of value (Rainey, 2006), necessitating any sustainable business strategy be approached from a value-creation perspective (Soyka, 2012). While the traditional model measures value in terms of increased performance, decreased costs, or both, the sustainable business model measures value in terms of increasing enhanced benefits and decreasing environmental impacts. The sustainable business value proposition encourages value creation and maximization for all current and future stakeholders. A successful sustainable business strategy increases performance and decreases costs for the business, simultaneously creating and maximizing sustainable value for all stakeholders (Beehner, 2017).

The World Commission on Environment and Development (WCED) concept of sustainability (1987) is often characterized by the triple bottom line (TBL) of economy, environment, and society (Elkington, Tickell, & Lee, 2007), referred to colloquially as the three Ps – profits, planet, and people (Seghezzo, 2009). One objection to the TBL approach is whether incorporation of environmental sustainability into the business model will be perceived as a legitimate function within the context of capitalist organizations (Springett & Kearins, 2001; Thomas, 2005). Moreover, Holthaus (2012) suggested the TBL concept is harmful to the sustainability movement, because we are categorically isolating humans from the environment, and the economy from both humans and the environment, wrongly suggesting that the economy is equal to and independent of humans and nature. However, progressive businesses are responding to the noticeable disconnect between financial and environmental performance, strengthening the belief that businesses can "do well by doing good" (Molnar & Mulvihill, 2003).

A change in consciousness to a state of connectedness (Pavez & Kendall, 2015) is essential for changing how businesses undertake social and environmental responsibility (Heaton, Schachinger, & Laszlo, 2016). Instead of viewing ourselves as separate from each other and from nature, focused only on maximization of personal gain, we can view ourselves as deeply connected to each other and to future generations (Heaton et al., 2016). According to Down and McKeown (2017), the characteristics of sustainable development include interconnectedness, a whole system approach, and working for the common good. The economic system at the dawn of the 21st century has placed tremendous pressure on the natural environmental system while only meeting the needs of approximately 25% of the planet's inhabitants. As population increases, and a greater proportion become consumers and producers, capitalist business models may become less profitable, necessitating business leaders to develop more innovative, sustainable products and services. The creation of innovative, new sustainable products and services will require complex interactions among many organizations (Dougherty & Dunne, 2011).

## Systems thinking in business

Systems thinking is an organizational management discipline based on interpreting an organization or sector as a system and examining relationships among the entirety of the system components (Tate, 2009). Systems thinking presents an alternative to the "silo" approach, offering a more comprehensive method for understanding the function of businesses within social-ecological systems (Williams, Kennedy, Philipp, & Whiteman, 2017). Systems thinking and several associated tools were examined in detail in Chapter 1. In addition, several systems thinking tools are appropriate for understanding and implementing sustainability at the business or organizational level. In this section, we will examine systems thinking from a business perspective and the related tools of enterprise thinking, life cycle thinking, and biomimicry. We will also explore the fields of industrial ecology and biocomplexity as useful for understanding business sustainability from a systems perspective.

Enterprise thinking characterizes a business organization or industry as a complete, interconnected system, rather than a collection of separate, unconnected components (Rainey, 2006). Application of enterprise thinking for business sustainability requires sustainability not be viewed as an isolated objective, but instead it should permeate the entire organization, influencing all business activities. The advantages of examining business sustainability with enterprise thinking are enhanced understanding of the relationship of the business with other organizations, flexibility in addressing customer and stakeholder requirements, increased organizational effectiveness resulting from an integrated approach, comprehensive waste reduction, and enhanced cross-department communication and relationships (Rainey, 2006).

Life cycle thinking (LCT) is a systemic approach to the production and consumption of products and services from a whole system perspective. LCT tools such as life cycle analysis, also known as life cycle assessment (LCA), are used to identify, quantify, and evaluate the environmental impacts of a product, service, or process, from cradle to grave (Srinivas, 2015), and may be useful in improving sustainable product development between firms (Gmelin & Seuring, 2014; Luthe, Kägi, & Reger, 2013). The application of LCA encourages preventative and proactive environmental management instead of reactive and responsive approaches. LCA can be a complicated and lengthy process, consisting of the following steps:

- Goal and scope definition is the step in which the purpose of the LCA is defined, the assumptions and boundaries are identified, and the scope of the assessment is clarified.
- Analysis involves identification, classification, and measurement of the impacts of energy, materials, emissions, and other attributes of the product, service, or process.
- Assessment is the step in which the environmental impacts of the product, process, or activity are assessed.
- Interpretation/evaluation describes the process of interpreting or evaluating the results to identify opportunities for environmental improvement and determine value (Srinivas, 2015).

Biomimicry is a revolutionary science in which nature is analyzed to discover best practices to be adapted for human use (Benyus, 1997). The goal of biomimicry is to construct products, processes, and procedures that are well suited to long-term life on earth. Proponents of biomimicry recognize that nature has solved most of the problems currently faced by humankind (Biomimicry Institute, 2019). From an evolutionary viewpoint, business structures imitate natural systems on multiple levels: on a business level as a social unit and entity, on a broader level as an actor in a trade system, and the trade system as a component of both social and environmental systems (Kassel, 2014). Examples of biomimicry include photovoltaic cells structured like plant leaves, steel fibers woven like spider webs, cancer cures provided by chimpanzees, computer signaling that mimics living cells, and a closed-loop economy that learns from coral reefs and redwood and oak-hickory forests (Benyus, 1997).

Biocomplexity is the study of complex networks and behaviors resulting from interactions of living organisms within systems. The field of biocomplexity emerged as an attempt to better understand sustainable systems (Colwell, 1998). The complexity, dynamics, and nonlinear nature of interdependent systems suggest sustainability does not exist in a steady state of equilibrium (Fiksel, 2006). Because technological, geopolitical, and climatic forces inevitably disrupt the rhythm of material and energy flows, it is useful to view ecosystems and industrial systems as dynamic, open systems that exist in disequilibrium and display nonlinear and often disorderly behavior (Fiksel, 2006). Achieving sustainability will require a transition from existing systems to resilient, adaptive industrial and social systems that mimic the dynamic characteristics of ecological systems (Fiksel, 2006). System leaders will be necessary to influence and integrate the diversity of stakeholders and subsystems across multiple boundaries.

The field of industrial ecology is used to examine energy and materials flows within industrial systems to understand the systemic behavior of integrated socio-ecological systems (Williams et al., 2017). Eco-industrial parks are socio-ecological systems that provide multiple benefits to the community and the participating businesses. Eco-industrial parks are industrial developments in which businesses collaborate with each other and the local community to increase economic growth and improve environmental quality (Hein, Jankovic, Farel, & Yannou, 2015). The benefits of eco-industrial parks are waste and pollution reduction; efficient utilization of information, energy, infrastructure, and resources; and attainment of sustainable development (Hein et al., 2015). Eco-industrial parks accomplish these benefits by geographically consolidating businesses whereby flows of resources, energy, and information can be better coordinated and integrated. Eco-industrial parks may also serve a broader purpose as tools for executing sustainable policies within a region (Cerceau et al., 2014).

The study of industrial ecology could benefit from a more integrated systems approach (Ashton, 2009; Hoffman, 2003; Metson, Aggarwal, & Childers, 2012), which could assist in expanding the field from a collection of tools for understanding material and energy flows to confronting more serious socio-technical issues (Allenby, 2009). Acknowledging the interconnectedness of business decisions, Birkin (2000) suggested the need for an expansion of or alternatives to systems thinking to better understand the relationships among business processes and components. Understanding the interconnections among industrial ecosystems can improve industrial synergy (Tsvetkova & Gustafsson, 2012). A combination of industrial ecology and systems thinking can improve understanding of the socio-technical environment, enhancing business leader decision-making to better solve complex sustainability problems (DeLaurentis & Ayyalasomayajula, 2009; Ehrenfeld, 2007).

## System leadership in business

Achieving business sustainability will require leaders capable of connecting multiple, often unrelated stakeholders toward a common purpose. These leaders will be able to influence diverse stakeholders to act toward the common good of humankind, in a manner that may at times seem counter to their traditional roles and expectations. However, action toward sustainability must be balanced with maintenance of profitability for businesses to continue to exist. Balancing the previously discussed TBL will require a unique combination of leadership, resources, and innovation.

Innovation will be an essential requirement of system leadership for sustainability in the business sector. To focus on system-level challenges and influence transformational change, revolutionary innovation in products, services, business structures, and business models is necessary (Boons & Lüdeke-Freund, 2013; Boons, Montalvo, Quist, & Wagner, 2013; Loorbach & Wijsman, 2013; Williams et al., 2017; Winn, Kirchgeorg, Griffith, Linnenluecke, & Günther, 2011). Businesses possess both the financial and human resources to achieve the necessary sustainability innovation. However, business innovations must extend beyond the perspective that technology will solve all problems by offering opportunities to significantly alter how businesses create, deliver, and secure value (Bocken, Short, Rana, & Evans, 2014). Business leaders must proactively seek innovative solutions to current sustainability challenges that consist of more than superficial, short-term remedies or postponement of existing problems to some future date. Organizational networks should be created to encourage interactions among firms to connect dissimilar ideas for the development and sharing of innovative knowledge and resources (Dougherty & Dunne, 2011). Sustainability innovation is a systemic, dynamic, nonlinear, and uncertain process (Foxon & Pearson, 2008), requiring leaders possessing the skills and competencies of a system leader.

Doppelt (2017) affirmed that for industry to transition from the existing linear "take – make – waste" system to a circular "borrow – use – return" system, organizational members at all levels must be deliberately engaged in organizational planning and decision-making. In contrast with traditional, unsustainable leadership styles, leaders in highly sustainable organizations recognize that the transition to a circular economic system requires complete commitment of all organizational members and stakeholders. Skilled leadership is necessary to transform the structure, production processes, management system, and culture of an organization. Effective sustainability leaders can maintain an organizational focus on accomplishing a higher purpose, while concurrently managing multiple, often contradictory, activity flows (Doppelt, 2017).

Because achieving sustainability is dependent upon complex interactions among governments, industries, and stakeholders (Deshpande, 2010), system leadership will be necessary to influence members of these diverse organizations and sectors to participate in a collaborative, cooperative network. Business leaders must be able to negotiate win-win outcomes in which their businesses are able to prosper without adversely impacting the economic and environmental prosperity of the communities in which they operate. At the industry level, high sustainability businesses may exert pressure on businesses with lower sustainability performance to innovate in response to increased insecurity over social and regulatory governance risks (Jänicke, 2008). Because many government and consumer advocates are frequently skeptical of the motives of business leaders, transparency will be a necessary component of any collaborative effort. Business leaders who are able to demonstrate effective system leadership may find that this core competency will produce a competitive advantage, compared with businesses that continue to operate in a defensive posture with government and policy leaders.

## System leadership for project management

The achievement of a sustainable future will require businesses, governments, and nongovernmental organizations to undertake a multitude of projects. As such, successful project management will be essential for success. However, research suggests project success is equally dependent on technical components and the individual and collective characteristics of leadership, teamwork, and collaboration (Hauschildt, Gesche, & Medcof, 2000). Because many projects fail or exceed time and resource budgets, research has identified several factors leading to project success. Effective and efficient project management is dependent upon project manager demonstration of appropriate leadership skills (Sumner, Bock, & Giamartino, 2006; Zimmerer & Yasin, 1998), such as balance, expertise, perseverance, logical decision-making, creativity, vision, values, integrity, trust, and authenticity (Maylor, 2003). While project managers are accustomed to a structured, predictable, logical, and standardized environment (Srica, 2008), projects are frequently characterized as imprecise and unpredictable, challenging the ability of project managers to coordinate and control a broad group of specialists, over whom they may have limited direct authority (El-Sabaa, 2001). These contradictory project characteristics may make leadership one of the most challenging roles in project management (Irani, Sharif, & Love, 2005).

The primary sources of project failure are poor estimating, poor scheduling, insufficient stakeholder governance, and inadequate risk management (Nelson, 2007). System leadership can be useful in addressing all three areas of project failure. Estimating and scheduling can be better managed from a systems perspective through understanding the characteristics of and actions among multiple functions, organizations, and systems that impact costs, activities, and ultimately, project success. Stakeholders can be better influenced and managed from a boundaryless, systems approach. The holistic understanding inherent among system leaders may provide a better understanding of risks and their origins, and how to influence or obtain the resources necessary for risk mitigation. Moreover, the collaborative nature of system leadership may be useful when negotiating project deadlines, contracts, and modifications. This will be especially important when collaborating among stakeholders with diverse perspectives of and requirements for sustainability.

## Application of system leadership for business sustainability

To achieve organizational transformation through incorporation of sustainability as a core value, business leaders must first recognize how sustainability differs from other types of business initiatives (Goleman & Lueneburger, 2010). First, the focus of sustainability is with operational reality before public perceptions, because business leaders who attempt to exaggerate, or "greenwash", their sustainability accomplishments may seriously damage their business reputations. Second, business initiatives are primarily commercially focused, wherein costs are reduced, markets are expanded, and pricing is commoditized. Finally, other business initiatives may be a component of a larger sustainability strategy, because while initiatives may focus on one department, sustainability applies to the entire organization, requiring comprehensive operational and cultural changes. While many business leaders acknowledge that sustainability is primarily about achieving sustainability in their own organizations, they infrequently make the transition to a more sustainable model, because they try to manage sustainability just like any other business initiative (Goleman & Lueneburger, 2010).

There are three phases in implementing sustainability initiatives, each requiring distinct leadership abilities and organizational capabilities (Goleman & Lueneburger, 2010). The first phase requires leaders make the case for change, demanding leaders that can promote collaboration and influence others to become reactive in response to sustainability challenges. At this stage, critical but often ill-defined risks and opportunities must be immediately identified. The second phase involves converting vision into action, thereby enabling the organization to deliver strong commercial results, resulting in sustainability becoming commercially embedded in the business. This stage requires business leaders capable of distinguishing between the concept of sustainability and the sustainable objectives of the organization, who view sustainability as one method of reaching those targets. In the third phase, leaders must anticipate and evaluate long-term sustainability trends, identify new opportunities, and develop strategies to shift the organization to benefit from these new opportunities. These leaders must expand boundaries, think long term, and develop intricate and at times unorthodox relationships with external stakeholders previously considered to be adversarial (Goleman & Lueneburger, 2010).

System leaders are capable of operating at these phases because they are capable of influencing change, achieving collaboration, and influencing both internal and external stakeholders. The systems perspective enables these leaders to convert vision into action, which may both produce commercial results and embed sustainability into the commercial core of the business. Moreover, these leaders have a long-term perspective and are therefore capable of anticipating and evaluating long-term sustainability trends, identifying potential opportunities, and developing strategies to achieve organizational benefit from new opportunities. Finally, the collaborative ability of system leaders enables development of intricate and creative relationships across boundaries with external stakeholders with whom they may not have previously considered collaboration.

## Global perspectives of system leadership in business

While trade between nations has occurred throughout most of recorded human history, global trade has increased exponentially since the middle of the 20th century. Global trade totaled US$59 billion in 1950, increasing to over US$17,000 billion in 2017 (World Trade Organization, 2018), an increase of nearly 29,000%. The expansion of global business has also contributed to the unsustainable conditions currently experienced. The challenges to global trade occurring as this text is being published are the result of nationalist interests among several large trading partners. Workers and politicians in a growing number of developed nations fear the loss of jobs to lower-wage developing nation workers. Moreover, the decision by the Trump administration to withdraw the United States from the Paris Climate Accord may have been partially influenced by concern among some workers and business leaders about unfair pollution limitations imposed on the United States compared with several large developing nations.

Exercising system leadership across industry, sector, and national boundaries will be both challenging and necessary. Laws, regulations, and customs vary among nations, and trade policies and regulations are subject to constant change as the dynamic nature of the US-China trade dispute influences trade and trade policy decisions in other nations. Moreover, environmental and sustainability standards and regulations vary by nation, with the US currently undergoing a reversal of prior environmental policies and regulations. Sustainability action and influence will vary by nation and industry, with individuals and organizations in some nations apprehensive or even skeptical of attempted external influence. The skills and competencies necessary for system leadership may need to be strongest among system leaders within the global business sector.

## Barriers and challenges to system leadership in business

Several barriers exist to the application of system leadership within business. Because the nature of capitalism suggests a free, competitive market with limited regulation, one of the barriers to system leadership for business is the competitive aspect of business. Competitive businesses are reluctant to collaborate or cooperate across organizations and industries because of concern for the possible loss of competitive information or position. Moreover, businesses may also resist collaboration or cooperation out of fear of being accused of collusion or engaging in monopolistic activities. While business collaboration may be supported in some nations, in other nations, such as the United States, regulations may limit businesses within the same industry from engaging in behavior that might be construed as monopolistic or collusive.

Business leaders in the United States are often skeptical of government and actively resist and lobby against regulation within their industries. Business leaders in Europe and Asia are more accustomed to cooperative arrangements with government. Moreover, national boundaries not only represent physical barriers, but also cultural and legal barriers to exercising business system leadership. This has become especially critical since nationalist attitudes have become more prevalent after the 2015 Brexit vote in the United Kingdom and the 2016 US presidential election.

The development of sustainable innovations can provide opportunities for problem solving and information movement (Dougherty & Dunne, 2011). However, inflexible organizational structures can inhibit the development of sustainable innovations (Dougherty & Dunne, 2011) and the individual sustainability agendas of organizational members (Hahn, Pinske, Preuss, & Figge, 2015). Individuals in these organizations may feel pressured to abandon sustainability innovations and objectives to maintain profitability or employment. System leaders will be required to encourage collaborative innovation within and between businesses and industries.

The combination of economic, environmental, and social objectives forming the foundation of business sustainability requires a broader perspective of the function of business in contemporary society (Bondy, Moon, & Matten, 2012; Gitsham, 2012). According to this broad perspective, the economic aspect of business is interconnected with the challenges of the long-term existence of and benefits provided by natural systems, unsatisfactory social conditions existing in communities globally, and the capacity of local and global economies to produce a small amount of wealth and benefit for all individuals (Ferdig, 2007). These challenges complicate the work of leaders who are responsible for establishing business strategies that respond to the challenges (Coleman, 2013). First, integrating these diverse objectives is challenging for business leaders because of the latent stresses (Haney, Pope, & Arden, 2018) among competing objectives (Margolis & Walsh, 2003), and between the conventional short-term targets of business decision-making and the long-term perspective necessary to respond to significant societal challenges (Hahn, Preuss, Pinkse, & Figge, 2014). Second, sustainability challenges are complicated, ill-defined, and lack obvious solutions (Lans, Blok, & Wesselink, 2014). Therefore, decision-making based upon past events to identify and manage future events are increasingly proving insufficient (Ferdig, 2007; Rieckmann, 2012; Sterling, 2011; Wesselink, Blok, van Leur, Lans, & Dentoni, 2015), because existing knowledge structures may inhibit recognition of innovative alternative solutions (Benner & Tripsas, 2012; Tripsas & Gavetti, 2000). Finally, managing these challenges requires collaboration with stakeholders espousing dissimilar perspectives of the problem (Lans et al., 2014) and of the preferred goals or objectives (Goleman & Lueneburger, 2010). The system leadership core competencies of being able to see the overall system, cultivate reflection and more innovative conversations, and transform the collective attention away from reactive problem solving to co-creation of the future (Senge, Hamilton, & Kania, 2015) will be essential for business sustainability leaders to overcome these challenges and barriers.

In managing the challenges created at the intersection of economic, environmental, and social objectives, business leadership that promotes sustainability outcomes through business activities (Visser & Courtice, 2011) is both essential (Eccles & Perkins, 2012) and dissimilar to conventional business leadership (Gitsham, 2012). Although the focus of most business literature has been with the institutional and organizational dimensions of sustainability (Aguinis & Glavas, 2012), there is an increasing interest in the role of and challenges faced by individual business leaders (Allen, Marshall, & Easterby-Smith, 2015) and the potential for these leaders to think and behave individually in the sustainability context (Hahn & Aragón-Correa, 2015). System leadership may provide the method for individual leaders to overcome the challenges presented by sustainability within the business sector.

## Conclusion

Several scholars have suggested that a paradigm shift is necessary to achieve sustainable development (Seiffert & Loch, 2005; Shin, Curtis, Huisingh, & Zwetsloot, 2008). Paradigm shifts in business management are typically influenced by broader shifts at the societal level (Valente, 2010), with dissatisfaction about the function of business in society driving the current paradigm shift towards sustainability (Valente, 2012). Gladwin, Kennelly, and

Krause (1995) proposed the promising evolution of an integrated "sustaincentric" paradigm, which is a combination of the technocentric and ecocentric worldviews, because neither worldview offers a suitable foundation for sustainable development. Moreover, because both current paradigms are in contention, they remain in a state of mutual contempt and contradiction (Myers & Simon, 1994) and, therefore, fail to benefit development or preserve nature (Gladwin et al., 1995). The concept of a sustaincentric worldview for sustainable development can be accepted as a controversial outcome of this competitive contest.

Although previous scholars have attempted to "green" the existing technocentric paradigm, the integration of ecocentrism and technocentrism is highly improbable (Wilber, 1995). The sustaincentric paradigm presents an alternative mechanism to explore the integration of the two existing paradigms. Sustaincentrism is established on an understanding of the universality of life, the stewardship doctrines prevalent among major religions, the field of ecological economics (Costanza, Daly, & Bartholomew, 1991), natural resource conservation and management (Norton, 1991), and scientific theories based on the complexity and self-organizing characteristics of nature (Botkin, 1990; Prigogine & Stengers, 1984; Wheatley, 1992).

Building a comprehensive business sustainability foundation requires fundamental organizational changes (Hui, 2008), which require new perspectives for how we depict organizations and the planet on which they function and exist. The transition to sustainability organizations must be viewed and managed as integrated whole systems, with each department having detailed knowledge of how all departments operate (Doppelt, 2017). Moreover, when we visualize the planet as a machine, we experience alienation because we cannot identify ourselves within the machine. However, the planet is not a machine; it is a living system full of life and history (Wheatley & Kellner-Rogers, 1999). Instead of behaving as if we intend to control the planet and all of the interconnected systems, humankind must begin to behave in a more holistic and harmonious manner toward nature. Although the planet naturally seeks organization, it needs no assistance from humankind (Wheatley & Kellner-Rogers, 1999).

In Chapter 2 we discussed the various leadership styles appropriate for sustainability, including servant leadership. Many successful business leaders are integrating sustainability and servant leadership to maintain a competitive position, while simultaneously improving organizational performance (McCann & Holt, 2010). Although servant leadership can happen anywhere and involve anyone, servant-leadership in business can have a broader impact because business leaders have the potential to affect more people globally than many other individuals (Graham, 1998). Moreover, strategic actions and decisions made at the most senior level of an organization can impact numerous individuals, both internal and external to the organization. However, it is at this organizational level that ethically based decision-making approaches still have had limited effect (McCann & Holt, 2010).

## Personal interview summary

World of Walas is an example of a company achieving sustainability through its operations and mission. World of Walas was founded in 2010 by Gerben van Straaten, who was inspired by the Earth Charter, UN Habitat3, the New Urban Agenda, and UNESCO, as well as individuals such as economist Jan Pen and urbanist Jane Jacobs to provide a platform to initiate change. Under van Straaten's leadership, Walas employees recognize that the existing practice of urban development is characterized by a succession of highly specialized stakeholders, with short-term involvement for the sole purpose of rapid profit maximization. This short-term perspective only benefits the developers, while the development beneficiaries are faced with rampant property development, inflated prices, and high vacancy (World of Walas, 2019a).

Walas has demonstrated models that retain the DNA of communities with significantly less initial investment and financial returns that are comparable to or exceed traditional development. With operations primarily located in North America and Europe, Walas continues to expand exponentially through ongoing projects, partnerships, and acquisitions. Walas moves beyond real estate and area development to achieve the activities, desires, and interests of individuals and cities for an energetic, vibrant whole. Their core business is effective, sustainable programming in close cooperation with the inhabitants and users of the cities, producing development of economic, social, cultural, sustainable, ecological, and financial values (World of Walas, 2019a). Walas works cautiously to balance all the components of urban development and redevelopment to provide places for people of all ages to live, work, shop, relax, learn, create, grow, develop, and be productive (World of Walas, 2019a).

After studying law and economics at the National University of Groningen, Gerben van Straaten worked as a project manager, business developer, and entrepreneur in Canada and Europe (World of Walas, 2019b). Van Straaten has more than 25 years of experience working with cities, higher education, governments, and industry on major, complex developments. He expanded into the areas of project development, real estate, and sustainable urban development, forming partnerships and alliances globally. After the financial and real estate crisis significantly altered the business landscape, he founded World of Walas in 2010 to conceptualize new sustainable business for cities and purchase, develop, redevelop, and manage real estate (World of Walas, 2019b).

Van Straaten believes that many contemporary societal problems can be solved through collective, collaborative initiatives around urban community developments. "He has 'radical hope' for the future, and believes that it all starts with an ethical reset" (World of Walas, 2019b). Together, Van Straaten and Walas establish intelligent, comprehensive combinations of convenient innovations, developing them into comprehensive, holistic sustainable development solutions (World of Walas, 2019b). Van Straaten is an example of a system leader who influences across multiple industries and sectors to achieve urban sustainability.

Van Straaten provided additional insight into his understanding and application of system leadership in an interview with this author on July 5, 2019. Van Straaten described himself as able to understand and "feel" complex systems and how they behave, even if he cannot calculate or "see" how the system operates. He noted the importance of recognizing the parts of a system you can control and the parts you cannot control, regardless of how hard you try. He tries to address both in his role as a sustainability system leader. He noted that part of systems thinking is building influence so that people can achieve something that is much larger than their immediate impact. He also understands the human aspects of systems and how groups of people or human interests evolve. He believes system leadership can be developed by telling a story, because stories are better understood than systems or algorithms, and by supporting that story with an understanding of how the new business model could work. He believes that it is "essential to understand evolutionary development versus planned development". An evolutionary way of thinking is necessary to understand those systems we want to change (G. van Straaten, personal communication, July 5, 2019).

He credits his success to his diverse combination of trained skills and the community-oriented culture in which he grew up. He believes his interdisciplinary background of economics, law, and project development provides him with a diverse skillset to perform his work. He encourages his employees to develop interdisciplinary skills, because schools have become so "siloed" in their teaching. He believes that when employees experience topics outside of their core skills like theater and local history, their understanding grows exponentially because they can "fold that around what they need to do with core skills". By encouraging this in his employees, he sees growth as professionals and in personal life, which is a huge asset for a company that wants to be a sustainable business (G. van Straaten, personal communication, July 5, 2019).

He tries to build capacity in people by showing them where they can go, making them think, and guiding them through mistakes, even though you may see them coming. He believes that if you can afford to let people make mistakes, the learning curve is so much higher. People may not always recognize it, but they grow faster if they can learn from mistakes. Encouraging this behavior requires that you inspire people, show them the field they are working in, let them have a look around, and make them feel safe. He also believes that because his employees are in the middle of the communities and cities they create, they cannot expect the community to grow unless they are a part of it, and they can see that the cities they are developing move from a bad situation to a new situation. He believes that urban communities are going through the same things that his people, company, and community are going through (G. van Straaten, personal communication, July 5, 2019).

The challenge or barrier he and his team faces in their work is that everyone else says that it cannot be done. Too many people think that there is only one way to develop cities, and they try to influence his employees, business partners, and infrastructure partners into believing that what they are doing will not work. He recognized when he started Walas that he was going against big industry with big interests who worked to prove that their system is the only one that will work. In addition, despite higher occupancy rates than nonsustainable developments, real estate appraisals are a problem, because property appraisers do not understand how to appraise their projects, which results in difficulty obtaining bank loans. He and his team have overcome this barrier by proving that what they are trying to do can be accomplished, noting that "every project gets a little easier". He also works to influence change through policy, paraphrasing Dutch Nobel Prize–winning economist Jan Tinbergen that every policy needs a tool, and without tools policies are meaningless. He believes that this involves two parts: let policy makers understand that they need to make tools, and then show them how they can do it. Van Straaten believes the success of Walas was based on being on the global stage and demonstrating that it can be done (G. van Straaten, personal communication, July 5, 2019).

Van Straaten recognized when he began sustainable urban development that there was no way he could make an impact by himself. His closing comments reinforced the system leadership skill of collaboration, noting that his slogan is "collaborate or die". Having grown up in Holland, much of which has been below sea level for 2,000 years, he noted, "it doesn't help if you build a dike in front of your own house, if your neighbor doesn't also build one. You must collaborate". Collaboration will work if people understand the interests they can reach by working together, and recognize that 1 + 1 = 3. Regarding change, he noted that if you want to drive system change you must really understand what you want to change and why. His appeal to anyone who wants to change systems is to find others who want to achieve change, build a movement, and see if together they can bring that to the next level, and bring it within the urgency that we need. The challenge is that many people who want to make change are doing so for a good reason like climate change, "so we must speed it up" (G. van Straaten, personal communication, July 5, 2019).

## Chapter reflection questions

1. The subject of the personal interview in this chapter was from the Netherlands, a nation that is likely more progressive when approaching sustainability, especially with approximately one-third of the land located below sea level. Do you think applying system leadership for sustainability would be more difficult with businesses located in nations that are less affected by climate change or are not as environmentally progressive? Why or why not?
2. While many nations are accustomed to business and government cooperation and collaboration, other nations, such as the United States, resist such efforts. What actions would you take as a system leader to encourage closer business and governmental collaboration and cooperation in your nation?
3. The business case for sustainability may be easier to influence when there are readily apparent impacts to financial performance. What actions would

you take as a system leader to influence a business to embrace sustainability absent any quantitative proof that there were benefits to participation in sustainability and costs for not participating?

## References


Accenture. (2016). *The UN global compact: Accenture strategy CEO study*. Retrieved from www.accenture.com/us-en/insight-un-global-compact-ceo-study

Aguinis, H., & Glavas, A. (2012). What we know and don't know about corporate social responsibility: A review and research agenda. *Journal of Management, 38*(4), 932–968. doi:10.1177/0149206311436079

Allen, S., Marshall, J., & Easterby-Smith, M. (2015). Living with contradictions: The dynamics of senior managers' identity tensions in relation to sustainability. *Organization & Environment, 28*(3), 328–348. doi:10.1177/1086026615575048

Allenby, B. (2009). The industrial ecology of emerging technologies: Complexity and the reconstruction of the world. *Journal of Industrial Ecology, 13*(2), 168–183. doi:10.1111/j.1530-9290.2009.00114.x

Andersen, M. S. (2007). An introductory note on the environmental economics of the circular economy. *Sustainability Science, 2*(1), 133–140. doi:10.1007/s11625-006-0013-6

Ashton, W. S. (2009). The Structure, function, and evolution of a regional industrial ecosystem. *Journal of Industrial Ecology, 13*(2), 228–246. doi:10.1111/j.1530-9290.2009.00111.x

Beehner, C. G. (2017, January). *Teaching sustainability to a traditional business audience*. Conference Proceedings of the International Academy of Business and Public Administration Discipline 14(1). Paper presented at IABPAD 2017 Conference, Orlando, FL (pp. 298–308).

Beehner, C. G. (2019). *Spirituality, sustainability & success: Concepts and cases*. London, England: Palgrave MacMillan.

Benner, M. J., & Tripsas, M. (2012). The influence of prior industry affiliation on framing in nascent industries: The evolution of digital cameras. *Strategic Management Journal, 33*(3), 277–302. doi:10.1002/smj.950

Benyus, J. M. (1997). *Biomimicry: Innovation inspired by nature*. New York, NY: William Morrow.

Berry, T. M. (1999). *The great work: Our way into the future*. New York, NY: Bell Tower.

Biomimicry Institute. (2019). *What is biomimicry?* Missoula, MO: Author. Retrieved from https://biomimicry.org/what-is-biomimicry/

Birkin, F. (2000). The art of accounting for science: A prerequisite for sustainable development? *Clinical Perspectives on Accounting, 11*, 289–309. doi:10.1006/cpac.1999.0367

Blowfield, M., & Murray, A. (2014). *Corporate responsibility*. Oxford, England: Oxford University Press.

Bocken, N. M., Short, S. W., Rana, P., & Evans, S. (2014). A literature and practice review to develop sustainable business model archetypes. *Journal of Cleaner Production, 65*, 42–56. doi:10.1016/j.jclepro.2013.11.039

Bondy, K., Moon, J., & Matten, D. (2012). An institution of corporate social responsibility (CSR) in multi-national corporations (MNCs): Form and implications. *Journal of Business Ethics, 111*(2), 281–299. doi:10.1007/s10551-012-1208-7

Boons, F., & Lüdeke-Freund, F. (2013). Business models for sustainable innovation: State-of-the-art and steps towards a research agenda. *Journal of Cleaner Production, 45*, 9–19. doi:10.1016/j.jclepro.2012.07.007

Boons, F., Montalvo, C., Quist, J., & Wagner, M. (2013). Sustainable innovation, business models and economic performance: An overview. *Journal of Cleaner Production, 45*, 1–8. doi:10.1016/j.jclepro.2012.08.013

Botkin, D. B. (1990). *Discordant harmonies: A new ecology for the twenty-first century*. New York, NY: Oxford University Press.

Cerceau, J., Mat, N., Junqua, G., Lin, L., Laforest, V., & Gonzalez, C. (2014). Implementing industrial ecology in port cities: International overview of case studies and cross-case analysis. *Journal of Cleaner Production, 64*, 1–16. doi:10.1016/j.jclepro.2014.03.050

Coleman, G. (2013). Sustainability as a learning challenge. *Journal of Management Development, 32*(3), 258–267. doi:10.1108/02621711311318292

Colwell, R. (1998). Balancing the biocomplexity of the planet's living systems: A twenty-first century task for science. *Bio-Science, 48*(10), 786–787. Retrieved from www.proquest.com

Costanza, R., Daly, H. E., & Bartholomew, J. A. (1991). Goals, agenda and policy recommendations for ecological economics. In R. Costanza (Ed.), *Ecological economics: The science and management of sustainability* (pp. 1–20). New York, NY: Columbia University Press.

Dean, T. J. (2014). *Sustainable venturing: Entrepreneurial opportunity in the transition to a sustainable economy*. Upper Saddle River, NJ: Pearson.

DeLaurentis, D. A., & Ayyalasomayajula, S. (2009). Exploring the synergy between industrial ecology and system of systems to understand complexity. *Journal of Industrial Ecology, 13*(2), 247–263. doi:10.1111/j.1530-9290.2009.00121.x

Deshpande, V. V. (2010). Environmental sustainability: Managing stakeholders through education. In P. M. Banerjee & V. Shastri (Eds.), *Social responsibility and environmental sustainability in business: How organizations handle profits and social duties* (pp. 99–110). Thousand Oaks, CA: Sage Publications.

Doppelt, B. (2017). *Leading change toward sustainability: A change-management guide for business, government and civil society*. Abingdon, England: Routledge.

Dougherty, D., & Dunne, D. D. (2011). Organizing ecologies of complex innovation. *Organization Science, 22*(5), 1214–1223. doi:10.1287/orsc.1100.0605

Down, L., & McKeown, R. (2017). *What is sustainable development?* San Jose, Costa Rica: Earth Charter Institute.

Eccles, R., & Perkins, K. (2012). How to become a sustainable company. *MIT Sloan Management Review, 53*(4), 43–50. Retrieved from https://sloanreview.mit.edu

Ehrenfeld, J. R. (2007). Would industrial ecology exist without sustainability in the background? *Journal of Industrial Ecology, 11*(1), 73–84. doi:10.1162/jiec.2007.1177

Elkington, J., Tickell, S., & Lee, M. (2007). *Sustainability: 20 years of global leadership [online]*. London: sustainability. Retrieved from www.sustainability.com

El-Sabaa, S. (2001). The skills and career path of an effective project manager. *International Journal of Project Management, 19*(1), 1–7. doi:10.1016/S0263-7863(99)00034-4

Ferdig, M. A. (2007). Sustainability leadership: Co-creating a sustainable future. *Journal of Change Management*, 7(1), 25–35. doi:10.1080/14697010701233809

Fiksel, J. (2006). Sustainability and resilience: Toward a systems approach. *Sustainability: Science, Practice, & Policy, 2*(2), 14–21. Retrieved from http://ejournal.nbii.org

Foxon, T., & Pearson, P. (2008). Overcoming barriers to innovation and diffusion of cleaner technologies: Some features of a sustainable innovation policy regime. *Journal of Cleaner Production, 16*(1), 148–161. doi:10.1016/j.jclepro.2007.10.011

Friedman, M. (1970, September 13). The social responsibility of business is to increase its profits. *New York Times Magazine, 32–33*, 122–124.

Gitsham, M. (2012). Experiential learning for leadership and sustainability at IBM and HSBC. *Journal of Management Development, 31*(3), 298–307. doi:10.1108/02621711211208925

Gladwin, T. N., Kennelly, J. J., & Krause, T.-S. (1995). Shifting paradigms for sustainable development: Implications for management theory and research. *The Academy of Management Review, 20*(4), 874–907. doi:10.5465/AMR.1995.9512280024

Gmelin, H., & Seuring, S. (2014). Determinants of a sustainable new product development. *Journal of Cleaner Production, 69*, 1–9. doi:10.1016/j.jclepro.2014.01.053

Goleman, D., & Lueneburger, C. (2010). The change leadership sustainability demands. *MIT Sloan Management Review, 51*(4), 49. Retrieved from https://sloanreview.mit.edu

Graham, J. (1998). Servant-leadership and enterprise strategy. In L. Spears (Ed.), *Insights on leadership: Service, stewardship, spirit, and servant-leadership* (pp. 145–156). Hoboken, NJ: John Wiley & Sons.

Green, D. (2016). *The world's top 100 economies: 31 countries: 69 corporations*. Washington, DC: The World Bank. Retrieved from https://blogs.worldbank.org/publicsphere/world-s-top-100-economies-31-countries-69-corporations

Hahn, T., & Aragón-Correa, J. A. (2015). Toward cognitive plurality on corporate sustainability in organizations. *Organization & Environment, 28*(3), 255–263. doi:10.1177/1086026615604446

Hahn, T., Pinske, J., Preuss, L., & Figge, F. (2015). Tensions in corporate sustainability: Towards an integrative framework. *Journal of Business Ethics, 127*(2), 297–316. doi:10.1007/s10551-014-2047-5

Hahn, T., Preuss, L., Pinkse, J., & Figge, F. (2014). Cognitive frames in corporate sustainability: Managerial sensemaking with paradoxical and business case frames. *Academy of Management Review, 39*(4), 463–487. doi:10.5465/amr.2012.0341

Haney, A. B., Pope, J., & Arden, Z. (2018). Making it personal: Developing sustainability leaders in business. *Organization & Environment*. doi:10.1177/1086026618806201

Harvey, M. (2001). The hidden force: A critique of normative approaches to business leadership. *SAM Advanced Management Journal, 66*(4), 36–48. Retrieved from https://samnational.org/sam-advanced-management-journal/

Hauschildt, J., Gesche, K., & Medcof, J. (2000). Realistic criteria for project manager selection and development. *Project Management Journal, 31*(3), 23–32. doi:10.1177/875697280003100304

Heaton, D., Schachinger, E., & Laszlo, C. (2016). Consciousness-development for responsible management education. In R. Sunley & J. Leigh (Eds.), *Educating for responsible management: Putting theory into practice* (pp. 211–232). Sheffield, England: Greenleaf Publishing.

Hein, A. M., Jankovic, M., Farel, R., & Yannou, B. (2015, August). A conceptual framework for eco-industrial parks. In *ASME 2015 international design engineering technical conferences and computers and information in engineering conference* (pp. V004T05A024–V004T05A024). New York, NY: American Society of Mechanical Engineers.

Hoffman, A. J. (2003). Linking social systems analysis to the industrial ecology framework. *Organization & Environment, 16*(1), 66–86. doi:10.1177/1086026602250219

Holthaus, G. (2012). *Learning Native wisdom: What traditional cultures teach us about subsistence, sustainability, and spirituality*. Lexington, KY: University Press of Kentucky.

Hui, L. T. (2008). Combining faith and CSR: A paradigm of corporate sustainability. *International Journal of Social Economics, 35*(6), 449–465. doi:10.1108/03068290810873429

Irani, Z., Sharif, A. M., & Love, P. E. D. (2005). Linking knowledge transformation to information systems evaluation. *European Journal of Information Systems, 14*(3), 213–228. doi:10.1057/palgrave.ejis.3000538

Jänicke, M. (2008). Ecological modernisation: New perspectives. *Journal of Cleaner Production, 16*(5), 557–565. doi:10.1016/j.jclepro.2007.02.011

Jones, P., & Upward, A. (2014). *Caring for the future: The systemic design of flourishing enterprises.* Proceedings of RSD3, Third Symposium of Relating Systems Thinking to Design, Oslo, Norway, 15–17 October. Retrieved from http://openresearch.ocadu.ca/id/eprint/2091/

Kassel, K. (2014). *The thinking executive's guide to sustainability.* New York, NY: Business Expert Press.

Lans, T., Blok, V., & Wesselink, R. (2014). Learning apart and together: Towards an integrated competence framework for sustainable entrepreneurship in higher education. *Journal of Cleaner Production, 62*, 37–47. doi:10.1016/j.jclepro.2013.03.036

Loorbach, D., & Wijsman, K. (2013). Business transition management: Exploring a new role for business in sustainability transitions. *Journal of Cleaner Production, 45*, 20–28. doi:10.1016/j.jclepro.2012.11.002

Luthe, T., Kägi, T., & Reger, J. (2013). A systems approach to sustainable technical product design: Combining life cycle assessment and virtual development in the case of skis. *Journal of Industrial Ecology, 17*(4), 605–617. doi:10.1111/jiec.12000

Marcus, J., Kurucz, E. C., & Colbert, B. A. (2010). Conceptions of the business-society-nature interface: Implications for management scholarship. *Business & Society, 49*(3), 402–438. doi:10.1177/0007650310368827

Margolis, J. D., & Walsh, J. P. (2003). Misery loves companies: Rethinking social initiatives by business. *Administrative Science Quarterly, 48*(2), 268–305. doi:10.2307/3556659

Maylor, H. (2003). *Project management* (3rd ed.). Upper Saddle River, NJ: Prentice Hall.

McCann, J. T., & Holt, R. A. (2010). Servant and sustainable leadership: An analysis in the manufacturing environment. *International Journal of Management Practice, 4*(2), 134–148. doi:10.1504/IJMP.2010.033691

Metson, G., Aggarwal, R., & Childers, D. L. (2012). Efficiency through proximity: Changes in phosphorus cycling at the urban-agricultural interface of a rapidly urbanizing desert region. *Journal of Industrial Ecology, 16*(6), 914–927. doi:10.1111/j.1530-9290.2012.00554.x

Molnar, E., & Mulvihill, P. R. (2003). Sustainability-focused organizational learning: Recent experiences and new challenges. *Journal of Environmental Planning and Management, 46*(2), 167–176. doi:10.1080/0964056032000070990

Myers, N., & Simon, J. L. (1994). *Scarcity or abundance: A debate on the environment.* New York, NY: Norton.

Nelson, R. R. (2007). IT project management: Infamous failures, classic mistakes, and best practices. *MIS Quarterly Executive, 6*(2). Retrieved from https://greenbay.usc.edu/csci577/spring2011/readings/ep/Project_mgnt_failures.pdf

Norton, B. G. (1991). *Toward unity among environmentalists.* New York, NY: Oxford University Press.

Opdebeeck, H. (2014). Spiritual sustainability management. In L. Zsolnai (Ed.), *The spiritual dimension of business ethics and sustainability management* (pp. 15–26). Heidelberg, Germany: Springer Nature. doi:10.1007/978-3-319-11677-8_20

Pavez, I., & Kendall, L. D. (2015, May). The arc of interconnectedness: A theory of the evolution of business towards flourishing. *7th Annual ARCS Research Conference.* Chicago, IL: Northwestern University

Prigogine, I., & Stengers, I. (1984). *Order out of chaos.* New York, NY: Bantam Books.

Rainey, D. L. (2006). *Sustainable business development: Inventing the future through strategy, innovation, and leadership.* New York, NY: Cambridge University Press.

Rieckmann, M. (2012). Future-oriented higher education: Which key competencies should be fostered through university teaching and learning? *Futures, 44*(2), 127–135. doi:10.1016/j.futures.2011.09.005

Rogers, M. (2016, March 29). *6 benefits of becoming a sustainable business*. Fort Collins, CO: Business Sector Media. Retrieved from www.environmentalleader.com/2016/03/6-benefits-of-becoming-a-sustainable-business/

Rosen, R. (1991). *Life itself: A comprehensive inquiry into the nature, origin, and fabrication of life* (1st ed.). New York, NY: Columbia University Press.

Seghezzo, L. (2009). The five dimensions of sustainability. *Environmental Politics*, *18*(4), 539–556. doi:10.1080/09644010903063669

Seiffert, M., & Loch, C. (2005). Systemic thinking in environmental management: Support for sustainable development. *Journal of Cleaner Production*, *13*(12), 1197–1202. doi:10.1016/j.jclepro.2004.07.004

Senge, P., Hamilton, H., & Kania, J. (2015). The dawn of system leadership. *Stanford Social Innovation Review*, *13*(1), 27–33. Retrieved from https://ssir.org/articles/entry/the_dawn_of_system_leadership

Shin, D., Curtis, M., Huisingh, D., & Zwetsloot, G. I. (2008). Development of a sustainability policy model for promoting cleaner production: A knowledge integration approach. *Journal of Cleaner Production*, *16*(17), 1823–1837. doi:10.1016/j.jclepro.2008.06.006

Soyka, P. A. (2012). *Creating a sustainable organization: Approaches for enhancing corporate value through sustainability*. Upper Saddle River, NJ: Pearson Education.

Springett, D., & Kearins, K. (2001). Gaining legitimacy? Sustainable development in business school curriculum. *Sustainable Development*, *9*, 213–221. doi:10.1002/sd.164

Srica, V. (2008). Social intelligence and project leadership. *The Business Review*, *9*(2), 189–200. Retrieved from www.velimirsrica.com

Srinivas, H. (2015). *Life cycle analysis*. Kobe, Japan: Global Development Research Center (GDRC). Retrieved from www.gdrc.org/sustdev/concepts/17-lca.html

Starik, M., & Kanashiro, P. (2013). Toward a theory of sustainability management: Uncovering and integrating the nearly obvious. *Organization & Environment*, *26*(1), 7–30. doi:10.1177/1086026612474958

Sterling, S. (2011). Transformative learning and sustainability: Sketching the conceptual ground. *Learning and Teaching in Higher Education*, *5*(11), 17–33. Retrieved from https://icdst.org/web/

Sumner, M., Bock, D., & Giamartino, G. (2006). Exploring the linkage between the characteristics of IT project leaders and project success. *Information Systems Management*, *23*(4), 43–19. doi:10.1201/1078.10580530/46352.23.4.20060901/95112.6

Tate, W. (2009). *The search for leadership: An organizational perspective*. Charmouth, England: Triarchy Press.

Thomas, T. E. (2005). Are business students buying it? A theoretical framework for measuring attitudes toward the legitimacy of environmental sustainability. *Business Strategy and the Environment*, *14*(3), 186–197. doi:10.1002/bse.446

Tripsas, M., & Gavetti, G. (2000). Capabilities, cognition and inertia: Evidence from digital imaging. *Strategic Management Journal*, *21*, 1147–1161. doi:10.1002/1097-0266(200010/11)21:10/11<1147::AID-SMJ128>3.0.CO;2-R

Tsvetkova, A., & Gustafsson, M. (2012). Business models for industrial ecosystems: A modular approach. *Journal of Cleaner Production*, *29–30*, 246–254. doi:10.1016/j.jclepro.2012.01.017

Valente, M. (2010). Demystifying the struggles of private sector paradigmatic change: Business as an agent in a complex adaptive system. *Business & Society*, *49*(3), 439–476. doi:10.1177/0007650310369376

Valente, M. (2012). Theorizing firm adoption of sustaincentrism. *Organization Studies*, *33*(4), 563–591. doi:10.1177/0170840612443455

Van Schalkwyk, A. (2011). Sacredness and sustainability: Searching for a practical eco-spirituality. *Religion and Theology, 18*(1–2), 77–92. doi:10.1163/157430111X613674

Van Straaten, G. (2019, July 5). Personal interview.

Visser, W., & Courtice, P. (2011). *Sustainability leadership: Linking theory and practice.* doi:10.2139/ssrn.1947221

Walker, B., Barrett, S., Polasky, S., Galaz, V., Folke, C., Engstrom, G., & de Zeeuw, A. (2009). Looming global-scale failures and missing institutions. *Science, 325*(5946), 1345–1346. doi:10.1126/science.1175325

Waste and Resources Action Programme. (2018). *WRAP and the circular economy*. Banbury, Oxon, England: Author. Retrieved from www.wrap.org.uk/about-us/about/wrap-and-circular-economy

Wesselink, R., Blok, V., van Leur, S., Lans, T., & Dentoni, D. (2015). Individual competencies for managers engaged in corporate sustainable management practices. *Journal of Cleaner Production, 106*(Supplement C), 497–506. doi:10.1016/j.jclepro.2014.10.093

Wheatley, M. J. (1992). *Leadership and the new science: Learning about organizations from an orderly universe.* San Francisco, CA: Berrett-Koehler Publishers.

Wheatley, M. J., & Kellner-Rogers, M. (1999). *A simpler way*. San Francisco, CA: Berrett-Koehler Publishers.

Whiteman, G., Walker, B., & Perego, P. (2013). Planetary boundaries: Ecological foundations for corporate sustainability. *Journal of Management Studies, 50*(2), 307–336. doi:10.1111/j.1467-6486

Wilber, K. (1995). *Sex, ecology, spirituality: The spirit of evolution.* Boston, MA: Shambhala.

Williams, A., Kennedy, S., Philipp, F., & Whiteman, G. (2017). Systems thinking: A review of sustainability management research. *Journal of Cleaner Production, 148*, 866–881. doi:10.1016/j.jclepro.2017.02.002

Winn, M., Kirchgeorg, M., Griffiths, A., Linnenluecke, M. K., & Günther, E. (2011). Impacts from climate change on organizations: A conceptual foundation. *Business Strategy & the Environment, 20*(3), 157–173. doi:10.1002/bse.679

World Commission on Environment and Development. (1987). *Our common future.* Oxford, England: Oxford University Press.

World of Wala̲s. (2019a). *Our story*. Heerlen, Netherlands: Author. Retrieved from https://worldofwalas.com/about-us/our-story/

World of Wala̲s. (2019b). *Gerben van Straaten*. Heerlen, Netherlands: Author. Retrieved from https://worldofwalas.com/team/gerben-van-straaten/

World Trade Organization. (2018). *World trade statistical review 2018.* Washington, DC: Author. Retrieved from www.wto.org/english/res_e/statis_e/wts2018_e/wts2018chapter08_e.pdf

Zimmerer, T., & Yasin, M. M. (1998). A leadership profile of American project managers. *Project Management Journal, 29*(3), 31–38. doi:10.1177/875697289802900107

# 6 System leadership for sustainability in academia

## Introduction

System leadership originated within the field of education, with academic leaders seeking to sustain gains in literacy and math skills, while simultaneously introducing more fundamental reform in the entire educational system (Fullan, 2005). This chapter will focus on system leadership within the field of academia, with sustainability defined within the previously described context of sustainability as originating in the Brundtland Report (World Commission on Environment and Development, 1987). There are three areas in which sustainability is relevant within academia: implementing sustainability within facilities and operations, incorporating sustainability into the curriculum, and sustainability-focused research. System leadership is a useful method for achieving sustainability within all three roles and would be feasible to implement, given that formal system leadership began in the field of education. Moreover, system leadership is based on systems thinking, and Harwood (2019) suggested the first two roles would benefit from systems thinking.

After examining early system leadership within the field of academia, the next sections of this chapter examine systems thinking in the field of education. These sections are followed by discussion of education for sustainability, business sustainability education, and sustainability research. The sections that follow describe system leadership from a global perspective and barriers to system leadership for sustainability in academia. While some of the content specifically describes higher education, most of the content is applicable to all levels of educational institutions and programs. Concluding comments are followed by a personal interview summary of an academic sustainability system leader.

## Early system leadership within the field of education

As previously stated, system leadership originated within the field of education, wherein leaders recognized the need to preserve and expand gains in literacy and math skills, while simultaneously introducing more fundamental reform in the entire educational system (Fullan, 2005). The required systemic changes necessitated development of new types of leaders who could lead within their own schools, systems, or levels, while simultaneously connecting with and engaging the bigger picture. Changing organizations and systems requires leaders who are capable of connecting to other parts of the system, while concurrently developing additional leaders with similar qualities. Development of numerous system leaders was deemed essential for achieving the critical mass needed for system change; however, limited training was available for systems thinking educational leaders (Fullan, 2005). The proposed solution to the development of system leaders was to connect systems thinking with sustainability, with Fullan noting that if systems thinking training could be provided, the likelihood of systems change would improve.

Educational system leaders recognize that changing the broader system requires meaningful engagement and managing subsequent change at a local level (Hopkins & Higham, 2007).

System leaders have already emerged in the field of education, characterized as administrators who agree to assume system-wide roles to support advancement of other schools in addition to their own (Hopkins & Higham, 2007). System leadership is a contemporary emerging practice encompassing multiple responsibilities that are developed locally or within separate networks or programs that, when combined, have the capacity to enhance system transformation. While system leadership in education has primarily occurred within the context of developing and sustaining system transformation, the skills are relevant to achieving sustainability within educational curricula and facilities (Hopkins & Higham, 2007).

The argument for education system leaders shares three inherent assumptions (Hopkins & Higham, 2007): achievement of sustainable change in education must be accomplished by individuals at the school level, change must be systemic, and system leadership is an emerging method. Moreover, several observations have been made concerning educational system leadership. First, tension exists between whether system leadership should be a national policy or a professional movement. Second, while system leadership is an emerging professional practice, it is established within an abundant theoretical and research context. Finally, although most school administrators are engaged in some type of collaborative or networking activity (Hill, 2006), these efforts do not constitute system leadership (Hopkins & Higham, 2007). System leadership offered the potential to become a catalyst for systemic change by providing an initial conceptualization established on existing literature and education policy; introducing a nomenclature of current system leader roles based on input from educators, administrators, government officials, and professional associations; locating system leadership within systems thinking and leadership literature; introducing a potential model of system leadership; and exploring the constraints surrounding further conceptual development (Hopkins & Higham, 2007).

While system leadership within the field of education has primarily been applied in pursuit of educational improvement sustainability, the concepts and intent are similar to efforts for achieving social, economic, and environmental sustainability. The objective in either case is achieving beneficial, desirable objectives and sustaining the outcome over time. The field of education can serve a significant role in practice and promotion of sustainability through the application of and training in system leadership. While system leadership has been effectively applied in higher education, barriers do exist, which will be the topic of a subsequent section. Because systems thinking provides a foundation for system leadership, the following sections examine systems thinking within the field of academia.

## Systems thinking in education facility operations

Primary, secondary, and post-secondary institutions own or control considerable real estate, occupy countless buildings, and consume energy and natural resources. The environmental and social impact of these operations is significant. Therefore, educational institutions serve an essential role in sustainable development. The coordinated effort needed among academic institutions and systems requires leaders capable of understanding systems and influencing across boundaries. Systems thinking provides a framework for understanding the interconnection of individuals, buildings, land, natural resources, and organizational structures. This framework is useful for all three of the previously identified sustainability roles for academia: facilities, curriculum, and research. In this section, we will consider the application of systems thinking in education facility operations.

There is limited empirical evidence of holistic or systemic approaches to sustainability within university operations (Harwood, 2019). While recent research findings indicate that universities are increasingly engaged in sustainable activities, efforts are compartmentalized and lack comprehensive integration (Lozano et al., 2015). Examples of systems thinking integration in sustainable campuses exist, including components such as university-wide educational mandates, conferences, workshops, and outreach programs, with leadership and participation identified as the ingredients for success (Koester, Eflin, & Vann, 2006). Several of these sustainability initiatives include commitments to environmental stewardship by signing the Talloires Declaration (Koester et al., 2006) and the Earth Charter (Earth Charter Initiative, 2009). The importance of sustainability signatory commitments was examined by Lozano et al., who determined that institutions that signed declarations, charters, and initiatives were more highly engaged in implementing sustainability. An alternative method of incorporating systems thinking into academic operations is to incorporate an environmental management system in the institution (Ferreira, Lopes, & Morais, 2006), based on the International Standards Organization (ISO) 14001 standard (Fisher, 2003). However, while examples exist of ISO standard-based holistic approaches to sustainable development at university campuses (Zenchanka & Malchenk, 2017), systems thinking did not necessarily predicate implementation of those approaches (Harwood, 2019).

A model of a sustainable university, grounded in systems theory, was developed by Velazquez, Munguia, Platt, and Taddei (2006). Fundamental attributes of the model included the significance of governance frameworks, embracing vision and mission, and an institution-wide committee to establish policies and objectives, coordinate initiatives, and obtain funding. Moreover, Posner and Stuart (2013) demonstrated how systems thinking can enhance understanding of the complexity of universities, shifting focus from general, solitary activities to more effective integrated efforts for addressing high-impact leverage points. However, the study did not determine the mechanism by which leverage points were identified (Harwood, 2019). From a systems perspective, higher education institutions are neither open nor closed systems (Harwood, 2019); they are best described as semi-open or semi-closed systems (Lozano, Lozano, Mulder, Huisingh, & Waas, 2013) or as informationally open and operationally closed systems (Espejo, 1992).

## Systems thinking in the education curriculum

While there are many examples of successful secondary education sustainability programs, the number is not extensive, with a limited number of programs in the United States (Watson, 2017). Moreover, sustainability education scholars and practitioners suggest limited data exists about how students develop sustainability competences, further noting limited methods for measurement of those competencies (Van den Elzen, 2017). However, there is considerable agreement among sustainability educators that systems thinking offers a "holistic approach through recognizing the complex interconnected nature of all aspects of the world around us from an individual to a global level" (Feng, 2012, p. 36). Systems thinking has been identified as an essential sustainability competency (Wiek, Withycombe, & Redman, 2011). In a study of the impact of systems thinking on the development of sustainability competencies of Indian secondary school students, the results indicated:

1 Systems thinking influences the development of other sustainability capabilities, by increasing the ability to comprehend complex systems and their spatial, temporal, and functional components.
2 Experiencing systems thinking, through completion of practical exercises, is essential for systems thinking to increase sustainability competencies and achieve successful program outcomes.
3 Important factors in experiencing systems thinking processes were reflection, evaluation, and teacher guidance.

(Van den Elzen, 2017)

The increasing importance of sustainable development has increased higher education efforts to integrate sustainability into the curriculum (Harwood, 2019). There are four ways sustainability can be incorporated into a curriculum: addition to an existing course, a dedicated sustainability course, included as a topic within general courses, or offered as a program or degree specialization (Lozano, 2010). While sustainable development course delivery is often compartmentalized into one element of sustainability, integrating sustainability as a concept among multiple academic disciplines would enable graduates to better contribute to making societies more sustainable (Lozano, 2010). Systems thinking would be an appropriate component of such an integrated, interdisciplinary curriculum. Regardless of how sustainability is integrated into curricula, systems thinking is an essential feature for developing sustainability literacy (Dale & Newman, 2005) for the management of unpredictable and dynamic complex problematic circumstances (Harwood, 2019). Systems thinking should reinforce deep learning and improvement of analytical and independent thinking abilities (Warburton, 2003), through activities such as personal experience reflection, key concept clarification, and participative and problem-solving activities (Harwood, 2019).

Several scholars propose systems thinking and an interdisciplinary approach are essential elements of sustainable development education (Dieleman & Huisingh, 2006; Feng, 2012; Warburton, 2003). The call for a systemic, interdisciplinary approach to sustainability received considerable university leadership support at the 2009 G8 University Summit Torino Declaration on Education and Research for Sustainable and Responsible Development (Turin Declaration; International Association of Universities, 2009). The declaration called for an integrated, interdisciplinary approach to decision-making and problem solving (Harwood, 2019), with disciplinary thinking replaced by systems thinking (International Association of Universities). Examination of the interconnectedness of socio-ecological systems and identification of significant change methods requires transdisciplinary effort influenced by systems thinking from the fields of management and ecology (Starik & Rands, 1995; Whiteman, Walker, & Perego, 2013).

## Education for sustainability

Having introduced the application of systems thinking in educational operations and curricula, the following sections present a foundation of education for sustainability, and more specifically, sustainable business education. The term education for sustainable development (ESD) emerged after the 1992 Earth Summit in Rio de Janeiro, Brazil, as a more generally defined term than environmental education, incorporating cultural diversity, global development, and environmental and social justice concerns (Calder & Clugston, 2003). One of the ESD initiatives is to provide sustainability education to all workforce sectors so every public and private employee would have access to the knowledge and skills needed to make sustainable work decisions (UNESCO, 2012).

There are two primary forms of education for sustainability: incorporating sustainability into existing the curriculum and teaching sustainability as a stand-alone topic, course, or degree program. Much of the education for sustainability occurring within the K–12 and higher education systems has taken place within an environmental science curriculum. However, the amount of environmental literacy, civic engagement, and social responsibility content in higher education curricula increased significantly during the 1990s (Bridges & Wilhelm, 2008; Rowe, 2002). Sustainability should be taught in a variety of academic fields and levels as well as interdisciplinary courses and programs. Adoption rates of a sustainability curriculum may increase if the contribution to sustainable development can be validated (Watson, Lozano, Noyes, & Rodgers, 2013). Unfortunately, it is difficult to measure the contribution to sustainable development, because the social and political outcomes of educational change is difficult to measure due to the dynamic nature of change processes (Dlouha, Huisingh, & Barton, 2013).

Education for sustainability is emerging in higher education and adult learning as an interdisciplinary method to assist learners with critical analysis of unsustainable systems, developing creative problem solving and active citizenship skills, and becoming personally and intellectually engaged in urgent social, ecological, economic, and political challenges (Nolet, 2009; Sterling, 2001). The goal of education for sustainability is to provide learners with the skills, values, and perspectives necessary to shift toward a sustainable society (Voisey & O'Riordan, 1998). However, sustainability educators are challenged with developing leaders who can understand complex socio-ecological systems and the impact of their actions (Raivio, 2011; Watson et al., 2013). Moreover, university leaders in sustainability education frequently lack an integrated interdisciplinary approach (Lozano, 2010).

Several pedagogical approaches have been examined for developing the knowledge, skills, and values necessary for sustainability leadership, including active and problem-based learning (MacVaugh & Norton, 2012); critical, reflective thinking about sustainability worldviews (Stubbs & Cocklin, 2008); on-the-job training (Ferreira et al., 2006); decision-making tools (Lozano & Lozano, 2014); interdisciplinary approaches (Gombert-Courvoisier, Sennes, Ricard, & Ribeyre, 2014; Hull, Kimmel, Robertson, & Mortimer, 2016; Shrivastava, Ivanaj, & Persson, 2013); collaboration (Gombert-Courvoisier et al., 2014); and developmental approaches (Pappas, Pierrakos, & Nagel, 2013). However, while the contributions of sustainability education emphasize the significance of personal values for sustainability, this approach is disputed by those who believe colleges and universities are not the venue for moral agenda development (Butcher, 2007). The consensus is that sustainability education is not a process of knowledge transfer to the student, but rather a process of student-centered personal development based on experiential learning (Savage, Tapics, Evarts, Wilson, & Tirone, 2015).

Experiential learning is an active learning process in which learners experience and reflect on the content to be learned (Kolb, 1984). The experiential learning cycle components are concrete experience, reflective observation, abstract conceptualization, and active experimentation, with Kolb suggesting that all learning is experiential, and Illeris (2007) arguing that transformation is more likely to occur with experiential learning. Dawe, Jucker, and Martin (2005) suggested that a combination of holistic thinking and experiential learning was essential for sustainability education delivery. Svanström, Lozano-García, and Rowe (2008) suggested expected learning outcomes from a sustainable development course might include the ability to think systemically, in addition to development of interpersonal, intrapersonal, and change agent skills (Harwood, 2019).

Experiential learning programs (ELPs) have been found to help train managers to become sustainability leaders within their organizations (Haney, Pope, & Arden, 2018). While the programs examined were offered to a business audience, the outcome should be generalizable to organizational leaders outside of industry. In the study, sustainability ELPs were found to support the learning outcomes of understanding, personal connection, and empowerment to act. In addition, making sustainability personal for ELP participants resulted in deep learning in each of the three outcomes (Haney et al., 2018).

Understanding is the most prominent learning outcome, with a goal of assisting participants in making sense of sustainability (Haney et al., 2018). The sustainability ELPs provided an opportunity for participants to consider the connections between diverse social and environmental sustainability characteristics, thereby demonstrating systems thinking. The programs also fostered development of additional, more profound types of understanding, such as understanding their own role and leadership within their organizations regarding sustainability (Haney et al., 2018). Understanding was enhanced by providing participants opportunities to interact with and observe people encountering issues that might be unfamiliar to the participants, such as water scarcity. These encounters assisted in creating an immersive experience, in which participants engaged with people with whom they may not have otherwise been able to (Haney et al., 2018).

Personal connection describes an individual's perception of being personally connected to sense of self, to other organizational members, or to specific sustainability issues (Haney et al., 2018). This personal connection enables individuals to embrace sustainability more deeply than by simply understanding or recognizing the issues, instead allowing them to contemplate how their private self relates to the person they are at work. The reported experiences of ELP participants suggested a degree of deep personal transformation and self-redefinition as described by Sterling (2011). Other participants reported that the program offered a safe environment to discuss issues with peers that might otherwise be impossible. A personal connection was found to provide an important connection between participants' understanding and feelings of empowerment to act on sustainability (Haney et al., 2018). Empowerment to act added to understanding and personal connection and included specific moments when participants recognized changes to their engagement in sustainability, ability to act on that engagement, or both, as a result of program participation (Haney et al., 2018). The importance of observing practical solutions was noted by multiple participants as essential for developing this competency, with participants frequently referring to specific program components in which observing solutions motivated feelings of empowerment (Haney et al., 2018).

"Transformation through transformative learning" is a common theme in sustainability education literature, with researchers suggesting transformative learning is essential for modifying learner perspectives (Sipos, Battisti, & Grimm, 2008; Sterling, 2011; Wals & Corcoran, 2006). Learning consists of the development of abilities "within existing (mental) frameworks, norms, policies and rules" (Tosey, Visser, & Saunders, 2012, p. 292) and also challenges and transforms these frameworks, norms, and policies through a process described as conceptual change (Pintrich, Marx, & Boyle, 1993). Transformative learning offers a holistic learning model, respecting both the intuitive and rational minds by utilizing innovative and critical knowledge and skills, combined with active participation in the classroom, community, and environment to achieve significant change (Wright, Cain, & Monsour, 2015). The sustainability curriculum established in Mezirow's (1997) transformative learning theory stimulates, challenges, and conceivably changes learner perspectives and assumptions. Through transformative learning the learner encounters the sustainability dilemma, is provided opportunities for critical reflection, participates in discussion, and becomes motivated to act (Wright et al., 2015).

Habron, Goralnik, and Thorp (2012) offered a unique glimpse into the pilot of an undergraduate sustainability course delivered by a combination of faculty and expert guest speakers. Anticipated proficiency development included self-consciousness, community engagement, and systems thinking, while the latter proficiency was identified as needing additional development. A magazine article was used to assist students with developing systems models, based upon boundaries, relationships, and feedback loops. In addition, an interactive discussion forum was developed to evaluate individual participation in a group dialog, enabling participants to validate their learning. The variety of assignments enabled assessment of multiple competencies, such as interaction, problem solving, and systems thinking (Harwood, 2019). While several examples exist of the use of systems thinking to construct a sustainable development course, the pilot course by described by Habron and colleagues contributed exceptional examples of how systems thinking can be incorporated into sustainable development instruction (Harwood, 2019).

The Professional Practice for Sustainable Development (PP4SD) was introduced in 1999 (Martin & Hall, 2002), in collaboration with 14 professional institutions, to develop a universal sustainable development curriculum structure to analyze and distribute educational materials (Martin, 2005). The educational content targeted professionals from multiple areas, including business, academia, and consultancy. While the immediate target was current professionals, the program also considered future professionals studying within the university system who were seeking methods for teaching sustainability in undergraduate and postgraduate programs (Martin, 2005). The PP4SD sustainability framework is based upon the following assumptions of a sustainable society:

- Natural resource extraction and substance manufacture should not exceed planetary capacity to distribute, absorb, recycle, or eliminate harmful consequences to humans and the environment.

- Ecosystem diversity and performance should not be jeopardized.
- A healthy economy should be maintained while accurately representing the value of natural, human, social, and financial resources.
- Individual abilities, knowledge, and health should be developed and utilized for the greatest benefit.
- Social justice and progress should equitably represent the needs of present and future generations.
- Structures and institutions should encourage environmental stewardship and societal development.

(Martin, 2002, 2005)

The PP4SD program influences organizational culture and behavior through interventions and facilitated conversations between participants (Martin, 2005). Although cultural change requires that most of these conversations be transformed (Isaacs, 1999), most change programs are focused on modifying large-scale structures and systems, not conversations (Martin, 2005). The PP4SD process is beneficial for undergraduate and graduate environmental programs because it provides additional opportunities to improve dialog and analytical skills in an interdisciplinary, collaborative manner. Because disagreement exists concerning how to achieve sustainability, environmental programs must integrate productive communication, systems thinking and practice, sustainability principles, and individual and professional values and ethics and emphasize the necessity for achieving systemic change (Martin, 2005).

It is increasingly apparent that any sustainability education approach must differ from the existing conventional education and training being administered by academic institutions (Jucker, 2002; Sterling, 2001). Education for sustainability requires additional emphasis on action learning, conversation, inquiry, participation, and interprofessional collaboration (Scott & Gough, 2003). The approach should extend beyond teaching, knowledge transmission, and syllabus or curriculum adherence to issue and problem investigation through continuous, open-ended inquiry (Martin, 2005). Therefore, effective sustainability change methods must incorporate innovative learning focused on transforming organizational culture and behavior (Martin, 2005). This section has provided an oversight of education for sustainability, including several methods and pedagogies for sustainable education delivery. The following section will summarize sustainability education specifically targeting business and industry.

## Business sustainability education

Several arguments exist for including sustainability in business curricula. The incorporation of sustainability in business curricula is fundamental for developing business leaders who demonstrate a critical global perspective (Cezarino, 2016). However, while addressing future sustainability challenges requires environmentally literate managers, many business students graduate with no environmental understanding (Rowe, 2002). Although business schools are considered advocates of modern capitalism, business students should learn to examine the existing capitalist model and develop reasonable modifications or alternatives (Von Der Heidt & Lamberton, 2011). Moreover, the synthesis of environmental objectives with business objectives can produce strategies to improve both environmental and business performance (Jabbour, 2010).

Although the need for business sustainability education has been identified, there are challenges with the development and delivery of sustainable business content (Beehner, 2017). While sustainability has become an important global issue, business schools frequently delay response to contemporary trends such as sustainability (Bates, Silverblatt, & Kleban, 2009), with a limited number of business schools having fully identified the essential sustainable business competencies (Adomßent et al., 2014). Moreover, because business and commerce consume so much of our natural resources and contribute to so many adverse effects, teaching sustainable business is critical.

Preparing business students to become leaders capable of addressing contemporary problems requires that higher education demonstrates how businesses can simultaneously manage profitability and consider the environmental effects of business activity (Hoffman, 1999). One challenge with teaching sustainable business is justifying the requirement for and role of business participation in sustainability, necessitating sustainability be explained to business students using the language of business (Beehner, 2018). An example of communicating sustainability with business language is drawn from the field of finance and accounting, in which sustainability is compared with the retirement planning principle of living off investment interest, without drawing down the principle of an investment (Down & McKeown, 2017). Haney and colleagues advocate experiential learning programs as an appropriate method to develop knowledge, skills, attitudes, and values to catalyze learning and facilitate sustainability leadership development among business leaders (Haney et al., 2018).

It is essential for current and future business leaders to acquire sustainability expertise. Although the number of colleges and universities offering a sustainable business curriculum is growing, the success of business sustainability initiatives may be diminished by lack of sustainability awareness among entry-level employees and supervisors (Beehner, 2018). Therefore, sustainable business education should be delivered at all academic levels, including community colleges that prepare workers for entry-level vocational, supervisory, and professional positions at organizations that have developed, or may develop, sustainability initiatives (Beehner, 2018). Because the majority of Americans reside within a one-hour drive of a community college campus (AACC, 2012), these institutions offer a convenient, affordable platform for sustainable business education. However, the US community college system is often neglected in offering environmental and sustainable education (Potter, 2009), with a limited number of institutions offering sustainable business coursework (Beehner, 2018). As community college participation in sustainable business education increases, businesses may benefit from additional sustainability-focused entry-level employees, and society may benefit from the increased sustainability awareness and the potential benefits from businesses operating more sustainably (Beehner, 2018).

## Sustainability research

Scholars from multiple disciplines and viewpoints have attempted to explain the complicated nature of sustainability (Williams, Kennedy, Philipp, & Whiteman, 2017), with a considerable increase in interest within the disciplines of business, management, and organizational studies (Cullen, 2016). A well-developed comprehension of sustainability management requires researchers to adopt an interdisciplinary systemic view to appreciate the interconnectedness of economic, political, social, and environmental issues across physical and geographical dimensions (Williams et al., 2017). While a limited number of articles about systems thinking and sustainability management were published prior to 2000, the number published in the current century has increased exponentially (Williams et al., 2017). Moreover, the limited availability of business and organizational management literature addressing systems thinking and sustainability suggests that a systems perspective on sustainability management is limited to transdisciplinary research and systems thinking disciplines, such as environmental sciences and engineering (Williams et al., 2017). Additional research in the area of system leadership for sustainability is necessary, and further recommendations for future research are provided in Chapter 10.

## Barriers to system leadership in academia

Education for sustainability serves an essential role in the development and uniformity of sustainability actions in organizations and society (Baccarin, Cezarino, Fernandes, Liboni, & Martinelli, 2015). However, several institutional barriers can inhibit the development of sustainability curriculum: the disciplinary environment, the competitive environment, misguided evaluation criteria, and ambiguous priorities, decision-making, and authority (Moore, 2005). The disciplinary environment frequently hinders interdisciplinary collaboration or discourages students from taking courses outside their major, because educational programs contain a comprehensive curriculum, with limited flexibility for non-departmental electives. The competitive environment is characterized by students competing for grades, faculty competing for publication and grants, departments competing for students and funding, and institutions competing for prestige. Evaluation criteria are frequently defined at the faculty level by publication and research, at the student level by employment and salaries, and at the university institutional level by unclear evaluation processes for policies and plans. Unfortunately, a comprehensive metric does not currently exist for measurement of sustainability at the faculty, the student, or the institutional level. Finally, while support may exist for sustainability curriculum, multiple priorities and unclear decision-making criteria may produce uncertainty or disagreement concerning where in the hierarchy curriculum decision-making should occur (Moore, 2005). Barriers to sustainability in academia include perceived insignificance and insufficient expertise at the faculty level, overcrowding at the curriculum level, and limited commitment at the institutional level (Dawe et al., 2005).

The previously identified institutional barriers are equally relevant to system leadership implementation. The disciplinary climate can inhibit interdisciplinary collaboration, which is an essential element of system leadership in academia. Faculty and administrators in science disciplines may consider themselves experts in sustainability and resist leadership influence originating from other disciplines. Moreover, scholars of non-science disciplines may question the need to participate in environmental or social initiatives. The competitive environment can inhibit system leadership because teachers and administrators seeking to influence across systems may be in competition for grants or funding and reluctant to embrace influence from someone deemed a competitor. The absence of established metrics for assessing collaborative sustainability activities may inhibit system leadership initiatives. Moreover, multiple priorities, ambiguous decision-making standards, and confusion regarding the hierarchical level responsible for curriculum decision-making may adversely impact any attempts to influence system leadership curriculum development efforts.

Wiek, Farioli, Fukushi, and Yarime (2012) noted two fundamental challenges that sustainability scientists must consider concerning research. First, research and education are important but not the sole ingredient in solutions to sustainability problems. Second, collaboration and partnerships within and among multiple stakeholder groups are essential prerequisites for sustainability science and practical results (Blackstock, Kelly, & Horsey, 2007; Spangenberg, 2011; Talwar, Wiek, & Robinson, 2011; Whitmer et al., 2010). Addressing these challenges will require leaders capable of seeing the big picture and engaging in successful collaboration, both attributes of system leaders.

Harwood (2019) observed that university-level systems thinking instruction has been declining for several years, consequently resulting in a decline in its general comprehension. Because sustainability requires a systems thinking perspective, the decline in systems understanding can inhibit achievement of sustainable development (Harwood, 2019). Systems thinking education and training are important tools for developing system leadership and should be incorporated in sustainability education curricula. Absent systems thinking curricula, system leaders will experience limited formal educational opportunities for development of essential systems understanding.

## Conclusion

Academia serves a critical role in achieving a sustainable future for humankind. Because system leadership originated within the field of education, academics may be well suited for implementing system leadership to achieve the desired state of sustainability. Systems thinking is essential for effective higher education sustainable development, in terms of both development and implementation of institutional sustainability initiatives and delivery of student learning experiences. However, academic contributions of systems thinking and integrated approaches to sustainability appear to be limited concerning use of systems concepts, with the risk of misinterpretation when systems thinking is advocated (Harwood, 2019).

The increasing necessity for educational partnerships and networks that cross institutional boundaries calls for conceptual developments in leadership theory (Boylan, 2016). System leadership offers an alternative approach to both theorizing and promoting boundaryless educational collaboration. These leaders must exist at all levels of the educational system, including at the teacher level. Because system leadership has been successfully applied in the field of education, this model may prove to be familiar and therefore useful in expanding the role of education in sustainability (Boylan, 2016).

Although individual-level learning is essential for developing new competencies, limited research exists on corporate sustainability concerning how leaders can learn to respond to sustainability issues (Haney et al., 2018). Fullan (2004) suggested that a new type of leadership is needed to overcome the status quo. Because systematic forces have an advantage in preventing system change, energetic, persuasive efforts are required to change existing systems. Changing organizations and systems will require leaders to become adept in connecting other system components and to assist in developing other leaders seeking similar outcomes (Hopkins & Higham, 2007). System leadership offers a model for leaders to respond appropriately to the challenges and issues of sustainability.

## Personal interview summary

Robert Franco is the Director of the Office for Institutional Effectiveness at Kapi'olani Community College in Honolulu, Hawaii. His career at the college has included teaching (1985–2000) and institutional planning, research, and grants development (2000–present). He learned arithmetic and interpersonal skills as a youth while working at his father's grocery store in Napa, California (Kapi'olani Community College, 2019b). Franco is a cultural anthropologist, having earned his PhD at the University of Hawaii Manoa, specializing in Samoan diaspora and urban adaptation, specifically with education, employment, health, housing, and chiefly status. His publication topics include contemporary Samoan political and cultural change, traditional Hawaiian water management systems, and sociocultural factors affecting fisheries sustainability in Polynesia and Micronesia. The focus of his current research and training is with student and community engagement, reducing the minority academic achievement gap, and strengthening the liberal arts, workforce development, and civic mission of higher education (Kapi'olani Community College, 2019a). He currently oversees the college's Service and Sustainability Learning Program (Kapi'olani Community College, 2019b).

Throughout his career, Franco has been an advocate for indigenous, intercultural, and international education. He is the campus liaison to Hawaii's National Science Foundation (NSF) Established Program to Stimulate Competitive Research (EPSCoR) and has written and evaluated numerous successful NSF grants for his campus and other University of Hawaii (UH) campuses, including a Pre-Engineering Education Collaborative and the Louis Stokes Alliance for Minority Participation. He also served as the college's accreditation liaison from 1994 to 2012, and has led campus initiatives with the American Association of Community Colleges ("Building Community"), Association of American Colleges and Universities ("Greater Expectations"), and American Council on Education ("Global Competence" and "International Collaborative"). He has conducted training, provided technical assistance, and engaged in research dissemination at community colleges, universities, and academic conferences in 42 states. His research-based training is designed to improve course success, semester-to-semester retention, degree completion, and transfer rates through service-learning, community-based research, and authentic partnerships (Kapi'olani Community College, 2019a).

Franco has been most influential in the realm of community and civic engagement, having collaboratively developed the Carnegie Foundation's Campus-Community Engagement Classification in 2002–2005. Franco has been and continues today as a Senior Faculty Fellow for Community Colleges for National Campus Compact and Hawai'i -Pacific Islands Compact, a Science Education for New Civic Engagements and Responsibilities (NSF-SENCER) Leadership Fellow, and an advisor to SENCER Center for Innovation (SCI)–Western Region. In 2011, he was named one of 20 national "Beacons of Vision, Hope, and Action" by the Community College National Center for Community Engagement. In March 2019, he received the "Advancing the Field-Distinguished Leader Award" from the Western Region Campus Compact Consortium (Kapi'olani Community College, 2019b). He also participates in the East-West Center's International Forum on Education for the Year 2020, with 25 scholars from China, India, Malaysia, Thailand, and the Philippines (Kapi'olani Community College, 2019a).

Franco provided additional insight into his understanding and application of system leadership in an interview with this author on July 19, 2019. His understanding of system leadership is based upon his role as a leader within the University of Hawaii community college system. His job description has included the development of international education, service-learning, STEM, and sustainability initiatives within the ten-campus system, as well as building collaborative efforts such as the previously mentioned Carnegie Foundation engagement project. He has been particularly focused on how innovations become institutionalized in college campuses. Some of the systemic questions that he continually asks in his work are, what role do colleges play in building diverse, equitable, healthy and sustainable communities, locally and globally; how does this role integrate with faculty and student engagement; and how do we encourage innovation to become institutionalized in campuses? (R. Franco, personal communication, July 19, 2019).

Franco offered the following sequence for ensuring that innovation becomes institutionalized throughout an organization. First, a number of organizational members (in his example, faculty) must embrace the initiative, and then the institution needs to reward these new roles over time. Second, organizational members must work together to build capacity, progressing from capacity building to building quality. Finally, leadership must determine how to sustain the initiative. He added that there is a science of institutionalization in which researchers seek to understand institutions, how they move from innovation to institutionalizing, and how institutionalization is sustained and continuously improved. Within the context of this text, Franco noted that sustainability has a double meaning, in that we are trying to understand how to sustain or institutionalize sustainability at an institution level (R. Franco, personal communication, July 19, 2019).

In our discussion of system leadership skills, competencies, and abilities, Franco commented that there is a need for focus on attitude or philosophy. There must be a willingness or desire to make change. He is driven by both civic and moral purpose. If he were not engaged in the moral questions of globalization, he would not be doing this work. The civic aspect refers to how to draw people into this dialog about the moral question. It is important to understand how faith, schooling, and earlier role models influence a person. He believes system leadership emerges from pondering moral and civic questions and adding the moral dimension to these questions. He frequently used the phrase "willing and able" describing *able* as the skills, competencies, and abilities of a person, and describing *willing* as how a person confronts moral and civic challenges. He noted that the person who most influenced his career is Thomas Ehrlich at the Carnegie Foundation, with his focus on the civic and moral dimensions of issues, moral and civic judgment, and taking action (R. Franco, personal communication, July 19, 2019).

Franco noted that initiatives like sustainability can come and go and are often not institutionalized. He identified two factors that prevent an initiative from enduring: loss of key individuals and lack of mission commitment. Frequently, an academic initiative is driven by a small group of "green light" faculty, and he has seen powerful, successful initiatives lose their influence with the loss these key faculty. He recommends thinking about who will replace key faculty and what their responsibilities are, and then mentoring junior faculty to prepare for those roles. The mission statement cannot be just a catch phrase; there must be mission-driven messaging and actions to lead to coherence and innovation (R. Franco, personal communication, July 19, 2019).

When asked about the barriers and challenges faced when influencing outside of his college system, Franco stated that multiculturalism is the only way forward. However, he sees an attitudinal barrier with multiculturalism, in which some people seem to feel that if they believe in multiculturalism, they will somehow lose power. There is too much focus on "me, me, me". Multiculturalism is both a competency and a commitment, and he does not see enough of a commitment, especially within community colleges. He believes this is an area in which community colleges should speak up, because minorities make up a large part of the population they serve. He noted that many people are doing what he calls "turtling", which is essentially pulling in their heads and hoping they will get through whatever is going on, while other people are making their individual gain argument more forcefully. Without a long-term, institutional emphasis on multicultural understanding and respect, we will experience greater class, racial, and gender inequity, more community disintegration and violence, and a resulting need for greater policing and over-imprisonment. He believes we cannot handle the expanding global population with a judicial, punitive system, in which some people are being punished by this lack of commitment and rhetoric around what a multicultural world looks like. While he does not currently see a larger political, administrative, leadership commitment to multiculturalism, "we are all going to have to find a way forward together" (R. Franco, personal communication, July 19, 2019).

According to Franco, to develop system leadership we need to realize that we are preparing students for a world that is extremely different than the one many of us grew up in, not just in terms of sustainability but also technologically. System leaders must have a moral and civic compass and must see that the world we are destroying will be a challenge for future generations. He believes system leadership development should include more questions about moral issues, unfairness, and social injustices, not only being aware of them, but caring about them and being willing to take action (R. Franco, personal communication, July 19, 2019).

He believes that we have not differentiated enough between managing and leading, because many administrators today are only managing. He believes that leaders need to have a real philosophical frame for what leadership is. He does not think people employ their philosophical or educational orientation – they just become managers without a broader philosophical perspective, because they think it is inappropriate to bring their philosophical perspective into their work. He thinks developing system leadership in academia requires more of a focus on institutional identity: what is the campus known for, what do they want students to come there for, what kind of students do you want to send out into world? If someone is only looking at performance measures, "the conversation ends up focusing on money and not meaning", resulting in a campus lacking an institutional identity. He summarized that what is needed of system leaders within academia is a moral and civic focus and creation of an institutional identity (R. Franco, personal communication, July 19, 2019).

In summarizing his role as a sustainability system leader, Franco cited the broader philosophical frame that he brings to his work, which is based on his faith and his education. He is a demographer, and he believes that locally and globally we are confronting "both a Malthusian and Marxian dilemma". Global population growth continues only slightly abated, resources are unequally distributed and exploited, and governments are challenged to equitably manage the intersections of these two dilemmas. He believes that community colleges find themselves at this intersection, but they have not elevated into a position, or a philosophical willingness, to recognize this challenge. Regarding differences in faith and philosophy, he noted that if you do not have a general commitment to the welfare of all, then you might feel you are more deserving of something than others are. People need to recognize that if any individual is suffering, we are also suffering, and we need to build a democratic social fabric that reduces suffering and builds healthy and sustainable communities (R. Franco, personal communication, July 19, 2019).

## Chapter reflection questions

1 What challenges do you think Robert Franco faces as a Caucasian male trying to promote multiculturalism among indigenous and minority populations in Hawaii? How would you act to overcome these challenges?
2 Because sustainability initiatives are frequently "owned" or driven by one individual, how can those initiatives be institutionalized within organizations and sectors to achieve sustainable sustainability action?
3 What role does multiculturalism serve in achieving sustainability? How can sustainability be achieved globally when multiple cultures and peoples exist, each with competing needs and perspectives of what actions need to be taken?

## References

Adomßent, M., Fischer, D., Godemann, J., Herzig, C., Otte, I., Rieckmann, M., & Timm, J. (2014). Emerging areas in research on higher education for sustainable development: Management education, sustainable consumption and perspectives from Central and Eastern Europe. *Journal of Cleaner Production, 62*(1), 1–7. doi:10.1016/j.jclepro.2013.09.045

American Association of Community Colleges (AACC). (2012). *About.* Retrieved from www.aacc.nche.edu/AboutCC/Pages/default.aspx

Baccarin, G., Cezarino, L. O., Fernandes, V., Liboni, L., & Martinelli, D. P. (2015). *Aplicação do Soft System Methodology na gestão de resíduos perigosos em laboratórios.* Paris: Anais do XI Congresso Brasileiro de Sistemas.

Bates, C., Silverblatt, R., & Kleban, J. (2009). Creating a new green management course. *The Business Review, Cambridge, 12*(1), 60–66. Retrieved from www.jaabc.com/

Beehner, C. G. (2017). *Teaching sustainability to a traditional business audience.* Conference Proceedings of the International Academy of Business and Public Administration Discipline, 14(1). Paper presented at IABPAD Conference, Orlando (pp. 298–308).

Beehner, C. G. (2018). Expanding sustainable business education beyond business schools. In S. Dhiman & J. Marques (Eds.), *Handbook of engaged sustainability.* Heidelberg, Germany: Springer Nature. doi:10.1007/978-3-319-53121-2_51-1

Blackstock, K. L., Kelly, G. J., & Horsey, B. L. (2007). Developing and applying a framework to evaluate participatory research for sustainability. *Ecological Economics, 60*(4), 726–742. doi:10.1016/j.ecolecon.2006.05.014

Boylan, M. (2016). Deepening system leadership: Teachers leading from below. *Educational Management Administration & Leadership, 44*(1), 57–72. doi:10.1177/1741143213501314

Bridges, C. M., & Wilhelm, W. B. (2008). Going beyond green: The "why and how" of integrating sustainability into the marketing curriculum. *Journal of Marketing Education, 30*(1), 33–46. doi:10.1177/0273475307312196

Butcher, J. (2007). Keep the green moral agenda off campus. *Times Higher Education.* Retrieved from www.timeshighereducation.com/news/keep-the-green-moral-agenda-off-campus/310853.article

Calder, W., & Clugston, R. M. (2003). International efforts to promote higher education for sustainable development. *Planning for Higher Education, 31*(3), 30–44. Retrieved from www.researchgate.net

Cezarino, L. (2016). Teachers' opinion about sustainability on management education. *Business Management Dynamics, 6*(1), 1–8. Retrieved from www.ebscohost.com

Cullen, J. G. (2016). Educating business students about sustainability: A bibliometric review of current trends and research needs. *Journal of Business Ethics, 145*(2), 429–439. doi:10.1007/s10551-015-2838-3

Dale, A., & Newman, L. (2005). Sustainable development, education and literacy. *International Journal of Sustainability in Higher Education, 6*(4), 351–362. doi:10.1108/14676370510623847

Dawe, G., Jucker, R., & Martin, S. (2005). Sustainable development in higher education: Current practice and future developments: A report to the higher education academy, York, UK. Retrieved from www.heacademy.ac.uk/assets/York/documents/ourwork/tla/sustainability/sustdevinHEfinalreport.pdf

Dieleman, H., & Huisingh, D. (2006). Games by which to learn and teach about sustainable development: Exploring the relevance of games and experiential learning for sustainability. *Journal of Cleaner Production, 14*(9), 837–847. doi:10.1016/j.jclepro.2005.11.031

Dlouha, J., Huisingh, D., & Barton, A. (2013). Learning networks in higher education: Universities in search of making effective regional impacts. *Journal of Cleaner Production, 49*, 5–10. doi:10.1016/j.jclepro.2013.01.034

Down, L., & McKeown, R. (2017). *What is sustainable development?* San Jose, Costa Rica: Earth Charter Institute.

Earth Charter Initiative. (2009). *Florida gulf coast university and the Earth charter.* San Jose, Costa Rica: Author. Retrieved from http://earthcharter.org/news-post/florida-gulf-coast-university-and-the-earth-charter/

Espejo, R. (1992). Management of complexity in problem solving. *Transactions of the Institute of Measurement and Control, 14*(1), 8–16. doi:10.1177/014233129201400103

Feng, L. (2012). Teacher and student responses to interdisciplinary aspects of sustainability education: What do we really know? *Environmental Education Research, 18*(1), 31–43. doi:10.1080/13504622.2011.574209

Ferreira, A. J. D., Lopes, M. A. R., & Morais, J. P. F. (2006). Environmental management and audit schemes implementation as an educational tool for sustainability. *Journal of Cleaner Production, 14*(9–11), 973–982. doi:10.1016/j.jclepro.2006.01.003

Fisher, R. M. (2003). Applying ISO 14001 as a business tool for campus sustainability: A case study from New Zealand. *International Journal of Sustainability in Higher Education, 4*(2), 138–150. doi:10.1108/14676370310467159

Franco, R. (2019, July 19). Personal interview.

Fullan, M. (2004). *Systems thinkers in action: Moving beyond the standards plateau.* London and Nottingham, England: DfES Innovation Unit and NCSL.

Fullan, M. (2005). *Leadership and sustainability: System thinkers in action.* London, England: Sage Publications.

Gombert-Courvoisier, S., Sennes, V., Ricard, M., & Ribeyre, F. (2014). Higher education for sustainable consumption: Case report on the Human Ecology Master's course (University of Bordeaux, France). *Journal of Cleaner Production, 62*, 82–88. doi:10.1016/j.jclepro.2013.05.032

Habron, G., Goralnik, L., & Thorp, L. (2012). Embracing the learning paradigm to foster systems thinking. *International Journal of Sustainability in Higher Education, 13*(4), 378–393. doi:10.1108/14676371211262326

Haney, A. B., Pope, J., & Arden, Z. (2018). Making it personal: Developing sustainability leaders in business. *Organization & Environment*. doi:10.1177/1086026618806201

Harwood, S. (2019). Systems thinking and sustainable development. In W. Leal Filho (Ed.), *Encyclopedia of sustainability in higher education*. Cham, Switzerland: Springer. doi:10.1007/978-3-319-63951-2_399-1

Hill, R. (2006). *Leadership that lasts: Sustainable school leadership in the 21st century*. London, England: Association of School and College Leaders.

Hoffman, A. J. (1999). Environmental education in business school. *Environment, 4*, 41. Retrieved from www.proquest.com

Hopkins, D., & Higham, R. (2007). System leadership: Mapping the landscape. *School Leadership and Management, 27*(2), 147–166. doi:10.1080/13632430701237289

Hull, R. B., Kimmel, C., Robertson, D. P., & Mortimer, M. (2016). International field experiences promote professional development for sustainability leaders. *International Journal of Sustainability in Higher Education, 17*(1), 86–104. doi:10.1108/IJSHE-07-2014-0105

Illeris, K. (2007). What do we actually mean by experiential learning? *Human Resource Development Review, 6*(1), 84–95. doi:10.1177/1534484306296828

International Association of Universities. (2009). *2009 G8 university summit Torino declaration on education and research for sustainable and responsible development (Turin Declaration)*. Paris, France: Author.

Isaacs, W. (1999). *Dialogue and the art of thinking together*. New York, NY: Currency.

Jabbour, C. J. C. (2010). Greening of business schools: A systemic view. *International Journal of Sustainability in Higher Education, 11*(1), 49–60. doi:10.1108/14676371011010048

Jucker, R. (2002). *Our common illiteracy: Education as if the Earth and people mattered* (Vol. 10). Frankfurt am Main, Germany: Peter Lang Pub Incorporated.

Kapi'olani Community College. (2019a). *Biosketch: Robert Franco, PhD*. Honolulu, HI: Author. Retrieved from http://ofie.kapiolani.hawaii.edu/biosketch-robert-franco-phd/

Kapi'olani Community College. (2019b). *Robert Franco*. Honolulu, HI: Author. Retrieved from www.kapiolani.hawaii.edu/directory/bfranco/

Koester, R. J., Eflin, J., & Vann, J. (2006). Greening of the campus: A whole-systems approach. *Journal of Cleaner Production, 14*(9–11), 769–779. doi:10.1016/j.jclepro.2005.11.055

Kolb, D. A. (1984). *Experiential learning: Experience as the source of learning and development*. Englewood Cliffs, NJ: Prentice-Hall.

Lozano, F., & Lozano, R. (2014). Developing the curriculum for a new bachelor's degree in engineering for sustainable development. *Journal of Cleaner Production, 4*, 136–146. doi:10.1016/j.jclepro.2013.08.022

Lozano, R. (2010). Diffusion of sustainable development in universities' curriculum: An empirical example from Cardiff University. *Journal of Cleaner Production, 18*, 637–644. doi:10.1016/j.jclepro.2009.07.005

Lozano, R., Ceulemans, K., Alonso-Almeida, M., Huisingh, D., Lozano, F. J., Waas, T., . . . Hugé, J. (2015). A review of commitment and implementation of sustainable development in higher education: Results from a worldwide survey. *Journal of Cleaner Production, 108*, 1–18. doi:10.1016/j.jclepro.2014.09.048

Lozano, R., Lozano, F. J., Mulder, K., Huisingh, D., & Waas, T. (2013). Advancing higher education for sustainable development: International insights and critical reflections. *Journal of Cleaner Production, 48*, 3–9. doi:10.1016/j.jclepro.2013.03.034

MacVaugh, J., & Norton, M. (2012). Introducing sustainability into business education contexts using active learning. *International Journal of Sustainability in Higher Education, 13*(1), 72–87. doi:10.1108/14676371211190326

Martin, S. (2002). Sustainability, systems thinking and professional practice. *Planet, 8*(1), 20–21. doi:10.11120/plan.2002.00080020

Martin, S. (2005). Sustainability, systems thinking and professional practice. *Systemic Practice and Action Research, 18*(2), 163–171. doi:10.1007/s11213-005-4156-7

Martin, S., & Hall, A. (2002). Sustainable development and the professions. *Planet, 8*(1), 17–18. doi:10.11120/plan.2002.00050017

Mezirow, J. (1997). Transformative learning: Theory to practice. *New Directions for Adult and Continuing Education, 74*, 5–12. doi:10.1002/ace.7401

Moore, J. (2005). Barriers and pathways to creating sustainability education programs: Policy, rhetoric and reality. *Environmental Education Research, 11*(5), 537–555. doi:10.1080/13504620500169692

Nolet, V. (2009). Preparing sustainability-literate teachers. *Teachers College Record, 111*(2), 409–442. Retrieved from www.gcafh.org/edlab/Nolet.pdf

Pappas, E., Pierrakos, O., & Nagel, R. (2013). Using Bloom's Taxonomy to teach sustainability in multiple contexts. *Journal of Cleaner Production, 48*, 54–56. doi:10.1016/j.jclepro.2012.09.039

Pintrich, P. R., Marx, R. W., & Boyle, R. A. (1993). Beyond cold conceptual change: The role of motivational beliefs and classroom contextual factors in the process of conceptual change. *Review of Educational Research, 63*(2), 167–199. doi:10.3102/00346543063002167

Posner, S. M., & Stuart, R. (2013). Understanding and advancing campus sustainability using a systems framework. *International Journal of Sustainability in Higher Education, 14*(3), 264–277. doi:10.1108/IJSHE-08-2011-0055

Potter, G. (2009). Environmental education for the 21st century: Where do we go now? *Journal of Environmental Education, 41*(1), 22–33. doi:10.1080/00958960903209975

Raivio, K. (2011). Sustainability as an educational agenda. *Journal of Cleaner Production, 19*(16), 1906–1907. doi:10.1016/j.jclepro.2011.07.009

Rowe, D. (2002). Environmental literacy and sustainability as core requirements: Success stories and models. In W. Leal Filho (Ed.), Reprinted from: *Teaching sustainability at universities*. New York, NY: Peter Lang.

Savage, E., Tapics, T., Evarts, J., Wilson, J., & Tirone, S. (2015). Experiential learning for sustainability leadership in higher education. *International Journal of Sustainability in Higher Education, 16*(5), 692–705. doi:10.1108/IJSHE-10-2013-0132

Scott, W., & Gough, S. (2003). *Key issues in sustainable development and learning: A critical review*. London, England: Routledge Falmer.

Shrivastava, P., Ivanaj, S., & Persson, S. (2013). Transdisciplinary study of sustainable enterprise. *Business Strategy & the Environment, 22*(4), 230–244. doi:10.1002/bse.1773

Sipos, Y., Battisti, B., & Grimm, K. (2008). Achieving transformative sustainability learning: Engaging head, hands and heart. *International Journal of Sustainability in Higher Education, 9*(1), 68–86. doi:10.1108/14676370810842193

Spangenberg, J. H. (2011). Sustainability science: A review, an analysis and some empirical lessons. *Environmental Conservation, 38*(3), 275–287. doi:10.1017/S0376892911000270

Starik, M., & Rands, G. P. (1995). Weaving an integrated web: Multilevel and multisystem perspectives of ecologically sustainable organizations. *Academy of Management Review, 20*(4), 908–935. doi:10.5465/amr.1995.9512280025

Sterling, S. (2001). *Sustainable education: Revisioning learning and change*. Cambridge, England: Green Books.

Sterling, S. (2011). Transformative learning and sustainability: Sketching the conceptual ground. *Learning and Teaching in Higher Education, 5*(11), 17–33. Retrieved from http://dl.icdst.org/pdfs/files/0cd7b8bdb08951af53e5927e86938977.pdf

Stubbs, W., & Cocklin, C. (2008). Teaching sustainability to business students: Shifting mindsets. *International Journal of Sustainability in Higher Education, 9*(3), 206–221. doi:10.1108/14676370810885844

Svanström, M., Lozano-García, F. J., & Rowe, D. (2008). Learning outcomes for sustainable development in higher education. *International Journal of Sustainability in Higher Education, 9*(3), 339–351. doi:10.1108/14676370810885925

Talwar, S., Wiek, A., & Robinson, J. (2011). User engagement in sustainability research. *Science and Public Policy, 38*(5), 379–390. doi:10.3152/030234211X12960315267615

Tosey, P., Visser, M., & Saunders, M. N. (2012). The origins and conceptualizations of "triple-loop" learning: A critical review. *Management Learning, 43*(3), 291–307. doi:10.1177/1350507611426239

United Nations Educational, Scientific and Cultural Organization (UNESCO). (2012). *Education for sustainable development sourcebook.* Paris, France: Author. Retrieved from https://sustainabledevelopment.un.org/content/documents/926unesco9.pdf

Van den Elzen, F. C. A. (2017). *Systems thinking in education for sustainable development* (Master's thesis). University of Utrecht, Utrecht, Netherlands. Retrieved from https://dspace.library.uu.nl/bitstream/handle/1874/349773/Systems%20thinking%20in%20ESD%20-%20MSc%20thesis.pdf?sequence=2

Velazquez, L., Munguia, N., Platt, A., & Taddei, J. (2006). Sustainable university: What can be the matter? *Journal of Cleaner Production, 14*(9–11), 810–819. doi:10.1016/j.jclepro.2005.12.008

Voisey, H., & O'Riordan, T. (1998). Sustainable development: The UK national approach. In T. O'Riordan & H. Voisey (Eds.), *Agenda 21: The transition to sustainability: The politics of Agenda 21 in Europe* (pp. 156–173). London, England: Earthscan.

Von Der Heidt, T., & Lamberton, G. (2011). Sustainability in the undergraduate and postgraduate business curriculum of a regional university: A critical perspective. *Journal of Management & Organization, 17*(5), 670. doi:10.1017/S1833367200001322

Wals, A. E., & Corcoran, P. B. (2006). 14: Sustainability as an outcome of transformative learning. In *Drivers and barriers for implementing sustainable development in higher education* (Vol. 103). Paris, France: UNESCO.

Warburton, K. (2003). Deep learning and education for sustainability. *International Journal of Sustainability in Higher Education, 4*(1), 44–56. doi:10.1108/14676370310455332

Watson, A. (2017). *Sustainability education in primary and secondary schools: Great needs and possible solutions.* University of Tennessee Honors Thesis Projects. Retrieved from https://trace.tennessee.edu/utk_chanhonoproj/2026

Watson, M. K., Lozano, R., Noyes, C., & Rodgers, M. (2013). Assessing curriculum contribution to sustainability more holistically: Experiences from the integration of curriculum assessment and students' perceptions at the Georgia Institute of Technology. *Journal of Cleaner Production, 61*, 106–116. doi:10.1016/j.jclepro.2013.09.010

Whiteman, G., Walker, B., & Perego, P. (2013). Planetary boundaries: Ecological foundations for corporate sustainability. *Journal of Management Studies, 50*(2), 307–336. doi:10.1111/j.1467-6486.2012.01073.x

Whitmer, A., Ogden, L., Lawton, J., Sturner, P., Groffman, P. M., Schneider, L., . . . Bettez, N. (2010). The engaged university: Providing a platform for research that transforms society. *Frontiers in Ecology and the Environment, 8*(6), 314–321. doi:10.1890/090241

Wiek, A., Farioli, F., Fukushi, K., & Yarime, M. (2012). Sustainability science: Bridging the gap between science and society. *Sustainability Science*, 7(1), 1–4. doi:10.1007/s11625-011-0154-0

Wiek, A., Withycombe, L., & Redman, C. L. (2011). Key competencies in sustainability: A reference framework for academic program development. *Sustainability Science, 6*(2), 203–218. doi:10.1007/s11625-011-0132-6

Williams, A., Kennedy, S., Philipp, F., & Whiteman, G. (2017). Systems thinking: A review of sustainability management research. *Journal of Cleaner Production, 148*, 866–881. doi:10.1016/j.jclepro.2017.02.002

World Commission on Environment and Development. (1987). *Our common future*. Oxford, England: Oxford University Press.

Wright, M. F., Cain, K. D., & Monsour, F. A. (2015). Beyond sustainability: A context for transformative curriculum development. *Transformative Dialogues: Teaching & Learning Journal, 8*(2), 1–19. Retrieved from www.op.ac.nz/assets/Sustainability/3f438a62e0/Transformative-Curriculum-Development.pdf

Zenchanka, S., & Malchenk, S. (2017). Three "Gs" for campus sustainability development. In W. Leal Filho, M. Mifsud, & P. Pace (Eds.), *Handbook of theory and practice of sustainable development in higher education*. Cham, Switzerland: Springer. doi:10.1007/978-3-319-47877-7_20

# 7 System leadership for sustainability in government and intergovernmental organizations

## Introduction

Although local citizens, organizations, and other governments serve significant roles in developing and promoting sustainability, government administrators are essential sustainability actors, especially with sustainability initiative implementation (Wang, Van Wart, & Lebredo, 2014). System leadership will be essential for leaders within these entities to influence stakeholders in making the changes necessary to alter humankind's present unsustainable trajectory. Government administrators serve several important roles relative to sustainability: they assist in designing the specific processes and supporting systems, which may be complicated and require extensive revision; they mitigate internal organizational resistance to change; and they support the community with dynamic methods of enhancing policy effectiveness (Borins, 2000).

In this chapter, we will explore the roles of government agencies and intergovernmental organizations (IGOs) in sustainable development and sustainability. Because system leadership is rooted in the understanding and application of systems thinking, we will examine the role of systems thinking and the methods of implementing systems thinking in governments and IGOs as a precursor to examining system leadership within these sectors. We will then examine the role and importance of system leadership for sustainability within these institutions and departments. The field of urban sustainability within the context of the public sector will also be discussed. Global perspectives of system leadership in governments and IGOs, and the barriers and challenges faced in promoting system leadership for sustainability in these organizations, will be examined. The chapter will conclude with a personal interview summary of a sustainability system leader from the IGO sector.

## Government

Governments exist at many levels, including municipal, county, state, regional, federal, and tribal, with each serving a specific group of constituents. Governments assume several roles in the sustainability movement: sustainability within government departments, facilities, and infrastructures; regulation for sustainability; funding and programs to assist communities, organizations, and businesses with sustainability initiatives; and public-private partnerships (PPPs). However, while government mandates alone will not achieve sustainability, public servants can demonstrate leadership by encouraging sustainability routines that produce incremental change, further influencing nongovernmental stakeholders to take actions beneficial to sustainability (Malmberg, 2019). Moreover, public servants are in a unique position to influence those behaviors by increasing the collective awareness (Malmberg, 2019).

Beginning in 2017, the US presidential administration has acted to reduce environmental regulations in the United States and announced the intent to withdraw from the Paris Climate Accord. However, in the absence of national leadership on sustainability issues, numerous local and state government agencies have assumed an increasing role in sustainability actions and initiatives. Since June 2017, more than 230 mayors representing more than 70 million Americans have said "We Are Still In", committing to the principles of the Paris Agreement (Bloomberg Philanthropies, 2019a). These administrators agreed to these commitments because their cities are currently experiencing the adverse effects of climate change; their citizens desire more resilient, sustainable communities and economies; and the mayors recognize that future health, employment, and opportunities require immediate actions (Bloomberg Philanthropies, 2019a).

Michael Bloomberg introduced the American Cities Initiative as an expansion of his support for US cities which, while facing major challenges, are taking action to implement solutions to achieve national climate action (Bloomberg Philanthropies, 2019b). The initiative consists of multiple investments to empower cities to produce innovation and develop forward-moving national policy. The initiative benefits include additional grants, coaching and technical support, and opportunities for city leaders to share knowledge and best practices (Bloomberg Philanthropies, 2019b). The primary objectives of the initiative are encouraging bold leadership and effective problem solving; supporting essential policy actions, and empowering artists, citizens, entrepreneurs, and other stakeholders to improve cities and solve urban problems (Bloomberg Philanthropies, 2019b). The role of cities in sustainability and the need for system leaders at the municipal level will be further discussed in the "Urban sustainability" section of this chapter.

The transition from a national focus to numerous local, regional, and state sustainability efforts will require system leaders who can influence and collaborate across political and territorial boundaries. While government leaders may desire cooperation and collaboration, their primary function is to serve the constituents within their respective communities. Any activity outside their jurisdiction would require at least implied consent from constituents and governing bodies. Moreover, these leaders will be required to collaborate with citizens and businesses, negotiating with multiple, often diverse interests and requirements. The effort required to influence across political and jurisdictional boundaries requires a systems-based leadership model.

## Intergovernmental organizations

IGOs are institutions consisting of the governments of representative member states (Leverty, 2019) and are commonly organized according to their membership and purpose (Harvard Law School, 2019). They frequently have a formal, permanent structure with multiple departments or committees to achieve organizational objectives (Leverty, 2019). The three most common types of IGOs are regional, specialized, and general. Regional IGOs limit membership to states within a specific geographic area, and specialized IGOs are selective organizations that limit membership based on specific criteria, such as field or industry. General IGOs have may broad membership with expertise in multiple fields (Harvard Law School, 2019).

The United Nations (UN) is a global IGO, because all nations are permitted membership, and the largest IGO, with 193 of the current 195 nations belonging to it. The UN Charter is the treaty that established the UN in 1945, listing the main functions "as maintaining international peace and security, developing relations among nations, working to solve international issues, promoting human rights, and being a central place for harmonizing the actions of nations" (United Nations, 2018). The UN headquarters is in New York City, with additional offices located in Geneva, Switzerland; Nairobi, Kenya; and Vienna, Austria. The UN is subject to extraterritoriality, meaning the organization is exempt from local legal jurisdiction, and is regulated by diplomatic law (Leverty, 2019). Funding for the organization is provided by assessed and voluntary payments from member states.

IGOs differ from nongovernmental organizations in that NGOs are formed by individuals or groups instead of nations. NGOs normally function independent of governments, typically have nonprofit status, and receive at least a portion of their funding from private sources. In contrast, IGOs have the financial and political support of member states (Harvard Law School, 2019). Major regional IGOs include the Association of Southeast Asian Nations (ASEAN), the North American Treaty Organization (NATO), the African Union (AU), the European Union (EU), and the Organization of American States (OAS; Harvard Law School). Major specialized IGOs include the International Atomic Energy Agency (IAEA), the International Criminal Police Organization (INTERPOL), and the Organization of Petroleum Exporting Countries (OPEC).

The UN has demonstrated considerable leadership in sustainability by establishing and promoting the UN Sustainable Development Goals (SDGs), and Agenda 2030 (Leverty, 2019). According to the UN:

> the Division for Sustainable Development Goals (DSDG) in the United Nations Department of Economic and Social Affairs (UNDESA) provides substantive support and capacity-building for the SDGs and their related thematic issues, including water, energy, climate, oceans, urbanization, transport, science and technology, the Global Sustainable Development Report (GSDR), partnerships and Small Island Developing States.
>
> (United Nations, n.d.)

UN Agencies and committees involved in sustainability include the United Nations Environment Programme (UNEP), the Committee on Food Security and Sustainable Development, and UNESCO. Other IGOs involved in sustainability and sustainable development include the Intergovernmental Panel on Climate Change (IPCC), the Organization for Economic Cooperation and Development (OECD), the Organization of American States (OAS), and the World Bank (Penn State University Libraries, n.d.).

## Role of systems thinking in government and IGO activities

Because many of the problems and challenges faced by government and IGO leaders are systems based and interrelated, responses will likely cross functional, geographic, and political boundaries. Systems thinking is a necessary and useful skill for addressing interrelated economic, environmental, and social issues, which encompass much of the work of governments and IGOs. However, systems thinking is often not applied in political and government applications. As Ackoff and Gharajedaghi (1996) noted, "[i]n the political arena finding what is normally thought of as a solution to a problem, and getting it accepted and implemented, are usually treated separately rather than as necessary aspects of the problem" (p. 33).

Sanneh (2018) proposed using systems thinking theory as a solution-based approach to address the following areas: renewable and sustainable energy; access to safe drinking water; access to basic health care in communities; climate change adaptation; sustainable development; introduction of a recycling system for sustainable municipal solid waste management; shipment of used information and communications technology (ICT) products to developing countries; and underground tank storage systems (USTs), environmental management, and petroleum pollution control. Although the international community, organizations, and governments have sustainable policies and procedures, individual, compartmentalized approaches will not be as effective as a holistic approach. Promoting systemic collaboration among the diverse governmental and intergovernmental initiatives can significantly enhance sustainable development and mitigate poverty (Sanneh, 2018).

While systems thinking is appropriate for circumstances in which the quantitative dimension is dominant, this approach is often inadequate for complex, people-oriented government policy situations (Kalim, Carson, & Cramp, 2006). In addressing these "softer" social system activities, Kalim and colleagues proposed the use of soft systems management (SSM). Checkland (1981) and subsequent colleagues (Checkland & Scholes, 1990; Wilson, 2001) developed SSM as a sense-making approach for addressing wide-ranging situations in both the public and private sectors. SSM encourages exploration of how individuals create meaning of their world and act intentionally as a result of that achieved meaning. One advantage of SSM is that the objective is to achieve consensus among system participants possessing divergent perspectives. Such an approach is essential for politically charged government policy-making activity.

## Methods of implementing systems thinking in government

One proven method of implementing systems thinking in local government is the Vanguard® method, developed by John Seddon (1992), influenced by the works of Deming (1982), Ohno (1988), and Ackoff (1978), and applied in the public sector (Summers, 2011). The Vanguard® method has become so commonly used in United Kingdom local governments that systems thinking has become synonymous with Vanguard® in that sector (Summers, 2011). This method combines systems theory and intervention theory to transition organizations from command and control to systems thinking logic (Middleton, 2010). The method employs a three-step *check-plan-do* process (Middleton, 2010; Zokaei et al., 2010), based on the Shewart plan-do-study-act cycle and the six-phase interventionist model of Argyris and Schön (1978).

A study of local government use of the Vanguard® method in the UK revealed several findings (Summers, 2011). In the organizations studied, limited evidence existed to support improvement claims, with sporadic baseline measurement, and some reporting inaccurate data. Moreover, the method did not appear to have become organizationally embedded, implying a perception that the new method would become embedded simply by changing the thinking of a few organizational members (Summers, 2011). Although program staff gained substantial process knowledge, resulting in improved service delivery, the participating staff frequently demonstrated exclusivity, being dismissive of coworkers who did not understand the method, with some participants rejecting further training after mastering the Vanguard® method. One source of tension among staff was with use of terms such as *waste* and *failure demand*, which were interpreted as negative by staff who were informed that their work was wasteful (Summers, 2011). In the examined cases, the Vanguard® method was applied to single processes that were observed separate from other systems within the broader system, promoting thinking within narrow boundaries and from a solitary perspective. While this singular, limited perspective enables designers to manage demand and guarantee that the system operates within scope (Summers, 2011), the best method for viewing a process is from multiple perspectives prior to treatment method selection (Ackoff, 1994). Moreover, a narrow, singular perspective may produce undesirable consequences and seems contradictory to systemic thinking (Summers, 2011).

While the previous research findings identified potential issues with application of the Vanguard® method, the system has demonstrated success. Application of the Vanguard® method has made significant improvements in social care, food safety planning, refuse collection, and trading standards with no additional taxpayer cost (Vanguard Consulting Limited, 2014). Specific results in the public sector included a 6.5% reduction in resources while handling 33% additional work in public housing, cost reduction of 35% in disabled facility grants, and an 84% reduction in processing time for housing benefits claim (Vanguard Consulting Limited, 2014). The strengths of the Vanguard® method are recognition and design for customer demand, added customer value, systemic application within specific boundaries, fewer unexpected consequences, participants' introduction to systems thinking, and process simplification (Summers, 2011). Weaknesses include possible limited threshold, ignoring alternative stakeholder perspectives, boundary limitations, program sustainability concerns, supporters possibly becoming opinionated, and impeded measurements (Summers, 2011).

## Role of system leadership in government and IGO activities

Governments and IGOs perform varying functions and roles in sustainability, depending upon political, geographic, social, and economic factors. As sustainability issues and challenges become more pressing, governments and IGOs will require leaders capable of influencing across governmental and sector boundaries. Because system leadership is rooted in systems thinking, this model is appropriate for leaders seeking to influence sustainability efforts among governments and IGOs. More specifically, soft systems thinking, described in an earlier section, will be an essential tool for government and IGO system leaders.

Sanneh (2018) proposed several areas in which system-level actions may achieve sustainability in developing nations. First, energy should be transitioned from centralized, urban-focused, fossil-fuel based systems to decentralized renewable energy grids that would benefit remote and rural areas as well. For example, only 8% of the rural population and 51% of the urban population in sub-Saharan Africa have access to electricity. Second, most cities in developing nations lack adequate environmental sanitation, with the lack of proper collection and management of solid waste increasing the prevalence of local diseases. Moreover, because waste is not recycled, recovered, or reused, natural resource depletion is rapidly increasing (Sanneh, 2018). This is exacerbated by the e-waste management policies of many African countries, in which used ICT products are accepted from developed nations for disposal in landfills, posing significant environmental impacts (Sanneh, 2018), such as toxic chemical leakage into drinking water supplies. Finally, access to potable drinking water is decreasing, especially with the increasingly unpredictable occurrence of droughts and floods resulting from climate change. Increased access to safe drinking water improves rates of child mortality and disease, resulting in poverty reduction and sustainable development (Sanneh, 2018).

These systems-based issues require leadership capable of crossing geographic, governmental, and sector boundaries. The dissemination of renewable energy and the establishment of waste management, water, and sanitation infrastructures across developing nations will require financial capital, legal frameworks, and human resources (Sanneh, 2018). Securing the necessary financial resources will likely require influencing financial institutions and developed nations. Reversing unsustainable policies will require influencing government officials, corporations that negotiate these agreements, and consumers who purchase the products that end up in the landfills of developing nations.

Several types of hybrid organizations influence and interact with government and IGO leaders, the most common being public-private partnerships and parastatal organizations. A PPP is a cooperative association between public, private, and/or nonprofit organizations to achieve common, cooperative decision-making procedures for addressing a public policy issue (Steets, 2010). Government agencies and nongovernmental organizations frequently partner with businesses to engage in projects that could not be completed autonomously because of financial, expertise, or resource limitations. Governments benefit from the financial and knowledge resources controlled by business, while businesses benefit from the fees typically collected for operation and management of the completed project. While most PPPs address infrastructure policy issues such as transportation, energy, health, and education, PPPs could be deployed to address sustainability issues such as renewable energy, water treatment, and climate change resiliency measures.

A parastatal is a business enterprise substantially controlled by a government through total, majority, or significant minority ownership (OECD, 2014). While some parastatals operate independently of governments, these organizations directly or indirectly serve the interests of corresponding government. Common sectors in which parastatals exist include agriculture, education, healthcare, broadcasting and communication, and infrastructure. Parastatals are more common in developing nations, especially in Africa.

The hybrid nature of these organizations supports the need for system leadership in achieving objectives through influencing diverse stakeholders across the sectors and systems represented by these organizations. PPPs and parastatals exist across public and private sector boundaries, necessitating boundaryless collaboration, a demonstrated system leadership ability. Moreover, these organizations often function within broad systems, necessitating the systems thinking perspective required of system leaders. Managed and influenced by system leaders, PPPs and parastatals provide opportunities for governments and IGOs to collaborate with the private sector in achieving sustainability.

Many government agencies and IGOs are engaged in collaborative, cooperative efforts to ensure resilience in response to current and future climate change effects. Resilience describes the extent of change a system can handle while maintaining the same purpose, structure, and feedbacks (Walker & Salt, 2006). The East Central Florida Regional Planning Council is an eight-county area-wide association of governments located in the metropolitan Orlando, Florida, area (East Central Florida Regional Planning Council, n.d.). The Regional Resiliency Action Plan is a collaborative effort of the East Central Florida Regional Planning Council and public and private stakeholders to improve resiliency and teamwork among the local and regional governments (Florida's Coastal Resiliency Portal, n.d.). Similar collaborative efforts exist across the United States, as local and regional governments respond to the lack of political support at the national level at the time of this publication.

## Urban sustainability

In most American cities, buildings and transportation are the two largest consumers of energy and producers of carbon pollution, collectively accounting for

80% of urban emissions (Bloomberg Philanthropies, 2019a). While critics insist that cities are inherently unsustainable, advocates suggest a need for additional efforts to make cities sustainable (Davidson & Venning, 2011). Urban sustainability is essential for the future of humanity, because the UN has projected that 68% of the global population will live in urban areas by 2050, with Asia and Africa experiencing 90% of this increase (Department of Economic and Social Affairs, 2018). Cities will serve a crucial role in accelerating economic growth relating to the sustainable cities debate. The World Commission on Environment and Development (WCED) report stated that human settlements are essential for achieving sustainable development, because cities are at the center of accelerated economic growth (Ooi, 2005). However, the existing model of urban development is characterized by a series of highly specialized stakeholders, whose short-term involvement is designed to maximize profit (World of Walas, 2019a). This model does not benefit the communities and has resulted in excessive property development, inflated prices, and low occupancy rates, with the construction of buildings having become a self-perpetuating goal (World of Walas, 2019a).

Although poverty has predominantly been a rural occurrence, urban poverty is rapidly rising (Sanneh, 2018). This is especially true in developing nations where women are particularly disadvantaged, although regional wealth disparities are also evident. Income inequality in developing nations is high, suggesting that the benefits of global economic growth are unevenly distributed, instead disproportionately benefiting a small population segment (Sanneh, 2018). Poverty is a sustainability concern, because individuals living in poverty are more likely to engage in unsustainable behavior to survive. Significant poverty mitigation will require system leaders capable of collaboration and influence across boundaries.

Responding to the urban sustainability challenges resulting from growing population and expected climate change effects is becoming progressively more complicated, requiring more robust decision-making processes to enhance governance for sustainable outcomes (Davidson & Venning, 2011). Under conditions of increased resource demand and increased risk and uncertainty, decision-making processes containing a systems approach contribute to better informed sustainability decisions. When cities are perceived as complex adaptive systems, they can experience urban shifts towards sustainability, guided by entrepreneurial change agents (Block & Paredis, 2013; Uyarra & Gee, 2013). Although systems thinking has been demonstrated to support a framework to operationalize sustainability, systems features are seldom integrated into urban sustainability decision-making frameworks (Davidson & Venning, 2011). While multiple tools are available to support urban sustainability decision-making, many initiatives only integrate one or two essential systems elements (Davidson & Venning, 2011). Moreover, while the application of systems thinking improves understanding of the interrelationship of system components, a framework that does not fully acknowledge component connections will have limited capacity to guide effective urban sustainability decision-making (Davidson & Venning, 2011).

Several elements are necessary for US cities to demonstrate leadership in carbon pollution reduction: local innovation, wide-ranging efforts to increase public support for sustainability, and a determined focus from mayors and stakeholders for achieving results (Bloomberg Philanthropies, 2019a). To support this crucial cause, Bloomberg Philanthropies and partners initiated a $70 million investment in the American Cities Climate Challenge (Bloomberg Philanthropies, 2019a). The American Cities Climate Challenge is part of the American Cities Initiative (mentioned earlier in the chapter), offering 25 enthusiastic cities the ability to significantly enhance their activities for climate change mitigation and promote a sustainable future for their inhabitants (Bloomberg Philanthropies, 2019a). The winning cities were accepted into a two-year program in which they were provided with resources and support to assist with meeting or exceeding short-term carbon mitigation goals. The resources and support included a dedicated individual to expedite development and enactment of high-impact policies; data, design, and innovation resources to assist with program delivery; leadership development programs for key staff to maximize team performance; implementation coaching for outcome achievement; assistance with citizen engagement to expand community acceptance; polling and communications support; robust peer-to-peer learning and networking to encourage participating leaders to learn from and support each another; and rapid response grants to expedite results (Bloomberg Philanthropies, 2019a).

The participating cities commit to making the Paris Agreement goals real, focusing on high impact, creating community, serving as role models for the country by leading movements, and delivering results. Participating cities focus efforts on the two sectors with the highest emissions levels in US cities: buildings and transportation. Mayors and staff work with dedicated experts to implement plans, involve city departments, routinely review progress metrics, and continuously improve and innovate until goals are achieved (Bloomberg Philanthropies, 2019a).

Achieving urban sustainability will require system leaders capable of influencing stakeholders across multiple sectors. Business and real estate developers are significant stakeholders critical to the success of urban sustainability initiatives. World of Wal̲a̲s is an urban development company that was examined in Chapter 5. Led by Gerben van Straaten, World of Wal̲a̲s recognizes that urban development extends beyond real estate and land development and also considers the collective activities, desires, and interests of citizens and cities for a meaningful system. World of Wal̲a̲s provides effective, sustainable programs in cooperation with inhabitants and users of cities, resulting in the development of economic, social, cultural, sustainable, and ecological values (World of Wal̲a̲s, 2019a). Wal̲a̲s projects include Carbon6 in Heerlen, The Netherlands, and Dudoc Vancouver in Canada, the latter having become a center of excellence for urban design, sustainability, and innovation, influencing projects in Asia and Europe (World of Wal̲a̲s, 2019b).

Eco-industrial parks were described in Chapter 5 as industrial developments in which businesses collaborate with each other and the local community to increase economic growth and improve environmental quality (Hein, Jankovic, Farel, & Yannou, 2015). The benefits of eco-industrial parks are waste and pollution reduction; efficient utilization of information, energy, infrastructure, and resources; and attainment of sustainable development (Hein et al., 2015). Eco-industrial parks may also serve a broader purpose as tools for executing sustainable policies within a region (Cerceau et al., 2014). Establishing public urban zones for entrepreneurial activity offers a low-risk nexus for development of social and environmental innovations (Radywyl & Biggs, 2013). Cities can achieve sustainability by encouraging the development of these centralized urban entrepreneurial zones, with both local and global citizens benefiting from the resulting innovation and efficiency.

Network governance is one collaborative tool that can be used by system leaders to achieve urban sustainability. Network governance may enhance decision-making in urban transitions toward sustainability (Khan, 2013). Network governance describes an interorganizational structure characterized by an informal social system, rather than a traditional, formal bureaucratic structure (Jones, Hesterly, & Borgatti, 1997). Network governance consists of autonomous organizations voluntarily cooperating in the development and delivery of products and services, bound by social and not legal agreements. Three characteristics differentiate governance networks from hierarchical governmental control and competitive market regulation (Sørensen & Torfing, 2005). First, governance networks are characterized as multi-centered systems rather than unicentric systems (Van Kersbergen & Van Waarden, 2004), with multiple interdependent entities interacting to achieve an outcome (Sørensen & Torfing, 2005). Second, decision-making in governance networks is based on negotiation rationality instead of the substantial rationality of government rule and the procedural rationality of market-based competition (Scharpf, 1997). Finally, agreement is achieved through trust and political accountability, which is reinforced by self-established rules and norms (Nielsen & Pedersen, 1998).

## Local government system leader spotlight

Chris Castro was appointed the Director of Sustainability for the City of Orlando, Florida, in 2016 (O'Connor, 2016). Castro was born in Miami, Florida, and acquired his interest in sustainability and the environment while living on a palm tree farm operated by his parents (Daigneau, 2018). Prior to his role with the City of Orlando, Castro was engaged in the sustainability movement for over 10 years (O'Connor, 2016), having established a UN-accredited environmental nonprofit and co-created an urban agriculture program that has been replicated both nationally and globally (Daigneau, 2018). Fleet Farming is a hyperlocal agricultural initiative in which homeowners convert front yards into miniature farms, subsequently receiving 5%–10% of the harvest, with the remainder sold to local restaurants and farmers markets. Fleet Farming addresses the sustainability challenge of agriculture, which contributes one-third of global carbon emissions. Fleet Farming was a logical solution, because residential lawns are a major source of pollution in the United States, with 40 million acres of grass yards absorbing 3 million tons of chemical fertilizers and 30,000 tons of pesticides annually, and requiring 800 million gallons of gasoline annually for lawn mowing (Daigneau, 2018).

In addition to serving as Director of Sustainability and Resilience, Castro is Co-chair of the Smart Cities initiative for Orlando Mayor Buddy Dyer and the City of Orlando, where he works to transition Orlando toward a smart, resilient, and sustainable future (Barbone, 2018). Castro starred in the National Geographic movie *Paris to Pittsburgh* (Boedeker, 2018), named for US President Trump's comment when announcing the US withdrawal from the Paris Climate Accord, that he was elected to serve the citizens of Pittsburgh, not Paris (Woodall, 2017). He has also served as keynote speaker for a UN conference in Rio de Janeiro and has been labeled the "Guru of Green" by the *Orlando Business Journal* (Daigneau, 2018). Castro clearly demonstrates system leadership by influencing sustainability initiatives within and beyond his community, as well as nationally and globally.

## Global perspectives of system leadership in government and IGOs

Sustainability is a global issue with the impacts of unsustainable activity not respectful of geographic or political boundaries. Addressing sustainability issues will require government influence and involvement across multiple boundaries. Action to prevent environmental degradation or improve access to water, food, education, and healthcare in one nation or region will reduce the impact of economic and climate refugees in other regions. System leaders who can understand these systemic relationships and impacts are needed in governments and IGOs.

While sustainability action must be dramatically increased, efforts to adapt to climate change are essential for the survival of the billions of inhabitants of areas that are or will soon be threatened by climate change and corresponding sea-level rise. The increasing incidence of heat waves, floods, drought, and crop failure supports the necessity for climate change adaptation (Sanneh, 2018). Climate change obligates developing nations to adapt to increasingly severe and unpredictable weather. Comprehensive development that acknowledges the integral role of the environment, human development, and economic development is essential for climate change adaptation (Sanneh, 2018). National-level resiliency planning by developed and developing nations provides a foundational model for sustainability. Urban and regional resilience plans and initiatives, such as those described earlier in this section, must be scaled and replicated globally.

In responding to global sustainability issues, a multi-stakeholder approach is reasonable, appropriate, and scalable (Sanneh, 2018). Because no single actor possesses the resources necessary to solve our current unsustainable conditions, collaboration is necessary across organizational, sector, and geopolitical boundaries. System leadership is essential if multiple stakeholders are to collaborate across these diverse and often competing boundaries. System leaders must influence collaborative efforts that transcend the allocation of blame and shame for past actions, through development of a shared vision for local and global sustainability and genuine prosperity.

## Barriers and challenges

Several barriers and challenges exist, in both government and IGO activities, that impact the success of system leadership in achieving sustainability within these institutions and departments. These barriers originate in the mistrust by segments of society in governmental and intergovernmental institutions. While some of this mistrust may be based on legitimate concerns and experiences, a considerable portion of mistrust is based on misunderstanding or misinterpreting the roles, intentions, and actions of these institutions.

Businesses leaders and individuals are often skeptical of government initiatives and resist regulation. While business leaders in many developed nations are more comfortable with government collaboration and involvement, US business leaders often resist any attempt by government to influence or regulate business activity. Moreover, business leaders in nations with a history of political corruption may resist government involvement and possibly fear retribution for non-acceptance of government influence. According to the Edelman Trust Barometer, in 2017, governments were mistrusted by investors in 75% of nations (Edelman, 2017), and in 2019, 58% of the informed public (of which business leaders would likely belong) mistrusted government (Edelman, 2019).

IGOs are often mistrusted by political leaders and constituents who perceive their actions as a threat to their sovereignty. Individuals or groups with protectionist or nationalist inclinations typically reject or mistrust any form of globalism or global governance, which puts pressure on efforts of IGOs such as the UN. Specific to the sustainability movement, the Brundtland definition (World Commission on Environment and Development, 1987) is described by critics as affiliated with a neoliberal worldview (Clapp & Dauvergne, 2005). Recent protectionist and nationalist movements gained strength in the United Kingdom with the Brexit movement and in the United States after the 2016 presidential election. An example of nationalist mistrust of the UN played out in 2017, when US President Trump announced that the US would withdraw from the Paris Climate Accord, citing that the agreement "disadvantages the United States to the exclusive benefit of other countries" (Roberts, 2018). This action is consistent with the promises of his campaign in which he championed American dominance and the unwillingness to be influenced by foreign governments (Roberts, 2018).

Political partisanship in many nations has divided politicians and constituents in their perspectives on sustainability issues such as climate change and environmental regulation. Moreover, partisanship inhibits the likelihood of opposing political characters cooperating on policy matters. Because sustainability has multiple meanings based upon ideological perspective, standards must be clearly established to operationalize the concept and encourage enlightened debate among proponents with dissimilar perspectives (Davidson & Venning, 2011). These ideological barriers must be overcome if governments and IGOs are to perform their essential roles in ensuring a sustainable future for humanity.

Sustainability partnerships and alliances between industry and governments or IGOs are necessary and will require system leadership to bridge the gaps between the sectors. While industry has been moving toward a more collaborative approach, efforts have been limited to partnerships with individual NGOs or pre-competitive industry or sector alliances (Weinreb, 2015). However, the practice of industry-government partnerships is more common in some nations. PPPs provide an opportunity for multiple stakeholders to collaborate on sustainability initiatives. Leading across these organizational, industry, and sector boundaries will require system leadership.

PPPs were previously identified as a method of addressing sustainability issues such as renewable energy, water treatment, and climate change resiliency measures. However, implementing and managing PPPs can be challenging due to the differing objectives of stakeholders. PPP research in Jordan identified the following challenges in managing PPPs:

- Internal management difficulties.
- Human resource management difficulties.
- Lack of knowledge and experience in managing PPPs.
- External management difficulties.
- Changing circumstances.
- External pressures.
- Coordination and communication.

(Mistarihi, Hutchings, & Shacklock, 2013, p. 378)

Research findings on construction PPPs in the United Kingdom identified 18 critical success factors, with the three most important factors being "'a strong and good private consortium', 'appropriate risk allocation' and 'available financial market'" (Li, Akintoye, Edwards, & Hardcastle, 2005, p. 459). The critical success factors were clustered into five groups, identified as effective procurement, project implementability, government guarantee, favorable economic conditions, and available financial market.

Senior (2002) suggested that organizational behavior cannot be changed unless it is reinforced by changes in organizational policies and procedures, and training and development programs, that reorient the organization to the new vision and the changes necessary for vision attainment. In the previously discussed Vanguard method studies, there was limited evidence of the change being embedded in the organization or system, which is necessary for change to be sustainable. Moreover, while frequent references were made to changing how people think, there was no discussion about how to make this change permanent (Summers, 2011). System leaders in governments and IGOs will face challenges when changing how stakeholders think, and subsequently with embedding necessary change within their organizations.

## Personal interview summary

Florencia Librizzi served in management roles at the Principles for Responsible Management Education (PRME) initiative of the UN Global Compact from 2013 to 2019 (Librizzi, n.d.). In this role, she was instrumental in developing PRME into the largest organized relationship between the UN and business schools, including over 730 signatories in more than 90 countries, along with co-creating regional chapters, working groups, and numerous projects and activities focused on the sustainable development goals.

Prior to joining PRME, Librizzi worked as a research consultant for the International Center for Transitional Justice (ICTJ) focusing on "human rights issues, working in the intersection of truth and memory, justice, reparations as well as gender, children and indigenous peoples issues, when addressing post-conflict societies" (Librizzi, n.d.). She practiced law from 2006 to 2011, advising business and non-business clients on a broad range of sustainability and legal issues. She has taught courses and conducted seminars at Universidad Empresarial Siglo 21, Universidad Nacional de Córdoba (UNC), NYU School of Law, and the Columbia Institute for Study of Human Rights, and she is a member and active contributor at the UNC Institute for Environmental Law and Policy.

Librizzi earned her first law degree *magna cum laude* from Universidad Nacional de Córdoba, School of Law in Argentina, and earned her Master of Laws (LLM) at NYU School of Law, where she was awarded the Dean's Award and was distinguished as a Transitional Justice Scholar. She has served as a graduate editor for the *NYU Journal of International Law and Politics* and has published several articles, book chapters, and expert reports for NGOs and the UN. Her academic efforts focus on the regulatory elements of sustainability. In addition to her academic activities, Florencia facilitates workshops and speaks about sustainability and responsible management education and leadership to diverse audiences globally (Librizzi, n.d.). Immediately prior to this interview, she joined the SDG Academy at the UN Sustainable Development Solutions Network (SDSN) in New York City as Head of Program and Partnerships.

Librizzi provided additional insight into her understanding and application of system leadership in an interview with this author on July 15, 2019. Overall, her comments supported the interdisciplinary, holistic, collaborative, and systems thinking aspects of system leadership. Prior to our interview, she had not heard of the term system leadership. However, she was familiar with systems thinking and the importance of being a system thinker. She commented that the description provided of system leadership by this author seemed natural, or intuitive. Her success as a sustainability system leader is based on her background of having come from a business family, with a practical business mentality, and her legal education and career, in which she was interested in human rights issues and wanted to improve the world. She desired a more holistic career than her "siloed" career in law, one that encouraged a more expansive, holistic mindset. She explained that too many people are siloed, thinking that everything is "either this or that", which she feels is not a strength but a weakness. She had admired the UN since she was young and desired a career in which she could build a community working on the sustainable development goals. She also noted the importance of personally living sustainably and being aware of your positive and negative impacts (F. Librizzi, personal communication, July 15, 2019).

The skills she identified as beneficial to system leadership included interpersonal and communication skills, collaboration, inclusiveness, being holistic or comprehensive, systems thinking, and seeing the big picture. She noted the importance of recognizing that we all have different mindsets and different roles and of being able to complement and work together by bringing out each other's talents and strengths. You might be an expert in one area, but if you want your idea or concept to have traction, you must be able to articulate it in a way that everyone will understand, support, and help you refine to address the many different angles of the issue. System leaders need to be able to talk to other people, observe, and listen, because "we do not have all answers". She advised, "Don't take yourself too seriously. If you don't know something ask someone, no one has all the answers". She strongly believes in collaboration and co-creation. She added the importance of becoming more receptive and in tune with intuition, alongside employing our analytical mindset, since it helps to have a more accurate reading of reality and more effective interventions with other human beings (F. Librizzi, personal communication, July 15, 2019).

Librizzi cited the importance of collaboratively bringing people together, being clear about objectives and roles, and building trust. Clarity of expectations is essential and requires that everyone make sure they are on same page. When managing others, she believes in creating expectations, but also allowing flexibility, so she believe that using frameworks that provide clarity and alignment while allowing ownership and creativity are essential to instill purpose and drive collective action. Regarding inclusiveness, she noted that the term involves people, concepts, and ideas, especially with sustainability in which so many concepts and ideas are created. She believes in enabling other parties by providing them with a clear vision but allowing enough freedom so they bring their own creativity, leadership skills, and expertise to the process. This freedom helps empower people. She also emphasized the importance of allowing individuals to take ownership of their work. She noted the importance of recognizing how things are connected (things, people, concepts), because most things repeat themselves and have a pattern. Systems thinking requires not only seeing the big picture, but also moving back and forth within that picture. If you want to introduce a variable in a system, everything in that system will experience change, including other variables and the environment. Systems thinking requires that leaders look at all of the system variables and how they will be affected. Everyone has a different understanding of reality, as they might observe it from a different angle, perspective, or mindset; therefore, we need to learn to "translate" our messages to be able to advance together important causes (F. Librizzi, personal communication, July 15, 2019).

Librizzi identified several barriers and challenges to exercising system leadership within an IGO. Systems are complex by nature and often have too many moving parts, requiring that action be accomplished by talking and influencing other leaders and drivers that can help to mobilize a critical mass. One challenge was with trying to find a common collaborative strategy without being in a position of formal authority over members. The lack of formal authority often limits the ability to formally assign financial or human resources. Another challenge is that participants often are too constrained by their supervisors, objectives, and performance criteria. Participants must satisfy their separate (and often narrow) organizational goals and objectives while simultaneously trying to collaborate on projects outside their organizations. The UN Sustainable Development Goals require stakeholders to contribute to larger system changes, and as such, they require efforts that might go beyond our own institutions' key performance indicators or our own professional goals. Frequently, individuals also feel compelled to compete and think that collaboration might work against their personal, professional, or institutional objectives (F. Librizzi, personal communication, July 15, 2019).

She has often reminded people that organizations, just like human beings, have different DNA, and there is plenty of space for everyone to fulfill our mission and contribute to our societies. "It is important to look beyond ourselves and think what might be the goals that we can achieve together, that we wouldn't be able to accomplish separately." Ultimately, she notes, "achieving the SDGs would require extensive collaboration and multi-stakeholder partnerships articulated in a more inclusive and transparent fashion never seen before, to ensure that everyone in the planet can enjoy a more sustainable and just world". Another challenge cited was that collaborative IGO efforts require a lot of energy, resources, and a genuine concern for people's well-being. Individual barriers and challenges might include a variety of reasons from lack of knowledge and other resources, restrictive thinking, lack of political will or ambition, self-interested mindsets, lack of ethics, or a lack of trust (F. Librizzi, personal communication, July 15, 2019).

Librizzi suggested system leadership could be developed through education and mentoring. Once someone learns how to be a leader, that person should feel inclined to enable and influence others to lead. This comment echoes the servant-leadership model of Greenleaf (1977), who suggested that the ultimate measure of servant leadership was whether followers grow as individuals and eventually become servant leaders. She commented that mentors helped in her career, and she desires for her mentees to fully develop their talents to become leaders who deliver positive impact for our societies. Moreover, she stated that while becoming specialists in our own discipline is still key, it is important to be able to think like a generalist and keep a good understanding of the "big picture". She noted the importance of a broad, interdisciplinary background, noting that her having studied music, dance, and other topics outside of her discipline helped her understand patterns and complex realities in a simpler way. Librizzi noted several times during the interview that it was important to use both the left and right sides of the brain. Often when you begin a project, there is a tendency to become practical and rigorous (left brain). She advised that it was important to begin with creativity (right brain), and then balance later with left-brain thought. It is also important to be expansive and receptive yet precise and rigorous; they are not exclusive from each other. She concluded that "addressing the complex issues of sustainability and achieving the SDGs can only be done through inclusive collaboration and partnership that engage relevant stakeholders to work together in a holistic and interdisciplinary fashion" (F. Librizzi, personal communication, July 15, 2019).

## Chapter reflection questions

1 How can system leaders influence across business and government in nations in which business and government view each other antagonistically?
2 Nationalist and populist movements have been increasing in the United States and Europe. How can system leaders influence individuals and groups in those nations to collaborate? How can system leaders in IGOs such as the United Nations influence individuals and groups in these nations who may be skeptical of any form of global collaboration or influence?
3 Many local and national governments have experienced budget shortages, initiated austerity measures, or experienced significant financial crises. How can system leaders within these governments influence constituents to contribute additional money to sustainability efforts? How can these leaders influence leaders in other governments to collaborate when funding is limited?
4 The subject of the personal interview in this chapter was engaged in a UN initiative in which higher education institutions voluntarily agree to incorporate sustainability curriculum within their business and management programs. How much more difficult (or easy) would it be to apply system leadership in an initiative in which membership and participation was mandatory?

## References


Ackoff, R. L. (1978). *The art of problem solving*. New York, NY: John Wiley & Sons.

Ackoff, R. L. (1994). Systems thinking and thinking systems. *System Dynamics Review, 10*(2–3), 175–188. doi:10.1002/sdr.4260100206

Ackoff, R. L., & Gharajedaghi, J. (1996). Reflections on systems and their models. *Systems Research, 13*(1), 13–23. doi:10.1002/(SICI)1099-1735(199603)13:1<13::AID-SRES66>3.0.CO;2-O

Argyris, C., & Schön, D. A. (1978). *A theory of action perspective*. Boston, MA: Addison-Wesley Publishing Company.

Barbone, S. (2018, November 13). *Interview with Chris Castro, director of sustainability at city of Orlando*. Brussels, Belgium: Next Tourism Generation Alliance. Retrieved from https://nexttourismgeneration.eu/interview-with-chris-castro-director-of-sustainability-at-city-of-orlando/

Block, T., & Paredis, E. (2013). Urban development projects catalyst for sustainable transformations: The need for entrepreneurial political leadership. *Journal of Cleaner Production, 50*, 181–188. doi:10.1016/j.jclepro.2012.11.021

Bloomberg Philanthropies. (2019a). *American cities climate challenge*. New York, NY: Author. Retrieved from www.bloomberg.org/program/environment/climatechallenge/#overview

Bloomberg Philanthropies. (2019b). *Helping U.S. cities innovate, solve problems, and work together*. New York, NY: Author. Retrieved from www.bloomberg.org/program/founders-projects/american-cities-initiative/#programs

Boedeker, H. (2018, November 29). Orlando shines in "Paris to Pittsburgh" documentary. *The Orlando Sentinel*. Retrieved from www.orlandosentinel.com/entertainment/tv-guy/os-et-orlando-shines-in-paris-to-pittsburgh-documentary-20181129-story.html

Borins, S. (2000). Loose cannons and rule breakers? Some evidence about innovative public managers. *Public Administration Review, 60*(6), 498–507. doi:10.1111/0033-3352.00113

Cerceau, J., Mat, N., Junqua, G., Lin, L., Laforest, V., & Gonzalez, C. (2014). Implementing industrial ecology in port cities: International overview of case studies and cross-case analysis. *Journal of Cleaner Production, 64*, 1–16. doi:10.1016/j.jclepro.2014.03.050

Checkland, P. B. (1981). *Systems thinking: Systems practice*. Chichester, England: Wiley.

Checkland, P. B., & Scholes, J. (1990). *Soft systems methodology in action*. Chichester, England: Wiley.

Clapp, J., & Dauvergne, P. (2005). *Paths to a green world*. London, England: The MIT Press.

Daigneau, E. (2018). *Public officials of the year*. Washington, DC: Governing. Retrieved from www.governing.com/poy/gov-chris-castro.html

Davidson, K. M., & Venning, J. (2011). Sustainability decision-making frameworks and the application of systems thinking: An urban context. *Local Environment, 16*(3), 213–228. doi:10.1080/13549839.2011.565464

Deming, W. E. (1982). *Out of the crisis: Quality, productivity and competitive position*. Cambridge, England: Cambridge University Press.

Department of Economic and Social Affairs. (2018). *68% of the world population projected to live in urban areas by 2050, says UN*. New York, NY: United Nations. Retrieved from www.un.org/development/desa/en/news/population/2018-revision-of-world-urbanization-prospects.html

East Central Florida Regional Planning Council. (n.d.). *About us*. Orlando, FL: Author. Retrieved from www.ecfrpc.org/about

Edelman. (2017). *2017 Edelman trust barometer*. Orlando, FL: Author. Retrieved from www.edelman.com/research/2017-edelman-trust-barometer

Edelman. (2019). *2019 Edelman trust barometer*. Orlando, FL: Author. Retrieved from www.edelman.com/trust-barometer

Florida's Coastal Resiliency Portal. (n.d.). *Regional resiliency action plan*. Orlando, FL: Author. Retrieved from www.perilofflood.net/ecfresiliency

Greenleaf, R. K. (1977). *Servant leadership: A journey into the nature of legitimate power and greatness*. New York, NY: Paulist Press.

Harvard Law School. (2019). *Types of IGOs*. Cambridge, MA: Author. Retrieved from https://hls.harvard.edu/dept/opia/what-is-public-interest-law/public-service-practice-settings/public-international-law/types-of-igos/

Hein, A. M., Jankovic, M., Farel, R., & Yannou, B. (2015, August). A conceptual framework for eco-industrial parks. In *ASME 2015 international design engineering technical conferences and computers and information in engineering conference* (pp. V004T05A024–V004T05A024). New York, NY: American Society of Mechanical Engineers.

Jones, C., Hesterly, W. S., & Borgatti, S. P. (1997). A general theory of network governance: Exchange conditions and social mechanisms. *Academy of Management Review, 22*(4), 911–945. doi:10.5465/AMR.1997.9711022109

Kalim, K., Carson, E., & Cramp, D. (2006). An illustration of whole systems thinking. *Health Services Management Research, 19*(3), 174–185. doi:10.1258/095148406777888116

Khan, J. (2013). What role for network governance in urban low carbon transitions? *Journal of Cleaner Production, 50*, 133–139. doi:10.1016/j.jclepro.2012.11.045

Leverty, S. (2019). *NGOs, the UN and APA*. Washington, DC: American Psychological Association. Retrieved from www.apa.org/international/united-nations/publications

Li, B., Akintoye, A., Edwards, P. J., & Hardcastle, C. (2005). Critical success factors for PPP/PFI projects in the UK construction industry. *Construction Management and Economics, 23*(5), 459–471. doi:10.1080/01446190500041537

Librizzi, F. (n.d.). *Bio*. New York, NY: Author. Retrieved from http://florencialibrizzi.com/

Librizzi, F. (2019, July 15). Personal interview.

Malmberg, K. B. (2019). *The role of government regulation and leadership in increasing sustainability*. Washington, DC: The American Society for Public Administration. Retrieved from https://patimes.org/role-government-regulation-leadership-increasing-sustainability/

Middleton, P. (2010). *Delivering public services that work* (Vol. 1). Axminster, England: Triarchy Press.

Mistarihi, A., Hutchings, K., & Shacklock, A. (2013). Differing opinions do not spoil friendships: Managing public-private partnership (PPP) infrastructure projects in Jordan. *Public Administration & Development, 33*, 371–388. doi:10.1002/pad.1651

Nielsen, K., & Pedersen, O. K. (1998). The negotiated economy: Ideal and history. *Scandinavian Political Studies, 11*(2), 79–101. doi:10.1111/j.1467-9477.1988.tb00361.x

O'Connor, B. (2016, June 20). *City of Orlando names Chris Castro as new director of sustainability*. Orlando, FL: Bungalower. Retrieved from https://bungalower.com/2016/06/20/city-orlando-names-chris-castro-new-director-sustainability/

Ohno, T. (1988). *Toyota production system: Beyond large-scale production*. Boca Raton, FL: CRC Press.

Ooi, G. (2005). *Sustainability and cities: Concept and assessment*. Singapore: World Scientific Publishing.

Organisation for Economic Co-Operation and Development. (OECD). (2014). *The size and sectoral distribution of SOEs in OECD and partner countries*. Paris, France: OECD Publishing. doi:10.1787/9789264215610-en

Penn State University Libraries. (n.d.). *Sustainable development*. State College, PA: Pennsylvania State University. Retrieved from https://guides.libraries.psu.edu/sustainable-development/international

Radywyl, N., & Biggs, C. (2013). Reclaiming the commons for urban transformation. *Journal of Cleaner Production, 50*, 159–170. doi:10.1016/j.jclepro.2012.12.020

Roberts, T. (2018, June 1). *One year since Trump's withdrawal from the Paris climate agreement*. Washington, DC: The Brookings Institute. Retrieved from www.brookings.edu/blog/planetpolicy/2018/06/01/one-year-since-trumps-withdrawal-from-the-paris-climate-agreement/

Sanneh, E. S. (2018). *Systems thinking for sustainable development, climate change and the environment*. New York, NY: Springer. doi:10.1007/978-3-319-70585-9

Scharpf, F. (1997). Actor-centered institutionalism. In F. Scharpf (Ed.), *Games real actors play actor-centered institutionalism in policy research*. Boulder, CO: Westview Press.

Seddon, J. (1992). *I want you to cheat!* Buckingham, England: Vanguard Education.

Senior, B. (2002). *Organisational change* (2nd ed.). Harlow, England: Prentice Hall.

Sørensen, E., & Torfing, J. (2005). The democratic anchorage of governance networks. *Scandinavian Political Studies, 28*(3), 195–218. doi:10.1111/j.1467-9477.2005.00129.x

Steets, J. (2010). *Accountability in public policy partnerships*. New York, NY: Palgrave MacMillan. Creative Commons Public License (CC by-nc-nd). Retrieved from www.doabooks.org/doab?func=search&addFilter=utlic:%22CC%20by-nc-nd%22&template=&query=public%20private%20partnership

Summers, P. (2011). Systems thinking in local government. *Systemist, 33*, 88–111. Retrieved from www.researchgate.net/publication/262414621_Systems_thinking_in_local_government

United Nations. (2018). *UN objectives*. New York, NY: Author. Retrieved from www.un.org

United Nations. (n.d.). *Sustainable development goals*. New York, NY: Author. Retrieved from https://sustainabledevelopment.un.org/?menu=1300

Uyarra, E., & Gee, S. (2013). Transforming urban waste into sustainable material and energy usage: The case of Greater Manchester (UK). *Journal of Cleaner Production, 50*, 101–110. doi:10.1016/j.jclepro.2012.11.046

Vanguard Consulting Limited. (2014). *Public sector*. Buckingham, England: Author. Retrieved from https://vanguard-method.net/2014/10/public-sector/

Van Kersbergen, K., & Van Waarden, F. (2004). "Governance" as a bridge between disciplines: Cross-disciplinary inspiration regarding shifts in governance and problems of governability, accountability and legitimacy. *European Journal of Political Research, 43*(2), 143–171. doi:10.1111/j.1475-6765.2004.00149.x

Walker, B., & Salt, D. (2006). *Resilience thinking*. Washington, DC: Island Press.

Wang, X., Van Wart, M., & Lebredo, N. (2014). Sustainability leadership in a local government context. *Public Performance & Management Review, 37*, 339–364. doi:10.2753/PMR1530-9576370301

Weinreb, E. (2015). *5 core competencies of sustainability leadership*. Retrieved from www.greenbiz.com/article/5-core-competencies-sustainability-leadership

Wilson, B. (2001). *Soft systems methodology*. Chichester, England: Wiley.

Woodall, C. (2017, June 1). Trump: "I was elected to represent the citizens of Pittsburgh, not Paris". *Pennsylvania Real-Time News*. Retrieved from www.pennlive.com/news/2017/06/trump_i_was_elected_to_represe.html

World Commission on Environment and Development. (1987). *Our common future*. Oxford, England: Oxford University Press.

World of Walas. (2019a). *Our story*. Heerlen, Netherlands: Author. Retrieved from https://worldofwalas.com/about-us/our-story/

World of Walas. (2019b). *Gerben van Straaten*. Heerlen, Netherlands: Author. Retrieved from https://worldofwalas.com/team/gerben-van-straaten/

Zokaei, K., Elias, S., O'Donovan, B., Samuel, D., Evans, B., & Goodfellow, J. (2010). *Report for Wales Audit Office Lean and systems thinking in the public sector in Wales*. Cardiff, Wales: Lean Enterprise Research Centre, Cardiff University.

# 8 System leadership for sustainability in nonprofit and nongovernmental organizations

## Introduction

Many of the current sustainability initiatives are conceived in and implemented by nonprofit or nongovernmental organizations (NGOs). While the two terms describe similar organizations, there are slight differences between them. Nonprofit organizations, often referred to as charitable organizations or charities, provide a public benefit without a focus on profitability. The nonprofit sector is often referred to as the "third sector" after business and government. This sector consists of the vast multitude of charities, volunteer organizations, community associations, cooperatives, and social enterprises (Hodges & Howieson, 2017). The term nongovernmental organization describes a broad range of institutions including international charities, research institutes, religious entities, community-based organizations, lobby and special interest groups, and professional associations (Leverty, 2019). NGOs are typically value-based organizations, and much like nonprofits, NGOs are dependent wholly or partially on charitable donations and volunteer service (Leverty, 2019).

While businesses are increasingly becoming involved in the sustainability movement, nonprofits and NGOs will likely continue to provide considerable leadership and an avenue through which businesses can accomplish their sustainability initiatives. For example, many businesses "outsource" their sustainability initiatives through funding nonprofit and NGO activities in areas synonymous with business activities or corporate social responsibility (CSR) statements. However, nonprofit organizations and NGOs frequently face budgetary limits, and unlike businesses, are in less of a position to borrow capital or increase revenue. Therefore, these organizations rely on the ability to influence individuals, businesses, and governments to provide necessary funding. Leaders of these organizations must possess the ability to influence across system boundaries to accomplish objectives and acquire necessary funding.

Within the nonprofit sector, leadership is an approach described by followers as one that maintains organizational reputation, ensures obligations are met, motivates followers, and creates a positive environment (Hodges & Howieson, 2017). In their research, Hodges and Howieson identified the following nonprofit leadership attributes: influencing; motivating; inspiring; listening; observing; empowering others; having conversations with people; authenticity;

visibility; resiliency; empathy; courage; earning respect, trust, and credibility; and possessing strong values. Their research findings also indicated the significance of leadership attributes, which are essential for influencing policy (Hodges & Howieson, 2017).

In this chapter, we will examine the background of nonprofit organizations and NGOs and the role both serve in the sustainability paradigm. System leadership will be examined within the context of both types of organizations, and global perspectives of system leadership in both will be considered. The challenges and barriers to system leadership in these organizations and the future role of these organizations in sustainability collaboration will be discussed. The chapter concludes with an NGO sustainability system leader spotlight, concluding thoughts, and a case study about NGO sustainability system leadership.

## Nonprofit organizations

Nonprofit organizations provide a public benefit or service and are not profit-focused. While these organizations may receive income in excess of expenses, all money received is used in providing a service and associated administrative costs. In the United States, these organizations are usually tax exempt under Internal Revenue Code Section 501(c)(3). While these organizations may be tax exempt and receive other protections from government agencies, they are at least partially accountable to government agencies and constituents.

The three major trends affecting charitable nonprofits are resource limitations; increased demands, resulting from increased community needs; and the increasing recognition that every organization and board member must be an active, vocal proponent of the organization's mission to influence policies at both the community and the national level (National Council of Nonprofits, 2019). Other important trends within the nonprofit sector include:

- protecting nonprofit nonpartisanship;
- providing moral leadership for the values of diversity, inclusion, and equity;
- budget cuts;
- cybersecurity;
- changes in charitable giving;
- natural disasters: preparedness and recovery;
- more respectful relationships between grant makers and nonprofits;
- donor-advised funds;
- gender pay gap;
- peer-to-peer fundraising and "crowdfunding";
- board members as advocates: Stand for your mission; and
- wellness for nonprofits: Being sustainable is more than money (National Council of Nonprofits, 2019).

The broad nature of these trends supports the need for leaders who are capable of influencing across multiple boundaries and systems. Moreover, these trends affect all nonprofit organizations, regardless of whether the organization is sustainability-focused.

The nonprofit sector in Europe is undergoing dramatic change influenced by shifts in the social, political, and economic landscapes (Hodges & Howieson, 2017). Beginning with the global financial crisis in 2008, the sector has faced increased demand for services coupled with reduction in resources (Wilding, 2010). Subsequently, the focus of much nonprofit activity has been with survival and resilience, increased effort on collaboration, and increasingly urgent efforts to exhibit organizational impact and monetary value (Macmillan & McLaren, 2012). In addition, accountability demands have intensified, and increased transparency in reporting activity, spending, and measurable outcomes is expected (Salamon, 2010). Moreover, performance measurement standards have increased with nonprofit organizations facing greater pressure to understand and measure the impact of programs (Hudson, 2009). There has also been heightened government recognition that the nonprofit sector is in a better position than government to address some social problems (Hodges & Howieson, 2017), resulting in increased diversity of size, function, scale, and legal structure of nonprofit organizations (Hunter, 2009).

The changes taking place in the nonprofit sector have raised questions about whether this sector can continue to be categorized as one single sector (Alcock, 2010). Moreover, there is greater concern with what the sector will become in the future and the role it will serve, given the current political environment of austerity (Macmillan & McLaren, 2012). A sector-wide response to these questions is necessary to prevent nonprofit organizations from responding defensively by pursuing limited organizational interests, which may further perpetuate the issues faced by these organizations (Cook, 2012). While the previous content referred to the nonprofit sector in Europe, many of the points can be generalized to other regions. Inadequate leadership has been determined to be one of the top five constraints confronting the nonprofit sector (Green, 2009), with leadership ability and strategic and forward planning identified among the top ten skills absent in nonprofit organizations (Clark, 2007).

## NGOs

NGOs are described as nonprofit organizations that are independent of government (Leverty, 2019). The United Nations further defines an NGO as

> any nonprofit, voluntary citizens' group which is organized on a local, national or international level. Task-oriented and driven by people with a common interest, non-governmental organizations (NGOs) perform a variety of services and humanitarian functions, bring citizens' concerns to Governments, monitor policies, and encourage political participation at the community level.
>
> (Department of Public Information, n.d.)

The two common types of NGOs are operational NGOs, whose main function is planning and operation of development-related projects, and advocacy NGOs, which primarily advocate a particular cause and attempt to influence the policies and procedures of IGOs (Leverty, 2019). NGOs have become more influential in global affairs, with many NGOs having relationships or formal status with major intergovernmental organizations (IGOs) such as the United Nations (UN) or the Organization for Economic Cooperation and Development (OECD). IGOs are institutions consisting of the governments of representative member states (Leverty, 2019), previously discussed in Chapter 7.

The United Nations Economic and Social Council (ECOSOC) is the central platform of the organization for reflection, debate, and innovative thinking about sustainable development (Economic and Social Council, 2019). ECOSOC resolutions provide NGOs with various levels of consultative status: *general status* is assigned to large, international NGOs that specialize in multiple issues relevant to ECOSOC, *special consultative status* is assigned to NGOs that specialize in several of ECOSOC's issues, and *roster status* is assigned to NGOs that provide occasional contributions (Leverty, 2019). Many NGOs maintain relationships with UN departments and agencies, provide technical analysis and expertise, offer opinions on social and economic issues, and participate in meetings, sessions, and conferences relevant to their objectives (Leverty, 2019). According to the United Nations Development Program, there are approximately 40,000 NGOs globally, not including the more than 100,000 community-based organizations and over 2,800 hold consultative status with ECOSOC (Leverty, 2019).

## System leadership in nonprofit organizations

Contemporary approaches to nonprofit leadership are changing, with the usefulness of hierarchical leadership being questioned (Bligh, 2016; Hodges & Howieson, 2017). In the dynamically changing environment in which they operate, scholars and practitioners question the future direction of leadership in this sector (Jackson, 2012). Nonprofit leadership for organizational development and change is shifting from being an individual responsibility to more of a collective one (Hodges, 2016; Raelin, 2015), with the interactions among leaders and followers becoming more influential than the actions of either (Howieson & Hodges, 2014). Moreover, Dobbs (2004) suggested the importance of relationship building in nonprofit leadership (Howieson & Hodges, 2014). Kirchner (2007) developed a nonprofit leadership model wherein the leader manages upwards (governance), downwards (effective management of organizations and resources), and outwards (external representation of the organization). The previous nonprofit leadership research and models support the need for system leadership, wherein the focus of leadership is collective, crosses multiple levels, and extends beyond the organization being led.

Many nonprofit organizations are founded and managed by social entrepreneurs, who are individuals seeking to solve a societal problem through either a profit or nonprofit business model. The characteristics of successful social entrepreneurs include holistic and speculative thinking; initiative and perseverance; strong values; focus (Chambers & Edwards-Stuart, 2007); passion; a strategic outlook; networking and influencing; modesty; ability to motivate teams; resilience; self-confidence; being an idealistic, inspiring communicator; and encouraging collective decision-making (Cormack & Stanton, 2003). A common theme in the literature is the significance of a conversational "ambassadorial" element of leadership, along with references to networking, representation, articulating a vision both inside and outside the organization, and conversation (Hodges, & Howieson, 2017), with an emphasis on story-telling and narrative (Peck, Freeman, & Dickinson, 2009).

The environment in which nonprofits operate has changed significantly, and it will likely continue to change based upon influence from within and without the sector. Existing leadership styles and methods will be less effective in confronting dynamic, global issues, challenges, and forces. Sustainability leaders must be able to understand the entire system, and their role in that system, in order to implement meaningful change. Grint (2010) suggested that conventional thinking, which demands that leaders become problem-solvers, acting decisively and accurately, may not be appropriate when responding to complex situations that require reflective and calculated responses. In these situations, leadership may include offering and interpreting relevant information and asking difficult questions, rather than providing decisive answers (Hodges, & Howieson, 2017). Paton and Brewster (2008) suggested the importance of seeing the big picture in their conceptual framework of nonprofit leadership. System and field awareness, emotional awareness, and intuition are the three elements of the framework (Hodges, & Howieson, 2017). The skills and leadership style previously described is that of a system leader, once who is able to understand and influence beyond the scope of traditional individuals and organizational boundaries.

## System leadership in NGOs

Numerous NGOs are involved in specialized sustainable development and sustainability activities. At the US national level, the US Green Building Council (USGBC) and the Union of Concerned Scientists are two examples of organizations devoted to specific aspects of sustainable development. The USGBC works to transform the manner in which buildings and communities are designed, built, and operated, enabling an environmentally and socially responsible, healthy, and flourishing environment that enhances quality of life (USGBC, n.d.). This mission is accomplished through a broad community network, constant collaboration with industry experts, market research publications, and training of leadership in energy and environmental design (LEED) professional credentials. The Union of Concerned Scientists, founded in 1969 at the Massachusetts Institute of Technology (MIT), works with individuals across the United States to "combine technical analysis and effective advocacy to create innovative, practical solutions for a healthy, safe, and sustainable future" (Union of Concerned Scientists, n.d.).

On a global level, Greenpeace International and Oxfam International offer two diverse perspectives on the function of global NGOs working on specific aspects of sustainable development. Greenpeace International is an environmental NGO with offices in over 39 nations and a global coordinating group in Amsterdam, the Netherlands. The message of Greenpeace "is that a better world is possible, and that brave individual and collective action can make that world a reality" (Greenpeace International, n.d.). Oxfam International is an international NGO consisting of 19 organizations working with partners and local communities in more than 90 nations (Oxfam International, n.d.). Oxfam works globally to find practical, innovative ways for individuals to move out of poverty and flourish. Poverty is an often neglected aspect of sustainability, with many sustainable development advocates focusing primarily on the environmental aspects of sustainability. Oxfam campaigns assist those in poverty to influence the local and global decisions that impact them.

Although the previously identified NGOs, and indeed all sustainability NGOs, function within various dimensions of sustainability, the descriptions of their organizations suggest common activities and challenges supportive of a systems approach to leadership. These organizations work collaboratively across industry, sector, and geographic boundaries to influence individuals and groups who are frequently beyond their direct influence. The development of networks and partnership among stakeholders with diverse and often conflicting objectives and perspectives requires boundaryless leadership. These leaders must understand systems thinking to influence the diversity of actors in the broad systems they wish to influence. The system leadership model provides the framework for accomplishing these sustainability objectives.

NGOs have a recent history of collaboration with business; however, the majority of collaborative efforts have been partnerships with individual NGOs or in sector alliances (Confino, 2012). As mentioned in Chapter 5, businesses frequently "outsource" their sustainability activities to nonprofit organizations and NGOs who possess expertise in one or more sustainability specializations. Because businesses possess the resources necessary for significant sustainability impact, NGOs must work to leverage those resources through collaborative efforts. Although many NGOs seek corporate board positions or attempt to force shareholder votes on key social and economic sustainability issues, those efforts are often viewed as adversarial by businesses. While such efforts are often necessary to achieve change, collaborative, cooperative efforts may be more productive. System leaders within NGOs must develop collaborative relationships across corporate boundaries where limited control or influence exists.

## System leadership elements in nonprofit organizations and NGOs

In Chapter 3, we considered the eight elements of system leadership, within the context of education as defined by Fullan (2005): public service with a moral purpose; commitment to changing context at all levels; lateral capacity building through networks; new vertical relationships that are co-dependent, encompassing both capacity building and accountability; deep learning; dual commitment to short-term and long-term results; cyclical energizing; and the long lever of leadership (Fullan, 2005). I propose that the same elements apply within other contexts, including nonprofit organizations and NGOs, which are often tasked with achieving sustainability outcomes across a broad collection of stakeholders.

Nonprofit and NGO leaders serve the public and must do so with a moral purpose, which in this context is sustainability. Fullan (2003) suggested moral purpose must transcend the individual to become an organizational and system characteristic in which all members commit to moral purpose in all essential activities. These leaders must be committed to change at all levels and be capable of building both lateral networks and vertical relationships to develop the capacity necessary to achieve sustainability under challenging political, social, and financial conditions. These leaders must be committed to individual deep learning, as well as the promotion of learning organizations, and be better able to adapt to dynamic, uncertain situations. Long-term goal achievement will require successful management and achievement of shorter-term goals and objectives. Fullan noted that sustainability is cyclical for two important reasons: energy, and the occasions when additional time and talent are required to achieve the next adaptive improvement. Cyclical energizing requires organizations to become learning organizations that explore, learn, analyze, and develop improved solutions. The long lever of leadership is the element that unifies the other seven elements and will require system leadership skills to achieve success.

## Global perspectives of system leadership in nonprofits and NGOs

Sustainability is a global issue requiring leadership and action globally. Moreover, unsustainable actions by one organization, industry, or nation may impact distant individuals and groups, most notably manifest in the environmental transgressions of nations in the Northern hemisphere adversely impacting their neighbors south of the equator. However, while developing nations increasingly experience the adverse effects of unsustainable behavior, the developed nations possess the financial and often intellectual capital necessary to reverse those behaviors and the resulting effects. While NGOs based in developed nations frequently perform their work in developing nations, NGOs in developing nations must exert their limited influence across boundaries and systems to ensure that their best interests are addressed.

While numerous NGOs based in developed nations embark on sustainability and sustainable development activities in developing nations, many NGOs originate and operate in developing nations. The global collaboration and cooperation required to reverse unsustainable behavior and begin the regenerative healing process for humankind and the planet will require system leadership. Leaders of NGOs in developed nations must influence public and private leaders and individuals in developing nations to accept their aid, advice, and assistance. However, challenges and barriers exist with employing system leadership in these scenarios, which is the topic of the following section.

In exercising system leadership on a global scale, NGO system leaders will require cultural intelligence to influence across broad cultural and national groups. This cultural intelligence will require an understanding of diverse cultures, as described in the GLOBE research (House & Javidan, 2004) in Chapter 4. These leaders must also influence individuals and groups with differing, and even opposing, ideological and political perspectives. A systems approach will be an essential tool for finding agreement and developing collaboration among parties who may not normally agree. However, while system leadership may be an effective tool, challenges and barriers exist to successful system leadership for sustainability. These challenges and barriers will be examined in the next section.

## Challenges and barriers to system leadership in nonprofit organizations and NGOs

System leadership provides the framework for navigating the challenges of nonprofit leadership. Nonprofit organizations face multiple challenges: developing leaders of change; reflecting and embracing diversity; and collaboration, alliance, and partnership (Hesselbein, 2004). Strategic alliances must be formed between nonprofit organizations and among the nonprofit, government, and business sectors (Green, 2004). Moreover, nonprofit leaders face similar challenges, with the primary challenges being recovering from financial downturns, establishing collaborative relationships, remaining innovative and unique, establishing and developing capacity, and reinforcing sector legitimacy (Hodges & Howieson, 2017). NGO leaders face similar challenges to those of nonprofit leaders in influencing change for sustainability in a dynamic, unpredictable global environment. Most of these organizations are funded by voluntary financial contributions, membership fees, revenue from publications and training programs, and limited government funding. While these challenges are likely relevant within any nonprofit organization, regardless of geography, the focus of this section is with nonprofits and NGOs in the area of sustainability. Of the five challenges listed, building collaborative relationships is likely the challenge that would be most difficult for, and benefit most from, system leadership. In this section, we will first examine the importance of building collaborative relationships, followed by examining the barriers system leaders might face in their collaborative efforts.

Nonprofit leaders must identify with whom and in what manner they should collaborate (Hodges & Howieson, 2017). These collaborations should occur across the nonprofit sector, and with organizations in other sectors with the objectives of attracting funding, reducing costs, and creating value, while simultaneously competing for contracts with some of the organizations with which they are in collaboration (Hodges & Howieson, 2017). Nonprofit leaders face the challenge of strengthening sector legitimacy while preserving the assumption of the unique nature of "voluntary association". Moreover, politicians and policymakers have begun questioning the legitimacy of nonprofits that champion social issues, especially recipients of government funding. Nonprofit leaders operate under significant pressure because their sector is susceptible to social, economic, and political change and must be responsive to dynamic forces of change (Hodges & Howieson, 2017).

Based on their nonprofit leadership research, Hodges and Howieson (2017) emphasized the importance of the type of leaders required to address the challenges of the nonprofit sector. The future of the nonprofit sector will require more than identifying a few inherent leadership qualities or recruiting and developing additional leaders. The nonprofit sector is not in need of more leaders; rather, leadership at all levels is needed. Leadership relates to multiple organizational or system actors and is not dependent upon a single individual in a management role (Leslie & Canwell, 2010). The challenges these organizations face will require leaders who can work and collaborate across organizations and systems, including public and private sectors.

Regardless of the sector, organizational boundaries are becoming more obscure because of partnerships, collaboration, and commissioning. Throughout the entire nonprofit sector, there is a necessity for collaboration to cultivate the development of a nucleus of leadership talent (Hodges & Howieson, 2017). Boundary crossing, or the movement of leaders across sectoral boundaries, introduces the much-needed expertise of public and private sector leaders to the nonprofit sector (Buckingham, Paine, Alcock, Kendall, & Macmillan, 2014). Boundary crossing requires leaders to be focused on and aware of the external environment, adopting a more collaborative method of boundaryless cooperation (Hodges & Howieson, 2017). While these researchers have not named this suggested leadership style or model, what they have described is system leadership.

System leadership is clearly beneficial for addressing the challenges of the nonprofit and NGO sector; however, this model is not without challenges of its own (Hodges & Howieson, 2017). Findings indicate the need for improved effectiveness among leadership across the nonprofit sector. Some researchers suggest that the role of leadership is best measured in terms of how the organizational context is shaped, instead of the economic impact (Oldham & Hackman, 2010). Moreover, the capacity and significance of nonprofit leadership must be addressed, with regard to effects on performance effectiveness and influence on organizational life, described by Nohria and Khurana (2010) as meaning, integrity, and culture within the organization (Hodges & Howieson, 2017).

Many of the challenges faced by nonprofit organizations and NGOs are magnified by visible and invisible barriers that leaders must overcome. These barriers may be physical, legal, organizational, or societal in nature. Individuals and organizations can demonstrate territorial behavior, broadly resisting attempts from other individuals and organizations to influence or alter their position. This territorial behavior may be overt, in terms of physically and orally resisting outside influence, or it may become manifest in covert attempts to undermine leadership, actions, or activities. These barriers may be based upon sound reasoning, such as competition for valuable, limited resources, or competing and potentially contradictory goals and agendas of the actors. Identifying and breaking down these barriers will require a systems perspective to understand the purpose and function of the barriers, as well as interpersonal skills to influence the constructors and managers of these barriers of the need for and benefit of mutual collaboration and cooperation.

Some of these barriers may be culturally based, driven by misperceptions and misunderstandings about the motives of the actors or past experiences and disagreements between the parties. NGOs based in developed nations but operating in developing nations may face skepticism, with aid recipients questioning the motives of agents and benefactors from previously colonial nations. Poorer nations have been and continue to be frequently exploited for their natural resources, resulting in skepticism in poorer nations of any offer of assistance from richer nations. Development and exercise of system leadership will be essential for NGO leaders to successfully influence and collaborate across these cultural barriers and boundaries.

## Future role of nonprofits and NGOs in sustainability collaboration

Achieving sustainability requires alternative leadership methods and the engagement of business, citizens, nongovernment organizations, and other environmental stakeholders (Hartman, Hofman, & Stafford, 1999). Collaborative alliances among these stakeholders are essential to shift public policies and markets to guide the creativity, resources, technology, and global reach of the business sector toward sustainability (Hartman et al., 1999). The culture of environmental NGOs has been shifting from protest to practical solutions, with an increasing number of environmental NGOs collaborating with industries previously considered adversarial (Stafford & Hartman, 1998). However, NGOs participating in collaborative efforts with industry face possible risks to public credibility (Stafford & Hartman, 1998), including being perceived as "selling out" to powerful corporate interests.

Recent research indicates that a growing number of businesses are engaged in sustainability-focused collaboration with suppliers, NGOs, industry alliances, governments, and competitors (Kiron et al., 2015). Business leaders recognize that sustainability issues have become increasingly complex, global, and essential for success, with 90% of respondents agreeing that collaboration is essential for businesses to respond to sustainability challenges (Kiron et al., 2015). The interconnectedness of businesses, governments, and citizens has produced a world of interdependence, in which collaboration is essential for sustainability progress. The research findings indicate the corporate sustainability model is transitioning from ad hoc or opportunistic efforts that frequently result in strained relationships with the public sector to strategic and transformative initiatives involving multiple stakeholders.

The goals and benefits of these collaborations include potential influence with standard-setting authorities, increased resource access, and new market development. The key drivers of these sustainability efforts include increased brand reputation, improved product and service innovation, market transformation promotion, and risk mitigation (Kiron et al., 2015), consistent with previous research findings of the strategic drivers of corporate sustainability (Kiron, Kruschwitz, Haanaes, Reeves, & Goh, 2012). With business leaders increasingly seeking collaboration with nonprofit organizations and NGOs, leaders with the collaborative, boundaryless, systems thinking abilities of system leadership will be essential to the success of these multi-stakeholder collaborations.

## NGO system leader spotlight

Mirian Vilela has been the Executive Director of Earth Charter International since 1996. In this role, she has coordinated an international consultation process, as well as established partnerships with individuals and organizations who contributed to the consultation process and who continue to support the implementation phase of the Charter. She has developed and facilitated numerous global workshops and seminars about sustainability values and principles. Prior to joining the Earth Charter, Vilela worked for the United Nations Conference on Environment and Development (UNCED) in preparation of the 1992 UN Earth Summit, and she is currently a member of the UNESCO Expert Reference Group for the Decade of Education for Sustainable Development (DESD). Vilela is a faculty member of the University for Peace in San Jose, Costa Rica, and holds a Master of Public Administration (MPA) degree from the Harvard Kennedy School of Government, where she was an Edward Mason Fellow (Earth Charter, 2019).

In 2012, she was awarded the eAward by the Instituto-E, UNESCO, and Rio de Janeiro Municipality (Vilela, 2019), which acknowledges the most representative initiatives for social and environmental development (UNESCO, 2012). In 2014, she was awarded the Spirit of the United Nations Award (SUNA), offered by the NGO Committee on Spirituality, Values and Global Concerns of New York (Vilela, 2019). The award recognizes individuals "whose work is an expression of the core principles, spirit and vision on which the United Nations was founded" (CSVGC-NY, n.d.).

Vilela's perspective on the meaning of sustainability and the Earth Charter transcends how people frequently think about sustainability, by proposing a profound connectedness of life, self, education, environment, and wholeness (Luvmour Consulting, 2018). Vilela believes one of our greatest challenges is to shift away from fragmented approaches to achieving a change of mindset. She suggested that we are all educated in the reductionist, fragmented manner in which our organizations are established and organized. However, we need to look at one aspect of problems and challenges while seeing the connection with the other aspects. Vilela believes the core of sustainability lies in the need to shift away from fragmented mindsets to a more systemic and holistic mindset and approach, because life is so much about interconnections and relationships (Luvmour Consulting, 2018). This recognition of a systemic, holistic approach to sustainability supports the system leadership model proposed in this text. Vilela has demonstrated system leadership in her role at the Earth Charter Initiative by bringing together diverse stakeholders from multiple continents and sectors to work toward a sustainable future. She has accomplished this by recognizing and appealing to our common interconnectedness. She is one of numerous system leaders operating within nonprofit organizations and NGOs to achieve a sustainable future.

## Conclusion

Nonprofit organizations and NGOs will perform an essential role in driving the collaboration necessary to achieve sustainability. Leaders of these organizations must be able to influence larger, more powerful businesses and governments to modify collective behavior and work collaboratively for global solutions. However, these organizations must collaborate to overcome the barriers and challenges previously identified. System leadership provides a model and framework for leaders within these organizations to take the necessary actions to achieve sustainability. Many nonprofit and NGO leaders have demonstrated system leadership for sustainability without any prior knowledge of system leadership. However, more system leaders will be required if sustainability is to be achieved on a global level. In this chapter, we have described nonprofit organizations and NGOs, as well as the role of system leadership within those organizations. We also considered global perspectives of system leadership in these organizations and the corresponding challenges and barriers to development and implementation of system leadership. This chapter concluded with a spotlight of an NGO leader who has significantly impacted sustainable development through system leadership.

## Case study

The Caribbean Sustainability Organization (a fictional entity) is an NGO based in Miami, Florida, in the US that promotes sustainability and resilience in the small island developing states (SIDS) of the Caribbean region. Funding is provided by businesses within the US travel industry, at least partially motivated by the need to maintain the viability of the Caribbean islands as travel destinations.

The overall mission of the NGO is to develop local system leaders who are able to influence sustainability and resilience initiatives throughout within the Caribbean region. The five-year plan calls for the development of a network of system leaders from various SIDS, capable of collaborative sustainability activity throughout the region. The NGO has recently considered relocating their headquarters to one of the SIDS in order to increase presence in the region being serviced.

Scholars, practitioners, and other experts from the United States volunteer their services as mentors by providing training and advice to government and tourism leaders in the islands serviced by the NGO. Most of these volunteers spend at least one week annually in the field, often accompanied by family members, and stay in beachside resorts while volunteering. Most of the leadership trainees have been recruited from the various English-speaking governments and tourism companies in destinations most visited by Americans, such as the Bahamas, Jamaica, and the British Virgin Islands. However, the leadership trainees have not always been receptive to their American leadership mentors. In addition, while government and tourism leaders in non-English-speaking nations have requested assistance from the NGO, the volunteers and resources continue to be primarily directed toward English-speaking SIDS.

## Case study reflection questions

1 What challenges and barriers do the Caribbean Sustainability Organization volunteers face in providing training and advice in the Caribbean islands? How can these volunteers overcome these challenges and barriers?
2 What barriers and challenges will the NGO face in development of a collaborative network of system leaders within the region? What steps can leaders and volunteers at the NGO take to overcome these barriers and challenges?
3 What specific actions and training would be necessary to develop system leaders capable of influencing sustainability in these SIDS? Why do you think the leadership trainees have not always been receptive to their American leadership mentors?
4 What impact would relocating the headquarters to one of the SIDS have on the impact of the NGO? In which nation do you think the headquarters should be located, and why?

## Chapter reflection questions

1 How can nonprofit and NGO system leaders from developed nations influence individuals and groups in developing nations who may be skeptical of their motives?
2 If you were (or are) a nonprofit or NGO leader, how would (or can) you influence business, government, and other nonprofits and NGOs to work collaboratively with your organization to achieve sustainability?

3 Faced with reduced revenue, often simultaneously combined with increased demand for transparency and accountability, how can sustainability system leaders influence donors to contribute additional revenue and volunteers to work more hours?
4 How can system leaders influence individuals and groups in developing nations to act more sustainably when many developing nations are still behaving unsustainably?

## References

Alcock, P. (2010). A strategic unity: Defining the third sector in the UK. *Voluntary Sector Review*, *1*(1), 5–24. doi:10.1332/204080510X496984

Bligh, M. (2016). *How followers create and sustain leadership*. Research Seminar. London, England: Henley Business School, Greenlands Campus, Henley-on-Thames, 12 May.

Buckingham, H., Paine, A. E., Alcock, P., Kendall, J., & Macmillan, R. (2014). *Who's speaking for whom? Exploring issues of third sector leadership, leverage and legitimacy*. Birmingham, England: Third Centre Research Centre.

Chambers, C., & Edwards-Stuart, F. (2007). *Leadership in the social economy*. London, England: School for Social Entrepreneurs.

Clark, J. (2007). *Voluntary sector skills survey*. London, England: NCVO.

Committee on Spirituality, Values and Global Concerns of New York. (CSVGC-NY). (n.d.). *About SUNA*. New York, NY: Author. Retrieved from http://csvgc-ny.org/about-suna/

Confino, J. (2012, October 15). *The art of systems thinking in driving sustainable transformation*. Retrieved from www.theguardian.com/sustainable-business/systems-thinking-sustainable-transformation

Cook, S. (2012, January 10). New Deakin-style inquiry may be needed, says Joe Saxton. *Third Sector Online*. Retrieved from www.thirdsector.co.uk/new-deakin-style-inquiry-needed-argues-joe-saxton/policy-and-politics/article/1110900

Cormack, J., & Stanton, M. (2003). *Passionate leadership: The characteristics of outstanding leaders in the voluntary sector e what sector leaders think Initial research findings*. London, England: Hay Management Group for ACEVO.

Department of Public Information. (n.d.). *About us*. New York, NY: United Nations. Retrieved from https://outreach.un.org/ngorelations/content/about-us-0

Dobbs, M. D. (2004). Some thoughts about nonprofit leadership. In R. E. Riggio & S. Orr (Eds.), *Improving leadership in nonprofit organizations* (pp. 10–18). San Francisco, CA: Jossey-Bass.

Earth Charter. (2019). *Mirian Vilela*. San Jose, Costa Rica: Author. Retrieved from http://earthcharter.org/about/mirian-vilela/

Economic and Social Council. (2019). *About*. New York, NY: United Nations. Retrieved from www.un.org/en/ecosoc/about/

Fullan, M. (2003). *The moral imperative of school leadership*. Thousand Oaks, CA: Corwin Press and Toronto, Ontario Principals Council.

Fullan, M. (2005). *Leadership and sustainability*. Thousand Oaks, CA: Corwin Press and Toronto, Ontario Principals Council.

Green, F. L. (2004). Ten things nonprofits must do in the twenty-first century. In R. E. Riggio & S. S. Orr (Eds.), *Improving leadership in nonprofit organizations* (pp. 19–35). San Francisco, CA: Jossey-Bass.

Green, H. (2009). *State of the sector panel survey*. London, England: Cabinet Office.

Greenpeace International. (n.d.). *Our story*. Amsterdam, The Netherlands: Author. Retrieved from www.greenpeace.org/archive-international/en/about/our-story/

Grint, K. (2010). Wicked problems & clumsy solutions: The role of leadership. In S. Brookes & K. Grint (Eds.), *The new leadership challenge* (pp. 169–186). Basingstoke, England: Palgrave MacMillan.

Hartman, C. L., Hofman, P. S., & Stafford, E. R. (1999). Partnerships: A path to sustainability. *Business Strategy and the Environment, 8*(5), 255–266. doi:10.1002/(SICI)1099-0836(199909/10)8:5<255::AID-BSE214>3.0.CO;2-O

Hesselbein, F. (2004). Future challenges for nonprofit organizations. In R. E. Riggio & S. S. Orr (Eds.), *Improving leadership in nonprofit organizations* (pp. 3–9). San Francisco, CA: Jossey-Bass.

Hodges, J. (2016). *Managing and leading people through change*. London, England: Kogan Page.

Hodges, J., & Howieson, B. (2017). The challenges of leadership in the third sector. *European Management Journal, 35*(1), 69–77. doi:10.1016/j.emj.2016.12.006

House, R. J., & Javidan, M. (2004). Overview of GLOBE. In R. J. House, P. J. Hanges, M. Javidan, P. W. Dorfman, V. Gupta, & Associates (Eds.), *Culture, leadership, and organizations: The GLOBE study of 62 societies* (pp. 9–28). Thousand Oaks, CA: Sage Publications.

Howieson, B., & Hodges, J. (2014). *Public and third sector leadership: Experience speaks*. London, England: Emerald Group.

Hudson, M. (2009). *Managing without profit: Leadership, management and governance of third sector organizations*. London, England: Directory of Social Change.

Hunter, P. (Ed.). (2009). *Social enterprise for public service: How does the third sector deliver?* London, England: Smith Institute.

Jackson, E. (2012). *The contribution of a change in leadership philosophy in a public body in Scotland*. (Unpublished MBA Dissertation). The University of Stirling, Stirling, Scotland.

Kirchner, A. (2007). A leadership model for export. *International Journal of Leadership in Public Services, 3*(3), 49–55. doi:10.1108/17479886200700021

Kiron, D., Kruschwitz, N., Haanaes, K., Reeves, M., Fuisz-Kehrbach, S. K., & Kell, G. (2015). Joining forces: Collaboration and leadership for sustainability. *MIT Sloan Management Review, 56*(3), 1–31. Retrieved from https://sloanreview.mit.edu/projects/joining-forces/

Kiron, D., Kruschwitz, N., Haanaes, K., Reeves, M., & Goh, E. (2012). *The innovation bottom line: Findings from the 2012 sustainability & innovation global executive study and research report*. Retrieved from https://sloanreview.mit.edu/reports/sustainability-innovation/

Leslie, K., & Canwell, A. (2010). Leadership at all levels: Leading public sector organizations in an age of austerity. *European Management Journal, 28*(4), 297–305. doi:10.1016/j.emj.2010.05.006

Leverty, S. (2019). *NGOs, the UN and APA*. Washington, DC: American Psychological Association. Retrieved from www.apa.org/international/united-nations/publications

Luvmour Consulting. (2018). *Episode 32: Mirian Vilela*. Portland, OR: Author. Retrieved from www.remarkable-educators.com/podcast/2019/4/2/episode-32-mirian-vilela

Macmillan, R., & McLaren, V. (2012). *Third sector leadership: The power of narrative*. Birmingham, England: Third Sector Research Centre.

National Council of Nonprofits. (2019). *Nonprofit sector trends*. Washington, DC: Author. Retrieved from www.councilofnonprofits.org/nonprofit-sector-trends

Nohria, N., & Khurana, R. (2010). Advancing leadership theory and practice. In *Handbook of leadership theory and practice*. Cambridge, MA: Harvard Business Press.

Oldham, G. R., & Hackman, J. R. (2010). Not what it was and not what it will be: The future of job design research. *Journal of Organizational Behavior, 31*(2–3), 463–479. doi:10.1002/job.678

Oxfam International. (n.d.). *Who we are*. Nairobi, Kenya: Author. Retrieved from www.oxfam.org/en/about

Paton, R., & Brewster, R. (2008). *Making deeper sense in the midst of great busyness: A study of and with third sector CEOs*. Paper given at the 37th Annual Conference of ARNOVA, Philadelphia, USA, 20–22 November.

Peck, E., Freeman, T. P., & Dickinson, H. (2009). Performing leadership: Towards a new research agenda in leadership studies? *Leadership, 5*(1), 25–40. doi:10.1177/1742715008098308

Raelin, J. A. (2015). Rethinking leadership. *Sloan Management Review, 56*(4), 95. Retrieved from http://mitsmr.com/1HPlqqI

Salamon, L. M. (2010). The changing context of nonprofit leadership and management. In D. O. Renz (Ed.), *The Jossey-Bass handbook of nonprofit leadership and management* (pp. 77–100). San Francisco, CA: Wiley.

Stafford, E. R., & Hartman, C. L. (1998). Toward an understanding of the antecedents of environmentalist: Business cooperative relations. In R. C. Goodstein & S. B. MacKenzie (Eds.), *American marketing association summer educators' conference proceedings* (pp. 56–63). Chicago, IL: American Marketing Association.

UNESCO. (2012). *Instituto-E, UNESCO and Rio de Janeiro City Hall launch the E-Award to acknowledge outstanding sustainable initiatives from Eco-92 on*. Paris, France: Author. Retrieved from www.unesco.org/new/en/rio-20/single-view/news/instituto_e_unesco_and_rio_de_janeiro_city_hall_launch_the/

Union of Concerned Scientists. (n.d.). *About us*. Cambridge, MA: Author. Retrieved from www.ucsusa.org/about-us

United States Green Building Council (USGBC). (n.d.). *About us*. Washington, DC: Author. Retrieved from https://new.usgbc.org/about

Vilela, M. (2019). *Curriculum vita*. San Jose, Costa Rica: University for Peace. Retrieved from https://upeace.academia.edu/MirianVilela/CurriculumVitae

Wilding, K. (2010). Voluntary organizations and the recession. *Voluntary Sector Review, 1*(1), 97–101. doi:10.1332/204080510X497037

# 9 System leadership for individual sustainability

## Introduction

Although numerous industries, corporations, municipalities, and organizations are acting to create a sustainable future for humankind, organizational action alone is insufficient. As mentioned in Chapter 2, achieving the UN Sustainable Development Goals will require the combined efforts of the public and private sectors, society, and individuals (Iftakhar & Bahauddin, 2018). Organizations are composed of individuals, and it is with individuals that sustainability action must begin. However, individual sustainability is a critical perspective that is often missing from most sustainability conversations (Pappas, 2013). The focus of the previous chapters has been with the leadership of individuals within business, government, academia, and nonprofit and nongovernmental organizations. In this chapter, the focus will shift to individual leadership for sustainability that occurs, and should be occurring, outside of organizations. The role of individuals in sustainability and how to achieve individual sustainability will be discussed, followed by sections describing education and training for individual sustainability. System leadership at the individual level will be examined, along with a global perspective of and the barriers to system leadership at the individual level.

## The role of individuals in a sustainable future

Individuals can assume two roles in the achievement of a sustainable future. First, individuals can act to achieve sustainability within their personal lives, for example by taking individual actions and demonstrating personal leadership for sustainability. Second, individuals can demonstrate system leadership to influence individuals and organizations within their spheres of influence. In addition to being employees, individuals are members of families and institutions such as civic organizations, churches, mosques, synagogues, and homeowner associations. As members of these organizations and groups, individuals can influence sustainability on multiple fronts.

Demonstrating sustainability can begin with simple steps such as recycling, replacing appliances and lighting with energy-efficient devices, and making behavior and lifestyle modifications such as carpooling. Participation and membership in environmental and sustainability organizations, movements, and events are likewise easy sustainability actions. While these actions may not constitute system leadership, they prepare a foundation for influencing sustainability at a systems level. The next and necessary step is for individuals on a broad scale to influence other individuals and organizations to emulate their sustainability behavior.

The greatest opportunity for most individuals to demonstrate system leadership is within the individual's place of employment. The average working adult spends more than 30 hours per week in their vocation, providing the greatest single opportunity for influencing individuals and organizations to participate in sustainability efforts. System leadership can be applied within nearly any organizational role or function, from entry-level unskilled employees to senior management. The influence can be applied internally within the organization as well as externally with customers or suppliers.

Outside the workplace, individuals often belong to religious, civic, athletic, or community organizations. These venues provide opportunities for individuals to influence others, who may in turn exert their influence within their workplace and other organizations. Many religious and charitable organizations have committees consisting of members who volunteer time and expertise assisting the organization with specific tasks, objectives, and initiatives. For example, maintenance or facilities management committees provide oversight and support for governance of facilities, utilities consumption, and other operational functions. Participation in one of these committees might enable an individual system leader to favorably influence energy consumption patterns, which are not only favorable to the environment, but also reduce costs associated with waste and inefficiency for the organization.

Cavagnaro and Curiel (2012) suggest that while the role and possible actions and strategies of business, governments, NGOs, and multilateral institutions are widely discussed, a missing link exists in the sustainability conversation. They suggest that the individual dimension of sustainable development has been overlooked, and that sustainable societies cannot be created without dedicated individuals who accept an active role in the sustainability initiative. Moreover, the focus of business sustainability literature has been primarily with the organizational dimensions of sustainability and not the role of the individual business leader (Aguinis & Glavas, 2012). Because organizations are made up of individuals, it is these individuals who will need to drive organizations and society toward a more equitable and just world. Because business is the largest organizational sector with the most employees globally, individuals within business perform an essential role in any sustainability effort. In an earlier chapter, it was mentioned that for industry to make the transition from the existing linear economy to a circular economy, employees at all levels must be actively involved (Doppelt, 2017). The circular economy is characterized by obtaining maximum natural resource value through long-term retention, followed by recovery and regeneration of consumed products at end of product life

(Andersen, 2007; Waste and Resources Action Programme, 2018). Individual participation is essential for the success of the circular economy or any other collective sustainability initiative.

All global change begins with individuals, because one cannot accomplish for a community what one cannot accomplish for oneself (Pappas, 2013). At present rates of consumption, it will take the resources of three earths to allow the Chinese and Indian population to achieve American consumption levels, and another six earths to allow the remaining population to achieve those levels (Targowski, 2012). Reversal of this trend of ever-increasing resource consumption will require the action of countless individuals who are willing to modify behavior and consumption in a manner that will stabilize demand on our planet's limited capacity. Individual behavior provides the basis for sustainability action and potentially influences our capacity to work collectively to make life-enhancing decisions (Pappas, 2013). Moreover, individual alignment of day-to-day behaviors with values results in broader sustainable community action (Pappas, 2013). While some may question the ability of individuals to have any impact on sustainability, voluntary household behavior changes might reduce US GHG emissions by an estimated 7.4% (Dietz, Gardner, Gillian, Stern, & Vandenbergh, 2009).

While the focus of most industrial ecology literature is with organizational and inter-organizational level connections to industrial and social-ecological systems (Williams, Kennedy, Philipp, & Whiteman, 2017), Ramaswami and colleagues (2012) recognized the significant role of individuals in social-ecological systems. Within the context of urban infrastructure usage and impacts, the researchers acknowledged that social actors are the dominant change agents, and institutions are the mechanisms through which change is achieved. The three primary categories of social actors are individual users, consisting of households and businesses whose demand for utilities and resources necessitates the existence of urban infrastructures; infrastructure designers and operators, who design, operate, and maintain infrastructure; and policy actors, including elected, appointed, and civil government officials and numerous nongovernmental actors, who attempt to influence infrastructure administration (Ramaswami et al., 2012). While the focus of their research was with individual interactions to influence urban sustainability outcomes, the researchers demonstrate the role and importance of individuals in achieving sustainability. Moreover, the descriptions of the primary individual categories characterize how individuals often portray multiple roles within the sustainability conversation (e.g. an individual user might also be employed in an infrastructure career, and simultaneously be a member of a group seeking to influence sustainability policy). The theories influencing these categories of actors will be examined in the section of this chapter entitled "Individual system leadership for sustainability".

## How to achieve individual sustainability

Achieving individual sustainability does not require that individuals sacrifice standard of living. Rather, it requires conscious action to experience quality of life while not adversely impacting the quality of life of other current and future members of society. Living sustainably requires development of harmony, interconnection, and a keen awareness of personal values, beliefs, and behaviors, along with maintenance of control over physical, emotional, social, philosophical, environmental, and intellectual aspects of personal life (Pappas, 2013). The personal habits that reinforce individual sustainability include awareness, ambition, and the ability to intentionally participate in self-development. Individual sustainability also requires a comprehensive, established value system that recognizes the interconnectedness of all planetary ecosystems and our appropriate place in those systems (Pappas, 2013).

Scholars from multiple disciplines have observed the complexity of personality and how it is exhibited, with some suggesting that personality traits operate interdependently to cultivate highly functioning individuals (Pappas, 2013). These scholars recognize that personality is related to multiple factors that constitute a complex system. If individuals appreciate the complexities and interrelationship of their own sustainability frameworks, those individuals might apply a systems perspective to focus on community environmental, social, and economic problems (Dewey, 1910/1997; Durkheim, 1978). However, some individuals might find this response to be challenging, with personal development efforts impeded by personal, career, family, or psychological concerns (Pappas & Pappas, 2011).

Several scholars offer a systems perspective of personality based upon awareness of the interconnectedness of all phenomena (Capra, 1982) and the complexity of awareness, suggesting intelligence and understanding must exist in harmony with behavior and emotions to achieve harmony among objectives, desires, feelings, and experiences (Csikszentmihalyi, 1993). A sustainable personality has been described as demonstrating responsible citizenship, with an attitude of "empathy, relationships, critical skills, co-operation, self-awareness, equality, feeling concerned" (Thoresen, 2004, p. 8). One significant challenge with a systems thinking approach to personality is that the five sustainability contexts (emotional, social, health, economic, and intellectual) "influence each other in complex ways, and understanding these interactions requires increased awareness" (Pappas, 2013, p. 1635). Therefore, understanding individual sustainability requires a conscientious, comprehensive evaluation of a variety of human factors. Because sustainability factors constitute a complex system, a change in one factor may produce an unpredictable or even undesirable change in one or more of the other factors. However, limited research has been performed to understand and assess the reciprocal influences created by these complex systems (Pappas, 2013).

Resource consumption is influenced by the values and actions of individuals (Raivio, 2011); therefore, behavior modification is necessary because individual behavior combines to force collective systems dynamics (Marcus, Kurucz, & Colbert, 2010). Modification of individual consumption habits is essential based on planetary limitations (Vinkhuyzen & Karlsson-Vinkhuyzen, 2014), but existing behavioral modification efforts have been unsuccessful

(Doyle & Davies, 2013). Behavioral incentives that may motivate sustainable consumption are unclear (Vinkhuyzen & Karlsson-Vinkhuyzen, 2014), and existing research has not fully examined how consumption habits are embedded in social-cultural and technological systems (Doyle & Davies, 2013). However, research at the local community level indicates individuals can become collectively involved, and their behavior can be influenced based upon personal connection to their local environment (Nevens, Frantzeskaki, Gorissen, & Loorbach, 2013).

Achieving individual sustainability requires individuals be willing to modify existing consumption behavior, which may be deeply rooted in personality and culture. For example, the American culture is deeply rooted in consumerism, with individuals influenced by advertising and marketing efforts, as well as peer pressure to purchase products that may not be necessary or even desirable. British economist Tim Jackson summarized the individual sustainability dilemma in a TED talk video: "It's a story about us, people, being persuaded to spend money we don't have on things we don't need to create impressions that won't last on people we don't care about" (2010). Individual sustainability can be achieved when individuals begin questioning the reasons behind purchasing decisions and consciously decide to purchase products and services they truly need and desire for improved quality of life. This shift in thinking is contrary to the goals of business, which are to increase revenue and profitability by stimulating demand for products and services. Because individuals comprise the staff and customers of businesses, individuals are the ones capable of shifting the increasing consumption paradigm to a more sustainable worldview.

## Individual system leadership for sustainability

Individuals serve an important role in the achievement of a sustainable future, because all actions and behavioral changes must begin with the individual. The previous sections examined the role of individuals in sustainability and how to achieve individual sustainability. This section considers the role and importance of individuals demonstrating system leadership, absent a formal leadership role. Fulfilling many of the roles described in the previous sections will require individuals who understand systems and can influence across system components and boundaries.

Sustainability is a major challenge and issue, possibly producing a feeling of helplessness in terms of what impact one individual can have. However, history offers many examples of individuals who have demonstrated system leadership for sustainability. US Vice President Al Gore assisted in brining global warming into mainstream conversation through his book *Earth in the Balance* (1992) and subsequent book and documentary movie *An Inconvenient Truth* (2006). Moreover, while individuals such as Al Gore possess considerable power and influence, seemingly powerless individuals are also beginning to achieve results through system leadership. Greta Thunberg is a Swedish student who began protesting about climate change at the Swedish parliament at age 15 (Cohen &

Heberle, 2019), and has influenced student climate change strikes wherein more than one million students in 112 countries participated. Her broad influence among students has become known as the "Greta Thunberg effect" (Nevett, 2019). One individual is clearly capable of influencing across boundaries and systems to achieve sustainability.

African change-maker Farai Mubaiwa is an example of how one individual can exercise system leadership to accomplish sustainability on a major scale. In 2015, when the Charlie Hebdo attacks in Paris gained the attention of the international community, there were a series of terrorist attacks in Baga, Nigeria. However, while Africans took to the streets in support of Paris, no one stood in solidarity with Nigeria. In the aftermath of both events, Farai Mubaiwa and her friend, Reanne Olivier, founded the Africa Matters Initiative to equip African youth, especially girls and women, with the necessary skills and tools to change this narrative Africa Matters Initiative (n.d.). Prior to attending a workshop about sustainability and environmental issues, Mubaiwa believed that Africans had too many problems to be concerned about the environment. Her perception changed when she realized that all of the workshop attendees were "black people whose homes, schools, and health were being destroyed by toxic waste from multinational companies" (United Nations Environment Programme, 2018). She recognized that poor women of color are disproportionately affected by climate change, and that these women were the same women that they were trying to empower through Africa Matters. Currently, Africa Matters focuses on three topics: environmental issues, youth, and gender. Mubaiwa has demonstrated how one individual, not from a wealthy developed nation but from a developing nation, can influence entire systems for sustainability.

Ankit Kawatra was 22 when he quit his corporate job to focus on reducing food waste and hunger in India (United Nations, n.d.). According to Kawatra, "It all started after I attended a large wedding in the capital of India. I was appalled at how much food was going to waste in a country where 194 million are undernourished". In 2014, he founded Feeding India, a nonprofit organization focused on collecting excess food from parties, events, and weddings and redistributing the food to people in need. Feeding India started with five friends helping out, and it has expanded into a network of more than 2,000 volunteers operating in 28 cities across the country and having served more than one million meals. Kawatra and his all-youth team are focused on a sustainable model that continues to expand, with a goal of providing 100 million meals by 2020 (United Nations, n.d.). He is another example of a system leader, who at a young age began influencing systemic change, by transforming how waste food is managed to mitigate poverty in a nation where much of the population lacks access to sufficient, nourishing food.

In a previous section, three categories of social actors that influence change were identified: individual users, infrastructure designers and operators, and policy actors. There are several theories applicable for describing the interdependent behaviors of individuals within the three actor categories (Ramaswami et al., 2012), which are also helpful for understanding how individuals can demonstrate system leadership. For individual users, value belief norms theory proposes norms are shaped by a causal succession from selfless values to assumptions about the benefits of ecological actions, such as recycling program participation (Stern, 2000). However, the theory of social norms (Schultz et al., 2007) suggests peer behavior can influence adoption of environmentally friendly behaviors, regardless of personal values and beliefs. Diffusion of innovation, which examines how, why, and at what rate new ideas spread (Rogers, 2003), has been explored to engage the public through social networks to participate in sustainability strategies (Ramaswami et al., 2012).

Limited literature exists concerning why individual infrastructure designers and operators, such as architects and engineers, are innovative in areas such as green design and operations (Monroe, 2003). Application of club theory revealed several factors contributing to business participation in voluntary environmental programs, such as the potential for additional regulations and the influence of public opinion (Potoski & Prakash, 2009). Regulation and public opinion influence the other two categories of individual actors, further supporting the need for interactions among all three categories of actors as an important catalyst for change (Ramaswami et al., 2012).

At the local government level, the institutional collective action (ICA) framework (Feiock, 2007) might illustrate why policy actors develop cooperative agreements for environmental services such as water treatment and waste management, shaping the cross-boundary nature of municipal infrastructures (Ramaswami et al., 2012). At the national level, multiple streams theory was used to explain the adoption of cap-and-trade regulations in Germany (Brunner, 2008), wherein public opinion, problem definition, and policy solutions were aligned, resulting in a "window of opportunity" for policy change (Ramaswami et al., 2012). The advocacy coalition framework (ACF) provides a subtler perspective of the interactions between multiple policy actors (Sabatier, 1988) and has been used to explain how these actors participate in coalitions to influence policy change (Ramaswami et al., 2012).

The examples in this chapter demonstrate how one individual can impact entire systems for sustainability. The theoretical content describes how individual members of three categories of social actors influence broad systemic change. The ability of one individual to have an impact should never be underestimated. Having demonstrated the potential for and impact of individuals as system leaders for sustainability, the following section will examine how to develop system leadership for sustainability.

## Development of system leadership for individual sustainability

Because individual action is essential for sustainability, individual system leadership must be encouraged and developed. Chapter 3 described the system leadership skills, characteristics, and competencies necessary for system leadership, and Chapter 4 included information and training resources for their development. While the focus of this previous content was with development of system leaders within organizations, the content is likewise appropriate for development of individuals desiring to demonstrate system leadership absent any specific organized setting. Some of the previous content will be discussed in this section within the context of individual system leadership.

Research supports the importance of assisting sustainability program participants with making a personal connection with sustainability (Haney, Pope, & Arden, 2018). The personal component exists in all learning outcomes and is an essential component of personal connection, linking understanding with action. Allowing individuals to personally explore their relationships with sustainability issues and between potential sustainability solutions and their obligations with those solutions is essential (Haney et al., 2018). This personal focus connects with the *attitude-behavior gap*, which is often applied to consumer behavior, and describes the condition in which consumers do not purchase more sustainable products and services despite having adequate knowledge and the best of intentions to do so (Haney et al., 2018). Research on this phenomenon reveals the significance of emotional involvement and moral obligation to close the gap (Antimova, Nawijn, & Peeters, 2012; Kollmuss & Agyeman, 2002). Making sustainability personal establishes a foundation for individuals to feel committed to and empowered to act for sustainability within their organizations (Haney et al., 2018). This individual commitment and empowerment act has been clearly demonstrated by individuals such as Greta Thunberg, Farai Mubaiwa, and Ankit Kawatra.

Cavagnaro and Curiel (2012) developed the three levels of sustainability (TLS) framework, which addresses at least some of the weaknesses of a fragmented approach to sustainability. The TLS framework encompasses individual, organizational, and societal levels, providing a roadmap for development of the types of leaders required to achieve comprehensive sustainable development. Individuals exist in organizations, and organizations exist in society, and individuals are the creators of ideas and ideals and the recipients of process outcomes. The fundamental objective of sustainability is improved quality of life for all of humankind (Cavagnaro & Curiel, 2012). Individuals are essential for achievement of sustainability on a broad scale.

Human development theories reveal that individuals have the capability to accept values that go beyond the material values related to "me" (Cavagnaro & Curiel, 2012). This is a complex process where decreasing egocentrism is accompanied by increasing compassion, a process that is mirrored in the three dimensions of the inner level of the TLS. "Care for me" relates to the value of the individual human life. "Care for me and you" relates to the value of relationships. "Care for all" relates to the value of all living creatures and the universe. Creating value on the three dimensions of care characterizes leadership for sustainability on the individual level, making each person a potential leader with a unique way to participate in the transition toward sustainability (Cavagnaro & Curiel, 2012). The leadership for sustainability conversation must begin with the individual and determine the values necessary to influence individuals, organizations, and societies to achieve sustainability and improved quality of life for all (Cavagnaro & Curiel, 2012).

Development of leadership for sustainability requires transformation of perspectives and behaviors, beginning with profound personal change within the individual. Leaders who have realized their inherent capacity to care for themselves, their constituency, and others are well-positioned to transition toward sustainability and become sustainability leaders (Cavagnaro & Curiel, 2012). These concentric levels of care influence individuals to act selflessly to contribute to the broader benefit of humankind, because their desire to care for humankind begins with self-care. The philosopher Eric Fromm (1956) proposed that one cannot love others until one loves oneself, and that selfishness is the result of not loving oneself. By caring for oneself, an individual may be inclined to care for others as a result. This level of care and love may be channeled through system leadership to influence others to care and be cared for, resulting in a collective, collaborative effort to accomplish sustainability. Greta Thunberg, Farai Mubaiwa, and Ankit Kawatra clearly channel these levels of love to influence sustainability on a systemic level.

## Global perspective of system leadership for individual sustainability

While the average individual may believe they are unable to influence sustainability beyond their local community or nation, most individuals likely possess some degree of global influence. Social media has drastically reduced national and global boundaries, enabling individuals to connect and reconnect with friends, family, and colleagues, regardless of geographic location. While global communication prior to the 1980s consisted of expensive telephone calls or postal letters requiring days or weeks to reach their destination, subsequent generations have enjoyed instant global communication through email, social media, and numerous smart phone applications. While social media, the Internet, and mass communication are more prevalent in developed nations, their use is being rapidly proliferated throughout the globe.

Consumers regularly purchase products that have been grown, manufactured, or assembled in multiple nations. Through online purchasing platforms, these consumers influence and participate in the global economy, often without leaving their homes or offices. Individual consumers can influence multinational corporations and entire economies by demanding sustainable products and services, refusing to purchase unsustainable products and services, and changing consumption patterns to reduce the adverse impacts of their behavior on disadvantaged populations. While this suggestion may seem grandiose, it is worth repeating that all change begins at the individual level. Maurice Schweitzer, a professor of operations and information management at the Wharton School at the University of Pennsylvania, noted that very few boycotts have produced change. However, while noting that "[b]oycotts are rarely the precipitating factor for change", he has suggested that boycotts "bring attention to an issue and signal the magnitude and intensity with which a group feels a particular way" (Livingston, 2018). The actions and influence of individuals may bring sufficient attention to the systemic changes needed to achieve sustainability. The momentum currently exists, with numerous individuals joining the sustainability movement daily.

The transition from a linear economy to a circular economy provides an avenue for individuals to exercise sustainability system leadership. In a traditional linear economy, natural resources are extracted, produced, or constructed into a product, transported to distribution centers and ultimately retailers, consumed by consumers, and disposed of at end of life. Products provided by the linear economy often travel thousands of miles, with beneficiaries in wealthier societies frequently receiving products and profits at the expense of environments and societies in poorer societies. In a circular economy, the end-of-life disposal is converted to reuse, recycling, refurbishment, and reintroduction. Moreover, production and consumption processes are modified to encourage efficient, local production and consumption. However, reduced transportation distance does not necessarily suggest that a product is sustainable. Products assembled or manufactured in developing nations provide employment and often reduce demand on valuable local resources. The objective of the circular economy is for durable, reusable products to be produced with the least environmental and societal impact.

Individuals occupy a significant role in the transition to a circular economy, because the transition requires changes in individual behavior. Individual choices, when combined, influence the behavior of manufacturers of products. When demand for a product declines, manufacturers reduce production. Individuals can demand sustainable products from a circular economy, supplemented by influencing others to take similar action. This local action can have global ramifications, because many of the products purchased by consumers originate or were at least partially assembled in other nations. From a system leadership perspective, individuals can choose to like, endorse, review, or recommend sustainable products and services on social media. While the sustainability impact of one individual may seem trivial, the potential for one individual to influence systemic change was acknowledged in a previous section of this chapter. The following section describes the barriers and challenges faced by individuals seeking to exercise system leadership for sustainability.

## Barriers and challenges to system leadership at the individual level

Individuals seeking to exercise system leadership outside of an organizational setting will face barriers and challenges to their actions and influence. Many individuals believe that leaders are born and not made, evidenced by the phrase "natural born leader". Moreover, many individuals who hold positions of leadership might deny that they possess the ability to lead beyond their immediate system or circle of influence. System leadership not only requires the ability to understand and influence systems, but also acceptance that the individual possesses the ability to influence across boundaries. However, because the subject of individual sustainability can be contentious, individuals often struggle with aligning actual behaviors with their admirable sustainability values (Pappas, 2013).

Two barriers exist to individual-level system leadership: the individual and the people whom the individual is trying to influence. Individuals who do not occupy formal positions of authority may feel they are not capable of leading or qualified to lead. Their lack of self-confidence may consciously or subconsciously inhibit their success. Likewise, the people whom the individual is trying to influence must accept the influence of the leader, a process referred to as followership (Northouse, 2018). However, some individuals do not like being told what to do and may be especially resistant when the person leading possesses no formal authority.

Individual system leadership requires the willingness of others to be influenced by someone who may not possess a formal leadership role and may represent a sector or viewpoint outside that of the follower. In these circumstances, followership is as important, if not more important than leadership. Followership is divided into two broad categories: role-based and relational-based (Uhl-Bien, Riggio, Lowe, & Carsten, 2014). The role-based perspective focuses on the hierarchical roles of leaders and followers in traditional organizational settings. Relational-based followership focuses on the interpersonal processes of influence and the other person's response to that influence. Because many of the scenarios in which an individual may seek to demonstrate system leadership are not traditional hierarchical or organizational structures, it is important for the individual system leader to focus on relational-based followership.

There are several new followership perspectives that may be useful for individual system leadership on an informal basis. These include recognition that followers are the ones who actually do the work, should work in the best interest of the organization, can challenge leaders, support the leader, and learn from the leader (Northouse, 2018). Influencing followers who operate outside the authority of the leader requires collaborative and interpersonal skills, which are possessed by system leaders and have been discussed in previous chapters.

## Conclusion

History contains countless examples of solitary individuals accomplishing significant social change, both positive and negative. Mahatma Gandhi inspired hundreds of millions of Indians to achieve independence from Great Britain without one shot being fired. Martin Luther King Jr. inspired a civil rights movement, which while ultimately costing his life, resulted in significant improvements in the rights of minorities in the United States. Each signifies the ability of one individual to influence a broad range of stakeholders across established boundaries and systems for positive societal outcomes. Such broad and significant change is likewise necessary for humankind to achieve sustainability, reversing the damaging effects of centuries of unsustainable behavior. This change may be initiated by individuals who are capable of influencing across boundaries, absent any formal authority and often absent any formal organization. While this change may occur within organizations, governments, and the public and private sectors, it will and must also occur outside of organizational structures and bureaucracies. The power of one individual should not be underestimated, and when that power is exerted across boundaries and systems, the energy and influence are contagious. This chapter contained several examples of individuals who demonstrated system leadership to achieve significant social change and sustainability outcomes.

Embarking on a mission of individual system leadership for sustainability requires an individual move beyond tactical behavior to more strategic sustainability. While it is important for individuals to "walk the walk" by engaging in sustainable behavior, it is equally important that individual leaders embrace sustainability from a systemic, boundaryless perspective. The actions of an individual are important and should not be underestimated. Moreover, the actions of a collective group of individuals will have greater impact. Individual system leaders must continually seek avenues to introduce sustainability into conversations and organizations. Numerous opportunities exist, especially when sustainability is viewed as more than an environmental issue. The social and economic dimensions of sustainability provide additional opportunities for individuals to introduce and influence sustainability. Changing entire systems requires changing the context within which individuals operate (Fullan, 2005). Although changing context requires time and cumulative effort, once in motion, context change demonstrates a self-generating ability to continue (Fullan, 2005). However, whatever level of change is desired, collective change always begins with the individual.

## Case study

Florida Gulf Coast University (FGCU) is located in Southwest Florida between the Florida Everglades and the Gulf of Mexico. One-half of the 800-acre campus is preserved or restored nature, and both the campus and region serve as a living laboratory where life-enhancing discoveries are made (Florida Gulf Coast University, 2019a). FGCU's comprehensive undergraduate and graduate programs prepare students to excel and innovate, with students, alumni, faculty, and staff actively engaged and environmentally conscious citizens. They serve their communities and inspire others by leading, doing, and making a difference (Florida Gulf Coast University, 2019a). Since classes were first offered in 1997, enrollment has grown to 15,000, attracting students from 45 states and more than 85 countries, with student diversity increasing from 12.6% minority in 1997 to 30% in 2019 (Florida Gulf Coast University, 2019a).

FGCU has embedded sustainability in their mission statement, which states, "FGCU emphasizes innovative, student-centered teaching and learning, promotes and practices environmental sustainability, embraces diversity, nurtures community partnerships, values public service, encourages civic responsibility, and cultivates habits of lifelong learning and the discovery of new knowledge" (Florida Gulf Coast University, 2019b). The mission is achieved through the *University Colloquium: A Sustainable Future*, which is a three credit hour interdisciplinary course which all undergraduate students are required to take prior to graduation (Florida Gulf Coast University, 2019c). The colloquium course goals are:

- To provide a "sense of place" and an understanding of the unique ecological features of the environment of which you are a part;
- To assist in developing an ecological perspective and a commitment to community awareness and involvement in order for students to know the issues related to economic, social, and ecological sustainability, analyze and evaluate ecological issues locally and globally, participate in projects requiring awareness and/or analysis of ecological and environmental issues;
- To provide experiences to assist in moving toward achieving the university learning goals of effective communication skills and critical thinking skills as well as the university's stated mission of "practicing and promoting environmental sustainability and "encouraging civic responsibility";
- To enable a practical understanding of sustainability, of environmental education, and of ecological literacy.

(Florida Gulf Coast University, 2019c)

The student learning outcomes include demonstrating an understanding of environmental issues; critically analyzing environmental issues from economic, social, political, and ecological perspectives; describing the unique ecological features of Southwest Florida and analyzing the region's unique environmental and ecological challenges; and demonstrating a practical understanding of sustainability, sense of place, and ecological literacy (Florida Gulf Coast University, 2019c).

FGCU has structured the curricula to emphasize the interdisciplinary nature of knowledge and to provide students with the ability to think in whole systems. Although the colloquium is a writing-intensive course, one course component requires students complete ten hours of natural environment-related service-learning (Florida Gulf Coast University, 2019c). FGCU is committed to making environmental education an integral part of their identity, because the environment applies to our entire human and natural living space and interrelationships and is therefore relevant to all disciplines and professions. In the colloquium, students are not introduced to FGCU values, they participate in them (Florida Gulf Coast University, 2019c). While FGCU does not specifically include system leadership in the colloquium course, several system leadership skills and core competencies are clearly present within the curriculum.

## Case study reflection questions

1 What role do you think the sustainability mission of FGCU serves in attracting students who already have an interest in sustainability? Do you

think the colloquium impacts the sustainability perspective of students who are not enrolled in environmental majors? Why or why not?

2 Do you think the mandatory requirement of the colloquium course contributes to individual sustainability behavior that might not otherwise occur? Why or why not?

3 How do you think the colloquium course at FGCU contributes to development of system leadership at an individual level? How effective do you think the colloquium course is in developing system leaders with students who are enrolled in non-environmental majors?

## Chapter reflection questions

1 What actions can you take as an individual to influence sustainability within your circle of influence? To what organizations do you belong that might benefit by your influence?

2 What system leadership skills do you currently possess, and how could you use them to promote sustainability? What system leadership skills that you are lacking could be easily learned?

3 To what organizations do you belong in which you could apply system leadership for sustainability, and how? What organizations or areas could you potentially join or become involved in which you could exercise individual system leadership for sustainability?

## References

Africa Matters Initiative. (n.d.). *About us.* Johannesburg, South Africa: Author. Retrieved from www.africamattersinitiative.com/about-us

Aguinis, H., & Glavas, A. (2012). What we know and don't know about corporate social responsibility: A review and research agenda. *Journal of Management, 38*(4), 932–968. doi:10.1177/0149206311436079

Andersen, M. S. (2007). An introductory note on the environmental economics of the circular economy. *Sustainability Science, 2*(1), 133–140. doi:10.1007/s11625-006-0013-6

Antimova, R., Nawijn, J., & Peeters, P. (2012). The awareness/attitude-gap in sustainable tourism: A theoretical perspective. *Tourism Review, 67*(3), 7–16. doi:10.1108/16605371211259795

Brunner, S. (2008). Understanding policy change: Multiple streams and emissions trading in Germany. *Global Environmental Change, 18*(3), 501–507. doi:10.1016/j.gloenvcha.2008.05.003

Capra, F. (1982). *The turning point.* New York, NY: Bantam Books.

Cavagnaro, E., & Curiel, G. (2012). *The three levels of sustainability.* Sheffield, England: Greenleaf Publishing.

Cohen, I., & Heberle, J. (2019, March 19). Youth demand climate action in global school strike. *Harvard Political Review.* Retrieved from http://harvardpolitics.com/united-states/youth-demand-climate-action-in-global-school-strike/

Csikszentmihalyi, M. (1993). *The evolving self.* New York, NY: Harper Collins.

Dewey, J. (1910/1997). *The influence of Darwin on philosophy.* New York, NY: Prometheus Books.

Dietz, T., Gardner, G., Gillian, J., Stern, P., & Vandenbergh, M. (2009). Household actions can provide a behavioral wedge to rapidly reduce U. S. carbon emissions. *Proceedings of the National Academy of Sciences of the United States of America, 106*(44), 18452–18456. doi:10.1073/pnas.0908738106

Doppelt, B. (2017). *Leading change toward sustainability: A change-management guide for business, government and civil society*. Abingdon, England: Routledge.

Doyle, R., & Davies, A. R. (2013). Towards sustainable household consumption: Exploring a practice oriented, participatory backcasting approach for sustainable home heating practices in Ireland. *Journal of Cleaner Production, 48*, 260–271. doi:10.1016/j.jclepro.2012.12.015

Durkheim, E. (1978). *On institutional analysis*. Chicago, IL: The University of Chicago Press.

Feiock, R. C. (2007). Rational choice and regional governance. *Journal of Urban Affairs, 29*(1), 47–63. doi:10.1111/j.1467-9906.2007.00322.x

Florida Gulf Coast University. (2019a). *About FGCU*. Fort Myers, FL: Author. Retrieved from www.fgcu.edu/about/

Florida Gulf Coast University. (2019b). *Mission*. Fort Myers, FL: Author. Retrieved from www.fgcu.edu/about/#Mission

Florida Gulf Coast University. (2019c). *University colloquium 2019–2020 catalog year*. Fort Myers, FL: Author. Retrieved from https://www2.fgcu.edu/Catalog/colloquium.asp

Fromm, E. (1956). *The art of loving: An enquiry into the nature of love*. New York, NY: Harper & Row.

Fullan, M. (2005). *Leadership and sustainability: System thinkers in action*. London, England: Sage Publications.

Gore, A. (1992). *Earth in the balance: Ecology and the human spirit*. New York, NY: Plume.

Gore, A. (2006). *An inconvenient truth: The planetary emergency of global warming and what we can do about it*. Emmaus, PA: Rodale.

Haney, A. B., Pope, J., & Arden, Z. (2018). Making it personal: Developing sustainability leaders in business. *Organization & Environment*. doi:10.1177/1086026618806201

Iftakhar, N., & Bahauddin, K. M. (2018, January 10). *Why leadership is essential for achieving Sustainable Development Goals*. Seoul, South Korea: International Policy Digest. Retrieved from https://intpolicydigest.org/2018/01/10/why-leadership-is-essential-for-achieving-sustainable-development-goals/

Jackson, T. (2010, October 7). *Tim Jackson: An economic reality check* [video file]. Retrieved from www.ted.com/talks/tim_jackson_s_economic_reality_check/transcript?language=en

Kollmuss, A., & Agyeman, J. (2002). Mind the gap: Why do people act environmentally and what are the barriers to pro-environmental behavior? *Environmental Education Research, 8*(3), 239–260. doi:10.1080/13504620220145401

Livingston, M. (2018, March 1). *Here's when boycotts have worked: And when they haven't*. Los Angeles, CA: Los Angeles Times. Retrieved from www.latimes.com/nation/la-na-boycotts-history-20180228-htmlstory.html

Marcus, J., Kurucz, E. C., & Colbert, B. A. (2010). Conceptions of the business-society-nature interface: Implications for management scholarship. *Business & Society, 49*(3), 402–438. doi:10.1177/0007650310368827

Monroe, M. C. (2003). Two avenues for encouraging conservation behaviors. *Human Ecology Review, 10*(2), 429–434. Retrieved from www.jstor.org

Nevens, F., Frantzeskaki, N., Gorissen, L., & Loorbach, D. (2013). Urban transition labs: Co-creating transformative action for sustainable cities. *Journal of Cleaner Production, 50*, 111–122. doi:10.1016/j.jclepro.2012.12.001

Nevett, J. (2019, May 3). *The Greta effect? Meet the schoolgirl climate warriors*. London, England: British Broadcasting Corporation. Retrieved from www.bbc.com/news/world-48114220

Northouse, P. G. (2018). *Leadership: Theory and practice* (8th ed.). Thousand Oaks, CA: Sage Publications.

Pappas, E. C. (2013, October). Individual sustainability: Preliminary research. In *Frontiers in education conference, 2013 IEEE* (pp. 1631–1636). Oklahoma City, OK: Institute of Electrical and Electronics Engineers.

Pappas, E. C., & Pappas, J. (2011). A dispositional behavioral approach to teaching cognitive processes that support effective thought and action. *Innovative Higher Education, 36*(5), 359–372. doi:10.1007/s10755-011-9178-8

Potoski, M., & Prakash, A. (2009). *Voluntary programs: A club theory perspective.* Cambridge, MA: The MIT Press.

Raivio, K. (2011). Sustainability as an educational agenda. *Journal of Cleaner Production, 19*(16), 1906–1907. doi:10.1016/j.jclepro.2011.07.009

Ramaswami, A., Weible, C., Main, D., Heikkila, T., Siddiki, S., Duvall, A., . . . Bernard, M. (2012). A social-ecological-infrastructural systems framework for interdisciplinary study of sustainable city systems: An integrative curriculum across seven major disciplines. *Journal of Industrial Ecology, 16*(6), 801–813. doi:10.1111/j.1530-9290.2012.00566.x

Rogers, E. M. (2003). *Diffusion of innovations* (5th ed.). New York, NY: Free Press.

Sabatier, P. (1988). An advocacy coalition framework of policy change and the role of policy-oriented learning therein. *Policy Sciences, 21*, 129–168. doi:10.1007/BF00136406

Schultz, P. W., Schultz, P. W., Nolan, J. M., Cialdini, R. B., Goldstein, N. J., & Griskevicius, V. (2007). The constructive, destructive, and reconstructive power of social norms. *Psychological Science, 18*(5), 429–434. doi:10.1111/j.1467-9280.2007.01917.x

Stern, P. C. (2000). Toward a coherent theory of environmentally significant behavior. *Journal of Social Issues, 56*(3), 407–424. doi:10.1111/0022-4537.00175

Targowski, A. (2012). Spirituality 2.0: A condition for a wise civilization. *Dialogue and Universalism, 22*(2), 133–143. Retrieved from www.researchgate.net

Thoresen, V. W. (2004). *Cultivating sustainable lifestyles.* UNESCO, IEF Conference: At the University of Thessaloniki, Greece, April.

Uhl-Bien, M., Riggio, R. E., Lowe, K. B., & Carsten, M. K. (2014). Followership theory: A review and research agenda. *The Leadership Quarterly, 25*(1), 83–104. doi:10.1016/j.leaqua.2013.11.007

United Nations. (n.d.). *Young leaders.* New York, NY: Office of the Secretary-General's Envoy on Youth. Retrieved from www.un.org/youthenvoy/youngleadersmeettheleaders/

United Nations Environment Programme. (2018). *We are the ones we have been waiting for.* Nairobi, Kenya: United Nations Environment Programme. Retrieved from https://web.unep.org/youngchampions/stories/we-are-ones-we-have-been-waiting

Vinkhuyzen, O. M., & Karlsson-Vinkhuyzen, S. I. (2014). The role of moral leadership for sustainable production and consumption. *Journal of Cleaner Production, 63*, 102–113. doi:10.1016/j.jclepro.2013.06.045

Waste and Resources Action Programme. (2018). *WRAP and the circular economy.* Banbury, Oxon, England: Author. Retrieved from www.wrap.org.uk/about-us/about/wrap-and-circular-economy.

Williams, A., Kennedy, S., Philipp, F., & Whiteman, G. (2017). Systems thinking: A review of sustainability management research. *Journal of Cleaner Production, 148*, 866–881. doi:10.1016/j.jclepro.2017.02.002

# 10 Future of system leadership for sustainability

## Introduction

Numerous individuals, organizations, and communities are currently engaged in individual and collective activities to achieve a more sustainable future (Burns, Diamond-Vaught, & Bauman, 2015). Although society is experiencing the increasingly adverse effects of environmental and social injustices, more individuals are embracing sustainability, and an increasing number of businesses and organizations are incorporating sustainability into their mission, vision, and operations. Many of these sustainability actors accomplish their work through decentralized and non-structured leadership, by emphasizing innovation and creativity while focusing on issues that are important to them (Hawken, 2007). While many of these contemporary sustainability leaders are unaware of the term system leadership, they have become exemplary system leadership practitioners.

In the preceding chapters, I described system leadership, explained why it is appropriate for sustainability, and examined system leadership for a sustainable future within several organizational contexts. In this text, I proposed application of the system leadership model as a framework for the realization of sustainability. In this chapter, I will summarize the key concepts and themes of the preceding chapters and suggest future trends, research opportunities, and recommendations.

## Summary

The text began in Chapter 1 with an introduction to system leadership, the origins of system leadership, and recent system leadership literature. A system leader is a unique individual capable of seeing and comprehending the larger system and catalyzing collective leadership to proactively co-create the future (Senge, Hamilton, & Kania, 2015). System leaders influence stakeholders across boundaries inside and outside of their organizations, industries, and sectors. The subsequent sections described systems theory, systems thinking, and systems thinking as a foundation for system leadership. The sections that followed described systems thinking and sustainability, system leadership for sustainability, system leadership from a global perspective, and barriers to system leadership implementation.

In Chapter 2 I explored why system leadership is an appropriate method for providing sustainability leadership and identified the benefits of the development and application of system leadership to promote a sustainable future. System leadership for sustainability was proposed to be based on a natural environmental structure, transcending boundaries and barriers, and a demonstrating a holistic perspective. These propositions were explored in depth, providing a foundation for the proposed system leadership for sustainability model on which the remainder of this text is based.

In Chapter 3, I examined the characteristics, skills, and core competencies of system leaders. The core competencies of system leadership were described within the context of the three system leadership propositions outlined in Chapter 2. According to Timmins (2015), system leaders are distinguished from organizational leaders by their experience "working across" services and organizations, especially in situations involving considerable complexity. The eight elements of system leadership as identified by Fullan (2005) were described: public service with a moral purpose; commitment to changing context at all levels; lateral capacity building through network; new vertical co-dependent relationships; deep learning; dual commitment to short-term and long-term results; cyclical energizing; and the long lever of leadership. System leadership for creating change was discussed, and the chapter concluded with an examination of the various leadership styles appropriate for system leadership.

Chapter 4 explored how to develop the core competencies of system leadership within the context of the three system leadership propositions outlined in Chapter 2. This chapter built upon the tools proposed by Senge et al. (2015) and Fullan (2004) by examining system leadership methods and tools most appropriate for addressing sustainability issues among a broad base of diverse stakeholders, with diverse perspectives of environmental issues and priorities. Methods, strategies, and tools for developing system leadership were examined, along with several leadership theories and styles appropriate for system leadership. The global aspects of and barriers and challenges to system leadership development were also explored.

Chapter 5 marked a transition from a foundational study of system leadership to the practical application, by introducing the role and importance of sustainability in business. This chapter provided examples of how system leadership has been and can be applied within business to achieve sustainable outcomes. While examples of system leaders within existing literature is limited to the field of education (e.g. Fullan, 2005), many examples exist of individuals demonstrating sustainability system leadership within the private sector, without awareness that the leadership method being used is system leadership. Systems thinking and system leadership in business were broadly examined, along with a specific focus on system leadership in project management. Global perspectives of and barriers to system leadership for sustainability in business were also examined, and the chapter concluded with a personal interview summary of a global sustainability system leader within the field of urban development.

The focus of Chapter 6 was with system leadership in academia. This chapter provided examples of how system leadership has been and can be applied within academia to achieve sustainable outcomes. Systems thinking in educational facilities and curricula were discussed, followed by education for sustainability content, including business sustainability education. The role and importance of system leadership in sustainability research was also examined. Early system leadership literature in the field of education was explored, which while not focused on environmental sustainability is still relevant to the sustainability conversation. The development of system leadership for academia was discussed, along with global perspectives of and barriers to system leadership in academia. The chapter concluded with a personal interview summary of a sustainability system leader in the field of higher education.

The focus of Chapter 7 was system leadership for sustainability in government and intergovernmental organizations (IGOs). This chapter provided examples of how system leadership has been and can be applied within government to achieve sustainable outcomes. Examples were provided of individuals demonstrating sustainability system leadership in the public sector, without awareness that the leadership method being used is system leadership. The chapter began with descriptions of government and IGOs and their roles in sustainability, followed by a description of the role of systems thinking in both types of organizations. One section of this chapter examined urban sustainability and the appropriateness of system leadership for development of urban sustainability. Finally, global perspectives of and barriers and challenges to system leadership in government and IGOs were explored. The chapter concluded with a personal interview summary of a system leader who was formerly employed in a sustainability leadership role at the United Nations.

In Chapter 8 I examined system leadership in nonprofit and nongovernmental organizations (NGOs). This chapter provided examples of how system leadership has been and can be applied within nonprofit and nongovernmental organizations to achieve sustainable outcomes. Examples were provided of individuals demonstrating sustainability system leadership in the nonprofit and NGO sectors, without awareness that the leadership method being used is system leadership. The role of both organizations in sustainability was described, and global perspectives of and barriers and challenges to system leadership in nonprofit and NGOs were examined.

In Chapter 9 I explored system leadership for individual sustainability. The role of individuals in sustainability and how to achieve individual sustainability were considered. Examples of several individuals who have demonstrated system leadership for sustainability were identified. I also examined how to perform education and training for individual sustainability. System leadership for individual sustainability was then examined, followed by the global perspective of individual system leadership for sustainability and barriers to development of individual system leadership for sustainability. In this final chapter, we will discuss and summarize system leadership, including strengths and weaknesses, and the themes resulting from the personal interviews included in this book. Future recommendations, research, and trends will also be considered.

## Discussion

Sustainability scholars now widely acknowledge the view that sustainable development is a "process" and not a "project" (Nabavi, Daniell, & Najafi, 2016). Sustainability is not an outcome that can be achieved by following instructions on a blueprint or making specific decisions (Voss, Bauknecht, & Kemp, 2006). Sustainability is a pathway (Scoones et al., 2007) containing numerous learning cycles and an uncertain outcome. The learning process is systemic – for an organism or system to survive, it must learn from previous actions and from its environment. Sustainability is the pathway the human system must follow to survive. From this perspective, sustainability is the preferred state of being for the human system, and sustainable development is the process of achieving that state or condition (Nabavi et al., 2016).

We currently exist in an increasingly unsustainable world, in which sustainability is manifest as a complicated multi-stakeholder concern (Barile, Orecchini, Saviano, & Farioli, 2018). The complexity of sustainability is becoming increasingly difficult to address with our conventional response capabilities. The challenge for society is how to approach complexity in the journey toward a sustainable world that must be grounded in inclusion and equity (Espejo, 2018). Sustainability must explain the individual and collective social, environmental, and economic impacts of choices and actions through a systems perspective appreciation of the essence and interdependence of natural and artificial systems (Crofton, 2000).

Gibson (2005) suggested that because the traditional approach to policy, governance, and management is functional and expertise-focused, leaders often do not comprehend the ramifications of seemingly unrelated ecological, social, and economic evaluations and reports. This functional approach has limited development of an integrated sustainability measurement model (Davidson & Venning, 2011). Moreover, the functional approach satisfies existing stakeholders, because sustainability operationalization requires connecting activities that are nonexistent in the prevailing model (Spangenberg, Pfahl, & Dellar, 2002). Sustainability is a complicated phenomenon to evaluate and measure, a task that has become more complicated in recent decades with the integration of social, economic, and environmental attributes of sustainability (Davidson & Venning, 2011).

Individuals, organizations, governments, and societies can no longer operate from a business-as-usual approach. Sustainability is a systemic issue, and entire systems must be redesigned and reorganized to protect our present delicate socio-ecological systems. Leaders from all sectors are emerging, and will continue to emerge, intent on influencing the change necessary for human and planetary survival. While these leaders may have never heard of system leadership, they possess and are using the characteristics, core competencies, and skills described within this text. Hopefully, this text will inspire future system leaders and influence scholars to expand and enhance the system leadership for sustainability model proposed and examined in the previous nine chapters.

## Strengths of system leadership

There are several strengths with the system leadership model. Because sustainability is a system-level issue, a systems-based approach is most appropriate for addressing the challenges posed by sustainability. System leadership provides a model for influencing actors across multiple systems toward achievement of a common objective. An increasing amount of academic and practical literature is emerging related to the applicability of system leadership for broad societal-level issues and problems. The system leadership model has been examined and applied within several industries within the context of other societal problems and issues. Personal interviews included in this text supported the applicability of system leadership to sustainability within several sectors. Moreover, sustainability is an issue impacting every sector and system and therefore requires solutions and methods that will address sustainability from a multi-faceted systems perspective.

## Weaknesses of system leadership

There are several weaknesses with the system leadership for sustainability model. This model has only been consciously applied and examined at the industry or sector level within the education and healthcare fields. The application of system leadership within the context of broad social issues is supported in the literature (Senge et al., 2015), and within the context of sustainability is supported by interview findings in this text. However, literature examining system leadership for sustainability is limited, with existing research focusing on system leadership for the sustainability of organizations or activities, not the Brundtland definition of sustainability. Empirical research will be necessary to demonstrate the appropriateness and effectiveness of system leadership for sustainability across all sectors, and support, enhance, or revise the model proposed in this text.

## Personal interview themes and findings

Interviews were conducted with three system leaders in the process of writing this text: Gerben van Straaten, CEO and founder of the sustainable urban development corporation World of Wal<u>a</u>s (Chapter 5); Robert Franco, Director, Office for Institutional Effectiveness at Kapiʻolani Community College in Honolulu, Hawaii (Chapter 6); and Florencia Librizzi, former Senior Manager, PRME, at the United Nations Global Compact Office (Chapter 7). More detailed interview content is included in the chapters containing the interview summaries. While interviewing three subjects provides limited qualitative data, several common themes and findings emerged, which helped enhance understanding of the phenomenon and therefore deserve summary in this final chapter. Future researchers may expand upon the themes identified in the interviews and the theoretical claims proposed within this text.

The participants were asked the following seven questions:

1 What was your knowledge of the term system leadership prior to being contacted by this author?
2 How do you apply system leadership in the context of sustainability?
3 What skills, competencies, or abilities enable you to see and comprehend the larger system?
4 What skills, competencies, or abilities enable you to catalyze collective leadership to proactively co-create the future?
5 What barriers or challenges do you face when attempting to influence across boundaries and systems?
6 How would you recommend developing system leadership?
7 Is there any other information you would like to share about system leadership that we have not already discussed?

Prior to the interviews, each of the three participants described having some understanding of what the term system leadership described.

Several common system leadership themes were identified by the interviewees, with the following themes identified by all three participants:

- The importance of understanding systems and how they function.
- Their leadership was influenced by culture, community, or family.
- The importance of human, interpersonal communication skills.
- The importance of ethics and morals in leadership.

The following system leadership themes were identified by at least two of the participants:

- Education and careers have become "siloed", emphasizing the need for an interdisciplinary background and approach.
- The need for mentoring to develop future system leaders.
- The need for collaboration.
- The need for inclusivity and diversity.
- The desire for change.

Overall, the themes identified during the interviews, and the corresponding comments, supported the literature regarding leadership for sustainability core competencies, system leader core capabilities, and system leadership elements. The common core competencies of leaders for sustainability were previously identified as strategic thinking, systems thinking, and interpersonal competence (Ploum, Blok, Lans, & Omta, 2018). Strategic thinking and interpersonal competence or skills were both identified by all three of the interview participants. The core capabilities of system leaders were previously identified as the ability to see the overall system, cultivate reflection and more innovative conversations, and transform the collective attention away from reactive problem solving to co-creation of the future (Senge et al., 2015). The ability to see the overall system was cited by all three participants, and co-creation of the future is supported by two of the participants having cited the need for collaboration. Fullan (2005) described the eight elements of system leadership within the context of education as public service with a moral purpose; commitment to changing context at all levels; lateral capacity building through network; new vertical co-dependent relationships; deep learning; dual commitment to short-term and long-term results; cyclical energizing; and the long lever of leadership. The role of ethics or morals and the desire for change were cited by two of the interviewees, and lateral capacity building through network and new vertical co-dependent relationships are supported by two of the interviewee comments regarding collaboration.

Overall, the common themes identified during the interviews, and the corresponding comments, supported the three propositions in this text regarding system leadership for sustainability. The first proposition is that sustainability is a natural environmental concept, the promotion of which requires leadership approaches based upon the natural environment structure. The core capability of being able to see the larger system (Senge et al., 2015) and the sustainability competency of systems thinking (Ploum et al., 2018) were previously identified as supporting this proposition because understanding the natural environment requires a systems thinking perspective. The second proposition is that sustainability is a boundaryless concept, the promotion of which requires system leadership capable of transcending boundaries and artificial barriers, engaging multiple stakeholders both vertically and horizontally. The core capabilities of promoting reflection and more innovative conversation and transforming the collective focus from reactive problem solving to proactive co-creation of the future (Senge et al., 2015), combined with the sustainability competency of interpersonal competence (Ploum et al., 2018), were previously identified as supporting this proposition, because transcending social boundaries and barriers requires interpersonal abilities. Finally, the third proposition is that sustainability is a complex, global concept, requiring leadership capable of seeing the big picture and influencing the entire system. It was previously noted that the core capabilities of being able to see the larger system and transforming the collective attention away from reactive problem solving to co-creation of the future (Senge et al., 2015), and the sustainability competencies of strategic thinking and interpersonal competence (Ploum et al., 2018), supported this proposition. All three interviewees identified the need for systems thinking, the ability to see the entire system, and interpersonal competence (skills) in their interview discussion, and two of the interviewees identified the need for collaboration (co-creation). While additional research is needed, the themes that emerged from the interviews support the propositions for the system leadership for sustainability model and framework advocated within this text.

## Future recommendations

System leadership has been defined and described in the previous chapters. The competencies, characteristics, and skills of system leadership have been identified, along with recommendations for their successful development and implementation. The system leadership for sustainability model provides a framework for leaders across all sectors and industries to influence collaborative efforts toward sustainability. This section contains recommendations for future action and effort by system leaders to achieve significant sustainability outcomes.

The limited gains in industrial sustainability, combined with the challenges posed by biocomplexity and resilience, demonstrate that sustainability is a systems problem that requires collaborative solutions (Fiksel, 2006). Legitimate systemic change may only be accomplished by a coordinated global effort, with participation from organizations in all sectors. The difficulties encountered during previous global efforts suggest that large-scale coordination will be difficult, due to the numerous urgent environmental issues encompassing multiple complex local and regional ecosystems (Fiksel, 2006). Brett Scheffers, a global change ecologist at the University of Florida, echoed the need for cross-sector collaboration to prepare for and mitigate the effects of natural disasters. Scheffers noted that there is one action every state can take to prepare for natural disasters: Maintain intact and healthy ecosystems, because the severity of natural disasters can be reduced "when people live in a landscape with intact and healthy ecosystems" (Eschner, 2019). Scheffers suggested business can serve a role in creating sustainable landscapes by partnering with scientists and governments. According to Scheffers, "[t]he best way to deal with this highly uncertain future is to get businesses, scientists, managers and policymakers all in a room together and [problem-solve] together in a highly coordinated way" (Eschner, 2019).

While improving modeling methods and creating a robust science of sustainability are essential, excessive research may provide an excuse for postponing necessary political action, resulting in "paralysis by analysis" (Cohen & Howard, 2006). Advancement in theoretical research must be balanced with exploratory policy implementation to enhance our knowledge of systemic sustainability issues (Fiksel, 2006). Sustainability is a pressing global issue that cannot wait for further research before taking action. Any efforts, however limited or unproven, may likely be better than no action at all. System leaders will need courage and perseverance to overcome efforts to delay or limit necessary action.

According to Brown (2012), the broad development of meaning-making competence among leaders is crucial for achievement of the challenging global sustainability goals. Compared with leaders possessing conventional systems of meaning-making, leaders with post-conventional meaning-making are more likely to think strategically, engage in collaboration, solicit feedback, resolve conflicts, devote effort to follower development, and redefine challenges to benefit from their interconnections (Joiner & Josephs, 2007). Therefore, leaders with well-developed, post-conventional meaning-making systems may possess enhanced and additional capacities, strengthening their ability to respond to complexity, uncertainty, and complicated situations. System leadership development programs should include processes that encourage this level of deep psychological development (Brown, 2012).

System leadership development programs are needed to enable sustainability leaders to develop the skills and competencies outlined in Chapter 3 of this text. While Chapter 4 introduced methods for developing system leadership, the content simply provided a foundation on which others may build. Additional best practices, tools, and methods should be developed and proliferated across organizational, sector, and geographic boundaries. Organizations and educational institutions should implement programs for system leadership at all levels, from introductory to senior leadership. Finally, system leaders should mentor and develop other system leaders to reach the impact and scale necessary for achievement of global sustainability.

## Future research

In Chapter 6 it was noted that scholars from multiple disciplines and viewpoints have attempted to explain the complicated nature of sustainability (Williams, Kennedy, Philipp, & Whiteman, 2017), with a considerable increase in interest within the disciplines of business, management, and organizational studies (Cullen, 2016). However, research examining systems thinking and sustainability management in business and organizational management literature is still limited, with previous research primarily interdisciplinary in nature or within systems thinking disciplines, such as environmental sciences and engineering (Williams et al., 2017). Future research is needed to examine the systems approach to sustainability management within business and organizations.

Because the system leadership framework is still in the development stage, an abundance of system leadership research opportunities exist. Sustainable systems research is needed to develop modeling and decision-making methods to enhance dynamic, adaptive management, which will require further understanding of the implications of alternative choices and their appropriateness for enhancing system resilience (Fiksel, 2006). This research would be beneficial for system leaders to better understand sustainability from a systemic perspective and to enhance sustainability decision-making.

Sustainability management scholars may apply systems thinking to "identify the points at which a system is capable of accepting positive change and the points where it is vulnerable" (Holling, 2001, p. 392). Based on the complexity of connected systems, researchers should explore the concurrent application of multiple models representing diverse system or stakeholder perspectives (Fiksel,

2006). Such research would assist system leaders in development of more comprehensive and inclusive sustainability approaches, initiatives, and structures. However, to effectively address the challenge of sustainability, research must shift from a primarily descriptive, analytic mode towards a transformational mode (Barile et al., 2018). Moreover, research must build upon the proposed model and framework introduced in this text by examining and developing methods for practical application of system leadership for sustainability. This practical knowledge is essential, because urgent and significant action is necessary to address sustainability challenges and issues.

Williams and colleagues (2017) noted the need for future research to specifically understand social-ecological embeddedness beyond the boundaries of the organization, industry, and production levels, as well as the interconnections among multi-level, embedded social-ecological systems. Embeddedness describes the degree to which economic activity is inhibited by non-economic institutions (Polanyi, 1968). This research may be beneficial for system leaders seeking to influence across organizational and industry boundaries. Williams et al. further suggested future transdisciplinary research could address whether collaborative action improves understanding of complex interactions between social-ecological systems, and how systems thinking can be applied in understanding how multi-stakeholder programs produce scalable action. Research along these lines would support the application of system leadership in developing boundaryless, collaborative sustainability action.

Fullan identified eight elements of system leadership within the context of education (2005). One of the elements was cyclical energizing, proposing that sustainability is cyclical for two important reasons: energy, and the occasions when additional time and talent are necessary to achieve the next adaptive improvement. While acknowledging that a precise model of cyclical energizing does not yet exist, Fullan suggested the concept should be an essential element of sustainability strategy. Future research could develop and study a model of framework of cyclical energizing supporting system leadership for sustainability.

Because system leadership has been previously examined in the fields of education and healthcare, future research is needed in other fields and sectors to support the generalization of previous research findings and the model proposed in this text. Gray (2010) suggested that social-ecological system sustainability will be accomplished through individual, organizational, political, and collective efforts. Further research on the characteristics and success of system leadership at the individual, organizational, political, and collective levels is needed. While system leadership has been proposed as a viable sustainability leadership model throughout this text, further research is necessary to support this model and prescribe methods of achieving, developing, and supporting system leadership. The three personal interviews conducted within the context of this text were intended to provide themes supporting system leadership. Future researchers may perform qualitative multiple case studies or quantitative research to support, enhance, or even refute some of the theoretical claims in this text.

## Future trends

People, technology, and governance are three essential resources for achieving sustainability (Barile et al., 2018). System leadership is necessary because all three resources exist across multiple organizations, subsystems, and systems, often with competing or even contradictory objectives. System leaders will need to achieve and maintain balance among people, technology, and governance within dynamic, increasingly complex economic, social, and environmental systems. While an abundance of literature about managing people, technology, or governance exists, the system leader must influence all three across multiple boundaries, sectors, and systems. This model of leadership will require uniquely capable individuals as described in this text.

The human characteristics of systems management allows for psychological and social consideration of the interactions among humans, organizations, and other species in the environment (Barile et al., 2018). Interactions within and between organizations and their environments provides a mechanism to discuss the current inadequate governance and learning structure for considering the delicate environment and illogical decision-making of the Anthropocene era (Simon, 1991). Existing information technology provides useful tools to enhance intelligence in sustainability efforts (Aquino, Barile, Grasso, & Saviano, 2018). Effective communication and smart technologies enable organizational structures to become responsive to changing environments and better able to disseminate scalable solutions both locally and globally (Barile et al., 2018). Smart technologies will enable better monitoring and management of activities. Cognitive machines, algorithms, hierarchical learning, and big data are capable of enhancing human capabilities and potentially introducing environmental constraints to improve our responses to unrelated complexity (Barile et al., 2018). The continued proliferation of information, communication, and artificial intelligence should improve the sharing of local and global best practices and tools for achieving sustainability. However, the same advances in communication and artificial intelligence will also empower sustainability antagonists in their ability to share information.

As consumers increasingly demand sustainable products and services, businesses will likely respond with appropriate offerings. Consumers must be discerning in their purchasing habits to correctly identify truly sustainable products and services from those which have been "greenwashed". Greenwashing refers to efforts by businesses, organizations, or industries to misrepresent or exaggerate their activities as being green or sustainable. Some scholars define greenwashing as the deliberate misrepresentation about the environmental efforts or lack of efforts of a business (Alves, 2009; Furlow, 2010). Social media should continue to provide a platform through which consumers can share perspectives concerning experiences with products and services that are sustainable and expose alleged greenwashing. However, social media may also continue to be used as a medium for proliferation of misinformation concerning sustainability issues such as climate change.

Sustainable development in a dynamic global system demands resilience at multiple levels, including businesses and communities (Fiksel, 2006). Increased global complexity and unpredictability require transitioning from a maintenance model of sustainability to adaptive policies and strategies that enhance management of unexpected challenges, while balancing the need to flourish with long-term consideration of human and ecological welfare. Achieving sustainability calls for unprecedented global cooperation in developing alternative technologies and adapting to the impacts of unsustainable activity (Fiksel, 2006). This cooperation must transcend organizational, sector, and political boundaries for meaningful change to occur.

As discussed in Chapter 7, cities and counties are forming collaborative organizations to address sustainability and resilience issues. The focus of many of these groups is to develop plans and procedures to ensure local businesses maintain resiliency to resume operations after an environmental catastrophe such as a hurricane. There are at least two reasons why these organizations will serve an essential role in addressing sustainability and resiliency issues and concerns at a local and regional level. First, the effects of climate change and sea-level rise will not be uniformly experienced, necessitating differing levels and types of response across regions, nations, and the globe. Second, state and national governments may become overwhelmed by future climate events, limiting the state and national role in multiple resilience responses. System leadership will be essential to coordinate collaboration and cooperation among multiple governmental and political bodies and diverse business interests.

Resiliency initiatives are becoming more prevalent, especially in areas most susceptible to the effects of climate change and sea-level rise. The US state of Florida recently announced the addition of a chief resilience officer who will report to the governor's office and coordinate a statewide response to climate change. The creation of this position by Governor Ron DeSantis demonstrated a reversal from the anti-climate change position of the previous governor, Rick Scott (Powers, 2019). This action mirrors actions by several municipalities in Florida, which have either appointed resiliency personnel or added resiliency to the title and responsibilities of existing sustainability staff.

In 2013, the Rockefeller Foundation launched the 100 Resilient Cities (100RC) program to help more cities build resilience to the physical, social, and economic challenges that are a growing part of the 21st century (Rockefeller Foundation, 2019). Cities in the 100RC network were provided with the necessary resources to develop a resilience roadmap along four main pathways:

- Financial and logistical guidance for establishing an innovative new position in city government, a Chief Resilience Officer, who will lead the city's resilience efforts;
- Expert support for development of a robust Resilience Strategy;

- Access to solutions, service providers, and partners from the private, public and NGO sectors who can help them develop and implement their Resilience Strategies; and
- Membership of a global network of member cities who can learn from and help each other.

(Rockefeller Foundation, 2019)

While the program ended in 2019, more than 1,000 cities applied, and 100 cities were selected to join the network, representing more than 20% of the global urban population (Rockefeller Foundation, 2019). The program has been superseded by the Adrienne Arsht-Rockefeller Foundation Resilience Center, launched by the Atlantic Council with support from the Rockefeller Foundation, with the goal of enhancing the resilience of one billion people by 2030 (Wemer, 2019). Future trends will likely include additional collective and singular resilience initiatives, requiring skilled system leaders to collaboratively manage sustainability and resilience efforts locally, regionally, nationally, and globally.

As the predicted effects of climate change become more obvious, support for sustainability may increase, possibly making the work of system leaders less difficult. Sea-level rise and other adverse environmental events will likely result in social and political pressure for sustainability action. However, disparity in where those consequences occur may result in antagonistic social and political positions, with climate change refugees blaming wealthier nations for their plight and possibly demanding compensation and increased immigration. The resulting instability may interfere with system leadership efforts, while simultaneously demanding increased system leadership to address these challenges.

## Conclusion

A quotation frequently attributed to American humorist and novelist Mark Twain suggests that "history does not repeat itself, but it rhymes". While the planet has undergone several mass extinction events, the current potential mass extinction event will be the first influenced by humankind. Humankind has reached a critical crossroads. The journey thus far has been characterized by increased pollution and biodiversity loss, nature resource limitations, poverty, overpopulation, and adverse climate effects. The future direction will determine the short-term and long-term viability of the quality of life and lifestyle currently enjoyed by a disproportionate segment of the population and desired by future generations. Although many people acknowledge the need to progress to sustainable, resilient lifestyles, the possibility of such a transition is discouraging, because it requires new methods of identifying and solving complex problems (Siebert, 2018). Comprehensive adoption of systems thinking offers society a promising option for achieving significant progress towards this intimidating transition; however, few understand systems thinking (Siebert, 2018).

The most common definition of sustainability, originating with the Brundtland Commission (World Commission on Environment and Development, 1987), finds acceptance among pragmatic development professionals, planners, and government administrators (Ooi, 2005). However, this definition is frequently criticized as ambiguous, failing to identify the requirements or structures necessary to achieve sustainability (Castro, 2004). Policy architects who do not express their sustainability perspective within an established definition and collection of criteria generate challenges for operationalizing sustainability (Davidson & Venning, 2011). Individual perception of sustainability influences the range of issues included in sustainability assessment framework, with some policy architects advocating economic growth for sustainability of society and others viewing economic growth as important, but placing greater emphasis on equity, social justice, and environmental resources (Davidson, 2011; Davidson & Wilson, 2010).

Seghezzo (2009) suggested that the WCED sustainability model and the triple bottom line (TBL) approach may no longer offer a valid pattern for understanding and addressing the current environmental, social, and economic challenges. Seghezzo offered a more comprehensive, plural, and practical framework in which the three Ps of people, planet, and profits would be substituted with place, permanence, and persons. Place describes the physical, geographic, and culturally organized spaces where humans exist and interact. Permanence, which is essentially overlooked in the sustainability conversation, requires deeper consideration of the potential long-term effects of human activity. Persons describes humans from an individual perspective, rather than indistinguishable participants in society, a perspective essentially nonexistent in the current frameworks (Seghezzo, 2009).

A better understanding of systems thinking, including history and contemporary developments, will enhance the ability to think more creatively, firmly grounded in physical phenomenon, and be better able to overcome contemporary environmental and social crises (Siebert, 2018). Baue and Wood (2015) insisted that we need to transcend the limited sustainability paradigm and incorporate sustainability "into a new meta-paradigm that spawns systems designed to thrive, sustainably" (p. 279). While Holthaus correctly suggested that "sustainability is always more complicated than it seems" (2012, p. 38), system leadership offers a model and framework to understand sustainability as a complicated but understandable and actionable endeavor.

While the focus of this text has been the presentation of system leadership as a means of achieving sustainability, the context is not complete or the final word. Rather, the intent was to present a foundation for the system leadership for sustainability model and stimulate further discussion and research on the concept. The future may seem uncertain, but one aspect of the future is certain: now is the time to act! System leaders will continue to emerge across every sector, influencing and initiating action toward a sustainable future. The necessary actions will not be easy, and the roadmap toward sustainability is being continually drawn and revised as we progress on the journey. It is the hope of this author that this text will provide a framework for others to follow and expand upon, developing themselves and others into system leaders for sustainability.

This chapter (and text) concludes with a quote from Kalungu-Banda (2006), who described the ordeals endured by Nelson Mandela (known as Madiba in South Africa) as the Madiba paradox:

> Things are not always smooth. Life is a mixture of joy and pain, success and failure, vision and disillusion. As leaders we have the task of helping others to live successfully with these contradictions. We must firmly believe and show through our actions that current difficulties have to be confronted while we keep an eye on the end goals. This can be done by enquiring honestly into the circumstances we face, and sharing our fears and frustrations as well as the sources of hope and inspiration.
>
> (p. 95)

Mandela endured many of his ordeals alone. The current unsustainability conditions on the planet and the actions necessary to reverse direction are ordeals that we will endure together. Each of us must internalize the words of Kalungu-Banda "enquiring honestly into the circumstances we face, and sharing our fears and frustrations as well as the sources of hope and inspiration" (p. 95).

## Chapter reflection questions

1 Do you believe that system leadership has been sufficiently demonstrated in this text to be an effective method for achieving sustainability? Why or why not?
2 What additional strengths and weaknesses to system leadership for sustainability can you identify? What actions can system leaders (and researchers) take to capitalize on the strengths and mitigate or overcome the weaknesses?
3 What additional recommendations can you identify for future sustainability action and effort? What additional research opportunities can you identify to support the model and framework introduced in this text? What future trends may confront or support sustainability system leaders?

## References

Alves, I. M. (2009). Green spin everywhere: How greenwashing reveals the limit of the CSR paradigm. *Journal of Global Change and Governance*, *2*(1), 1–26. doi:10.1.1.458.3293

Aquino, R. P., Barile, S., Grasso, A., & Saviano, M. (2018). Envisioning smart and sustainable healthcare: 3D Printing technologies for personalized medication. *Futures*, *103*, 35–50. doi:10.1016/j.futures.2018.03.002

Barile, S., Orecchini, F., Saviano, M., & Farioli, F. (2018). People, technology, and governance for sustainability: The contribution of systems and cyber-systemic thinking. *Sustainability Science*, *13*(5), 1197–1208. doi:10.1007/s11625-018-0621-y

Baue, B., & Wood, R. (2015, August–November). Leveraging integral leadership to shift sustainability mindsets into a thriveability paradigm. *Integral Leadership Review*, 279–284. Retrieved from http://integralleadershipreview.com/

Brown, B. C. (2012). Leading complex change with post-conventional consciousness. *Journal of Organizational Change Management*, *25*(4), 560–575. doi:10.1108/09534811211239227

Burns, H., Diamond-Vaught, H., & Bauman, C. (2015). Leadership for sustainability: Theoretical foundations and pedagogical practices that foster change. *International Journal of Leadership Studies*, *9*(1), 88–100. Retrieved from http://citeseerx.ist.psu.edu

Castro, C. (2004). Sustainable development: Mainstream and critical perspectives. *Organisation & Environment*, *17*(2), 195–225. doi:10.1177/1086026604264910

Cohen, M., & Howard, J. (2006). Success and its price: The institutionalization and political relevance of industrial ecology. *Journal of Industrial Ecology*, *10*(1–2), 79–88. doi:10.1162/108819806775545394

Crofton, F. S. (2000). Educating for sustainability: Opportunities in undergraduate engineering. *Journal of Cleaner Production*, *8*(5), 397–405. doi:10.1016/S0959-6526(00)00043-3

Cullen, J. G. (2016). Educating business students about sustainability: A bibliometric review of current trends and research needs. *Journal of Business Ethics*, *145*(2), 429–439. doi:10.1007/s10551-015-2838-3

Davidson, K. M. (2011). Reporting systems for sustainability: What are they measuring? *Social Indicators Research*, *100*(2), 351–365. doi:10.1007/s11205-010-9634-3

Davidson, K. M., & Venning, J. (2011). Sustainability decision-making frameworks and the application of systems thinking: An urban context. *Local Environment*, *16*(3), 213–228. doi:10.1080/13549839.2011.565464

Davidson, K. M., & Wilson, L. (2010). *Advancing sustainability in a time of crises*. 11th Biennial ISEE Conference, Oldenburg, Germany, 22–25 August.

Eschner, K. (2019, July 10). *The most dangerous places to live in America that are prone to natural disasters*. New York, NY: CNBC. Retrieved from www.cnbc.com/2019/07/10/billion-dollar-natural-disasters-rising-these-states-better-prepare.html

Espejo, R. (2018). Introduction. In S. Barile, R. Espejo, I. Perko, & M. Saviano (Eds.), *Cybernetics and systems: Social and business decisions*. London, England: Routledge-Giappichelli.

Fiksel, J. (2006). Sustainability and resilience: Toward a systems approach. *Sustainability: Science, Practice, & Policy*, *2*(2), 14–21. Retrieved from http://ejournal.nbii.org

Fullan, M. (2004). *Systems thinkers in action: Moving beyond the standards plateau*. London and Nottingham, England: DfES Innovation Unit and NCSL.

Fullan, M. (2005). *Leadership and sustainability*. Thousand Oaks, CA: Corwin Press and Toronto: Ontario Principals Council.

Furlow, N. E. (2010). Greenwashing in the new millennium. *The Journal of Applied Business and Economics*, *10*(6), 22–25. Retrieved from www.na-businesspress.com/jabeopen.html

Gibson, R. (2005). *Sustainability assessment: Criteria and processes*. London, England: Earthscan.

Gray, R. (2010). Is accounting for sustainability actually accounting for sustainability . . . and how would we know? An exploration of narratives of organisations and the planet. *Accounting, Organizations & Society*, *35*(1), 47–62. doi:10.1016/j.aos.2009.04.006

Hawken, P. (2007). *Blessed unrest: How the largest movement in the world came into being and why no one saw it coming*. New York, NY: Penguin Group.

Holling, C. S. (2001). Understanding the complexity of economic, ecological, and social systems. *Ecosystems*, *4*(5), 390–405. doi:10.1007/s10021-001-0101-5

Holthaus, G. (2012). *Learning Native wisdom: What traditional cultures teach us about subsistence, sustainability, and spirituality*. Lexington, KY: University Press of Kentucky.

Joiner, B., & Josephs, S. (2007). *Leadership agility: Five levels of mastery for anticipating and initiating change*. San Francisco, CA: Jossey-Bass.

Kalungu-Banda, M. (2006). *Leading like Madiba: Leadership lessons from Nelson Mandela*. Lansdowne, South Africa: Double Storey Books.

Nabavi, E., Daniell, K. A., & Najafi, H. (2016). Boundary matters: The potential of system dynamics to support sustainability? *Journal of Cleaner Production, 140*, 312–323. doi:10.1016/j.jclepro.2016.03.032

Ooi, G. (2005). *Sustainability and cities: Concept and assessment*. Singapore: World Scientific Publishing.

Ploum, L., Blok, V., Lans, T., & Omta, O. (2018). Toward a validated competence framework for sustainable entrepreneurship. *Organization & Environment, 31*(2), 113–132. doi:10.1177/1086026617697039

Polanyi, K. (1968). The economy as instituted process. In E. LeClair & H. Schneider (Eds.), *Economic anthropology: Readings in theory and analysis*. New York, NY: Holt, Rinehart and Winston.

Powers, S. (2019, May 7). *Ron DeSantis tackling climate change with "Chief Resilience Officer"*. St. Petersburg, FL: Florida Politics. Retrieved from https://floridapolitics.com/archives/295872-ron-desantis-tackling-climate-change-with-chief-resilience-officer

Rockefeller Foundation. (2019). *100 resilient cities*. New York, NY: Author. Retrieved from www.rockefellerfoundation.org/our-work/initiatives/100-resilient-cities/

Scoones, I., Leach, M., Smith, A., Stagl, S., Stirling, A., & Thompson, J. (2007). *Dynamic systems and the challenge of sustainability*. Brighton, UK. Retrieved from http://opendocs.ids.ac.uk/opendocs/handle/123456789/2470

Seghezzo, L. (2009). The five dimensions of sustainability. *Environmental Politics, 18*(4), 539–556. doi:10.1080/09644010903063669

Senge, P., Hamilton, H., & Kania, J. (2015). The dawn of system leadership. *Stanford Social Innovation Review, 13*(1), 27–33. Retrieved from https://ssir.org/articles/entry/the_dawn_of_system_leadership

Siebert, M. (2018). *Systems thinking and how it can help build a sustainable world*. Corvalis, OR: Post Carbon Institute. Retrieved from www.resilience.org/stories/2018-07-11/systems-thinking-and-how-it-can-help-build-a-sustainable-world/

Simon, H. A. (1991). Bounded rationality and organizational learning. *Organization Science, 2*(1), 125–134. doi:10.1287/orsc.2.1.125

Spangenberg, J., Pfahl, S., & Dellar, K. (2002). Towards indicators for institutional sustainability: Lessons from an analysis of Agenda 21. *Ecological Indicators, 2*(7), 61–77. doi:10.1016/S1470-160X(02)00050-X

Timmins, N. (2015). *The practice of system leadership: Being comfortable with chaos*. London, England: The King's Fund. Retrieved from www.kingsfund.org.uk/sites/default/files/field/field_publication_file/System-leadership-Kings-Fund-May-2015.pdf

Voss, J.-P., Bauknecht, D., & Kemp, R. (2006). *Reflexive governance for sustainable development*. Cheltenham, England: Edward Elgar Publishing.

Wemer, D. A. (2019, April 29). *Atlantic Council launches Adrienne Arsht-Rockefeller Foundation Resilience Center*. Washington, DC: Atlantic Council. Retrieved from www.atlanticcouncil.org/blogs/new-atlanticist/atlantic-council-launches-adrienne-arsht-rockefeller-foundation-resilience-center

Williams, A., Kennedy, S., Philipp, F., & Whiteman, G. (2017). Systems thinking: A review of sustainability management research. *Journal of Cleaner Production, 148*, 866–881. doi:10.1016/j.jclepro.2017.02.002

World Commission on Environment and Development. (1987). *Our common future*. Oxford, England: Oxford University Press.

# Index

Note: Page numbers in *italic* indicate a figure on the corresponding page.

For Product Safety Concerns and Information please contact our EU representative GPSR@taylorandfrancis.com
Taylor & Francis Verlag GmbH, Kaufingerstraße 24, 80331 München, Germany

www.ingramcontent.com/pod-product-compliance
Lightning Source LLC
LaVergne TN
LVHW011131300926
849160LV00008B/606

* 9 7 8 1 0 3 2 0 8 3 5 7 5 *